1st ed.

85¢

ANN

D1159790

# BREAKFAST TABLE AUTOCRAT

Henry P. Crowell

You cannot study this photograph of Mr. Crowell in his eighty-eighth year without sensing he was kind, considerate, self-effacing, soft-spoken. Nor can you miss the fact that he was an executive. Eyes, mouth, hair, everything about him reveals it; even the careful grooming which with men of his kind becomes habitual as they grow older. You think, "That man knew where he was going." He always did know where he was going, but he never resorted to table pounding or bowled folks over getting there.

"Take your time," the photograph seems to say, "Take your time. Be sure to find the will of God. When folks do not agree with you, let them talk. Be quiet while they talk. When they've talked themselves out, they'll ask you what you think should be done. Tell them. They'll do it."

\* \* \*

Mr. Crowell smiled at the book title. "So, I am an autocrat?" "Yes, Mr. Crowell, you are an autocrat. But such an altogether amiable one!"

The world must have autocrats to get things done. And autocracy is sublimated if tempered to the will of God. (Author's "Ritornelle")

BOOKS BY

RICHARD ELLSWORTH DAY

---

THE SHADOW OF THE BROAD BRIM
(Life of Charles Haddon Spurgeon)

BUSH AGLOW
(Life of Dwight Lyman Moody)

MAN OF LIKE PASSIONS
(Vignette of Charles Grandison Finney)

THE BORROWED GLOW
(Daily Meditations)

BREAKFAST TABLE AUTOCRAT
(Life of Henry Parsons Crowell)

# BREAKFAST TABLE
# AUTOCRAT

The Life Story of Henry Parsons Crowell

by

Richard Ellsworth Day

Moody Press
Chicago
1946

"You don't imagine my remarks made at this table are like so many postage stamps do you—each one to be only once uttered? If you do you are mistaken. . . . A thought is often original though you have uttered it a hundred times. It comes over a new route, by a new and express train of associations." (Oliver Wendell Holmes, *The Autocrat* of *The Breakfast Table*.)

Everything you write, Good Friend of Beacon Street, has such an agreeable rattle! And this particular book title has a sound so fore and aft, it deserves to be uttered again. Let's bring it over a new route indeed! Let's give it a very new and express train of associations by conferring it upon the man who changed the breakfast habits of the world—Henry Parsons Crowell. (*Sketch Book*)

(Book plate presented to the Author by Fannie Green Clark, Historical Librarian, Berkshire Athenaeum, Pittsfield, Massachusetts.)

To

WILL H. HOUGHTON

PROTAGONIST

OF

THIS BIOGRAPHY

# CONTENTS

Ritornelle

## PART ONE
## CHRISTIAN BUSINESS MAN

## PART TWO
## CHRISTIAN STATESMAN

ix

# ILLUSTRATIONS

# RITORNELLE

Herein the Major Thesis is recorded. But we refuse to label it the "Preface." This rose by *any* other name . . . !

The lights go down, the singers are ready. But before their voices are heard, the orchestra leader lifts his baton for strings, wood-wind, and brass to sound out the Ritornelle. By your leave, it isn't in form to begin without a Ritornelle. That passage represents the burden of the entire composition. If those opening musical notes, for instance, set forth the gleam of the Evening Star, then the light of the Star shines through the entire performance, shaping and tempering every bar of music. (*Sketch Book*)

# RITORNELLE

I F THE significance of Henry Parsons Crowell could be set forth by a study of four sizable American enterprises, then the burden of this book would be to represent the Quaker Oats Company, the Perfection Stove Company, the Wyoming Hereford Ranch, and the Moody Bible Institute, together with appropriate photographs, impressive statistics, and frequent references to their symposiarch. But a portrait of Mr. Crowell cannot be fashioned with factory outlines. His likeness will not appear until we search out what he himself was. Though this book, therefore, will have much detail about his institutions, these institutions will be conceived as mill products; and our chief purpose will be to provide a look at the miller.

These pages will take you up to the General Offices of the Quaker Oats Company in Chicago's Board of Trade Building, followed by little journeys to the one hundred and one Quaker units scattered over the world. You will visit the Perfection Stove Company of Cleveland. You will go out to the fifty-five thousand acre Wyoming Hereford Ranch at Cheyenne. You will be conducted through cathedral-like Crowell Hall, and note the life of Chicago's Moody Bible Institute which it centers. Moreover, you are to be a guest at the Crowell Estates—Green Court in Augusta, Georgia, and the city home in Winnetka, Illinois. But none of the foregoing are primary in these pages.

You are also to look at another area for which the life of Mr. Crowell provides glowing material—the industrial application of personal talent. This is a curiously neglected side of American life. "In an era so alert as is this to the importance of the economic equation in history, it is surprising how little attention has been given to the study of particular industrial enterprises." The

3

foregoing sentence, in the first paragraph of Thornton's *The History of the Quaker Oats Company,* indicates the scope of his book.

Likewise, literature, while devoting reams to men whose personal talent was applied to art, science, government, war, and religion, has by-passed the men who valorously rode the money tides and created great estates. The reason may largely arise from a distrust of money-making. But the strength and continuity of American life cannot be fully known without the careers of her factory builders. Their stories are a Calaveras mother-lode for annalists who have the vision to see and the courage to record that big business is, after all, essentially a matter of generalship, and belongs to the literature of inspiration.

\*    \*    \*

But the premium is not to be placed on any of the foregoing. Our aim is to understand Mr. Crowell himself, this man who was such a good specimen of America at its best. More accurately, Mr. Crowell is to be seen in these pages as a representative man, the kind of a person who explains institutions. As Jean Paul Frederick Richter would have phrased it, Mr. Crowell had something in him which put empires on their hinges. And that something was a peculiar quality derived from a blending of business sagacity and Christian faith.

\*    \*    \*

On first thought, the book title may seem to be unfair to Mr. Crowell, a libel upon an amiable gentleman. But that is on first thought, only. For when you really came to know Mr. Crowell, you found he was conclusively an autocrat; an autocrat bound in velvet. The president of the Perfection Stove Company, who is by preference a big game hunter, sat in his office whose walls are heavy with mounted game-heads; "I've been with Perfection *just a short time,* thirty-three years. I know Mr. Crowell. What he wanted done was always done, though he was very quiet about it." On the day of the Crowell Memorial Service, Thomas S. Smith, of the Moody Board, brokenly reviewed forty years of fellowship with him; "He was an autocrat: make no mistake about it. I'd say 'a godly autocrat,' but an autocrat just the same."

So there you have it, whether you like it or not. No phrase more neatly encysts Mr. Crowell than a little transposition of Holmes' well-known title to read, "Breakfast Table Autocrat." The stride in which he proceeded to build a great cereal enterprise, and to change the breakfast habits of the world, was characteristic of the man in every other area. "Breakfast Table Autocrat" is a bonny label for representing his life-time of inflexible, but gentlemanly, executive action, after he had taken time to think things through and was certain of the wisdom of his conclusions.

The frontispiece photograph of Mr. Crowell, taken in his eighty-eighth year, has for months lain under the glass top of my desk at Cedar-Palms. Day by day, as in other biographical studies, I have scrutinized his features, trying to discern what manner of man he was. A biographer, so far as possible, is under obligation to see his man just as God sees him. Then, too, portraits, if brooded over sufficiently long, have a strange way of speaking to you.

"Well," said the Breakfast Table Autocrat in the Green Court Interviews, "has mine talked to you yet?"

"Oh yes, Mr. Crowell."

"What does it say?"

"TAKE YOUR TIME. TAKE YOUR TIME. THINK IT THROUGH. BE SURE TO FIND THE WILL OF GOD. KNOW WHAT OUGHT TO BE DONE. WHEN FOLKS DO NOT AGREE WITH YOU, LET THEM TALK. BE QUIET WHILE THEY TALK. WHEN THEY'VE TALKED THEMSELVES OUT, THEY'LL ASK YOU WHAT YOU THINK SHOULD BE DONE. TELL THEM. THEY'LL DO IT."

You cannot study the photograph of the frontispiece without sensing he was kind, considerate, self-effacing, soft-spoken. Nor can you miss the fact that he was an executive. Eyes, mouth, hair, everything about him reveals it, even the careful grooming which with men of his kind becomes habitual as they grow older.

You think "That man knew where he was going." He always did know where he was going; but oh, he was so gentlemanly about it! He always did know where he was going, but he never resorted to table pounding or bowled folks over getting there.

In the concluding interview, September, 1944, Mr. Crowell smiled over the book title:

"So I'm an autocrat."

"Yes, Mr. Crowell, you're an autocrat. But such an altogether amiable one."

\* \* \*

The world must have autocrats to get things done. And autocracy is sublimated if tempered to the will of God.

\* \* \*

The idea of writing Mr. Crowell's biography originated with President Houghton of Moody Bible Institute. In ten years of close association, Dr. Houghton knew the great man hidden behind Mr. Crowell's reserve and humility. At the same time, the President of Moody desired that the author of *Bush Aglow* undertake the biographical labor.

But neither subject nor writer had the slightest interest. Each time it was mentioned to Mr. Crowell, he quietly replied, "No. (Pause) No. (Pause) I can't give my consent to it." To the writer, the head of the Quaker Oats Company offered no biographical interest.

One fall day in 1941, Dr. Houghton arranged a meeting of subject and writer in the Quaker Oats Offices. For some time the writer, after introduction, sat waiting in front of Mr. Crowell's desk, gazing out of the lofty windows at the city towers. The interview began without amenities.

"Why do you want to write my biography?"

"Well, Mr. Crowell, in the first place, I had never thought of writing it: and in the second place, I never heard you wanted it written."

Mr. Crowell looked over his desk—just like the frontispiece picture. He smiled.

"Well, what would you do if you did write it?"

"If I did, I wouldn't flatter you. I'd find out all about you, then show what God could do with you in spite of it."

Another smile—just like the photo.

"That sounds good. But, do you think anyone would be interested?"

"I believe thousands of American business men would say, 'If

God can use Mr. Crowell, I want Him to use me. I would like to know just how Mr. Crowell went about the matter.' "

Mr. Crowell smiled again.

"I think you've got something there."

And the interview was over.

\* \* \*

According to his own formula, Mr. Crowell must now consider the idea of having his life written. He must "take his time, think it through, find the will of God." A solid, silent year went by. At September-end in 1942, the phone bell in a Chicago hotel room rang, and the green lights went up all along the Biographical Boulevard. A secretary at Quaker reported, "Mr. Crowell says if you wish to go ahead with the biography, he would be glad to co-operate."

\* \* \*

But the matter was not settled when the secretary at Quaker Oats announced Mr. Crowell's approval. You see, an adequate biographical enthusiasm arises from one or the other of two reactions: the author must either thoroughly detest his subject; or, he must admire him so deeply that his admiration requires a tight rein. Certainly neither of these attitudes was held towards Mr. Crowell. It would have been easy to have dropped the matter; and no doubt that would have been most agreeable to Mr. Crowell. But—there was still President Houghton! Finally, out of consideration for his enthusiasm, or perhaps out of apprehension of his tenacity, it seemed good to give the matter further consideration. This required a closer view of Mr. Crowell.

Therefore, the proper persons were contacted: "If this biography is undertaken, there are to be no locked doors: every detail must be open for inspection. Then, the author must be unhampered in his interpretations, even to the point of painting the moles, if there are any. Biography is not worth-while unless it is realistic."

These conditions were immediately approved.

"Then too, a few days of close contact with Mr. Crowell are highly necessary. Where is he going to be in December?"

"In Green Court."

"Very well, we will spend a week with him in Georgia."

He came down to the hotel in Augusta, where we were registering, insisting that we come right out to Green Court. He picked up Deborah's grip, and started for his auto. Deborah was amazed. The idea of *Mr. Crowell* carrying *her* grip: and he *eighty-seven years old!* The first strong impression of his character was made right then. There was something sterling about him. After three days in his home, admiration was completely captured. His strength was unmistakably of a kind with the greatest so far studied. Adequate biographical enthusiasm appeared rapidly. "Why, here is a man of international exploits, yet he is the most humble and self-effacing person I have ever met. He is one hundred per cent genuine." The Green Court Biographical Interviews began forthwith.

\*   \*   \*

The years 1942-1944 were devoted to nation-wide research, visiting great industrial enterprises, interviewing scores of people in all walks of life. There were side trips to many forgotten places simply because Mr. Crowell at some time had lived or labored there.

The subject himself gave time beyond expectation in co-operating upon the research. Innermost matters, confidential documents, hitherto veiled from the world, were disclosed. Boswell ended by losing his heart completely to the Breakfast Table Autocrat. He found himself beginning to say as his own critical junctures appeared,

"Take your time! Find what God wants!"

\*   \*   \*

At last the research was finished: finished save two or three bits of minor detail. In September, 1944, your scribe wired, "Research practically completed. Will be in Chicago the twenty-seventh. Could I have a little time?" The answer returned, "I have set aside the entire day for you and the next if you wish."

The outline of the book and chapter sketches were reviewed. In the intimacy that had grown during the enterprise, we laughingly recalled the circumstances under which the writing of the book began.

"Mr. Crowell, you know when the matter of your biography

first came up, you seemed just another rich man; and rich men, per se, do not rate very high."

He smiled: "And, *now?*"

"Well, Mr. Crowell, I seem to have no capacity for disliking you."

I did not want to tell him: never did! He would not have liked it. So I never told him he was all bound up in my bundle of life with Spurgeon and Moody. No, I never told him straight out. I was certain he knew without my saying so.

The nearest the final conversations ever came to such a declaration was a bizarre remark which jumped up like a rabbit out of the brush:

"Mr. Crowell, you know, with your private correspondence in my keeping, I am nauseated by some of the fulsome letters. They were written with their little palms extended for back-sheesh. Well, here's one man you never did anything for, and never will. The best you will ever do for me is what you are. *And that's plenty!*"

\* \* \*

The long hours of September twenty-seven and twenty-eight are a cherished memory, beginning first in the Quaker Offices; noon luncheon at the Union League Club with Mr. Crowell and his right hand man, George C. Lazear; continued conference in the afternoon and the next day; then an evening at city home in Winnetka. Late at night, Denton Bench drove up with the car. Mr. Crowell stood on the cool front terrace:

"Remember," he said, "You are to be in Green Court January 27, my ninetieth birthday! And bring Deborah."

\* \* \*

Yesterday was the twenty-seventh of January, 1945, but we were far from Augusta. Bittersweet fills our hearts. On my desk lies Mr. Crowell's 1944 Christmas greeting. Year by year, similar personal messages went to friends all over the world. So great was their excellence that one letter exclaims, "You must begin January first to prepare for the next Christmas!" The 1944 Greeting is an eight-page booklet, bound in royal purple covers, consisting of carefully selected Scripture verses upon the general theme of Christian Liberty.

There was also, loose within the lids, a small slip of paper, signed by "His Family," and reading as follows:

". . . the sudden home-going of Mr. Henry Parsons Cro-well, October 23, 1944 . . . his Christmas cards had already been completed . . . we felt he would like this message to go to you as usual. . . ."

And here are the closing words of his 1944 Greeting, an appropriate valedictory for the subject of this biography:

"Stand fast in the liberty wherewith Christ hath made us free. For in Him, and through Him, and to Him are all things: To Whom be glory forever! Amen."

*Richard E. Day*

*Cedar-Palms,*
*Sunnyvale, California*

# PART ONE
## CHRISTIAN BUSINESS MAN
## 1855 – 1898

ANCESTRY—YOUTH—DELIVERANCE—LILLIE AUGUSTA WICK
—THE QUAKER OATS COMPANY—THE PERFECTION STOVE
COMPANY

GEN.
MOSES CLEAVELAND
FOUNDER OF THE CITY
1796

Statue of Moses Cleaveland
Public Square, Cleveland, Ohio

Mr. Crowell's life was so largely centered about this City Park that
his biography, geographically viewed, could well have been titled
"Public Square,"

# I

# "THE YANKS ARE COMING!"

In which General Moses Cleaveland lays out a city in the Ohio wilderness, and makes ready for the Yankee Invasion.

The Yankee temperament seems to be resultant of forces between shrewd bargaining and a genius for faith. Faith kept bargaining from becoming sordid, and bargaining kept faith from becoming gullible. You can't help admiring these men. They were Puritans with a Mission Street education. They could deal with Scrooge to his disadvantage, and commune with Fenelon to his edification; yet neither function violated the other.

There was the matter of the Western Reserve for instance. The "Yanks" were delightfully clever in getting possession, and refreshingly altruistic in using their profits. Seven-eighths of the land, about thirty-five thousand acres, were sold to the Connecticut Land Company, and the proceeds ear-marked "Public Education." The remaining eighth was titled "The Fire Lands," and devoted to the relief of those who suffered from British depredations during the Revolutionary War.

Henry Parsons Crowell was a Yankee from Cleveland. You will never measure the sagacity with which he reared great enterprises, or the devotion of his walk with God until you take time to look at his fore-bears—the Yankees from Connecticut. (*Sketch Book*)

# "THE YANKS ARE COMING!"

W E NOW move up such slides, decorations, and fittings as seem convenient for making an open air theatre of a certain six hundred acres in downtown Cleveland. This theatre is to be the scene of a Pageant of Progress rich with thick-coming fancies. Hotel Cleveland and its Siamese sister, the Terminal Tower Building, will do for stage-center. Scribe a circle round about of half a mile. That is the arena. Now for a brief glance at its appearance in 1945.

Directly in front of the hotel, which has a northerly exposure, is the Public Square, on the north side of which, in fine centennial dignity, is the Old Stone Church. Continuing northward from the Public Square is a conventional huddle of American, big-city buildings, good, bad, and indifferent, which, after a few blocks, end at the waters of Lake Erie. A few doors east of the church is one of the buildings of the Western Reserve University. Running almost due east from the Public Square is Buffalo Road—pardon, "Euclid Avenue"; and forking southward from Euclid, about two-hundred feet from the Square is Fourth Street—but its name was once "Sheriff Street." No modern map of Cleveland will help you make this identification. So you say to an officer,

"Where is Sheriff Street?"

He replies, "Well, this is Fourth Street. But right down there at the end, is an old building with a sign 'Sheriff Street Market.' Say! do you suppose Fourth was once Sheriff Street?"

Yes, as a matter of fact, Fourth Street was once Sheriff Street; and you cannot walk along this little street running from Euclid Avenue to Prospect Avenue without considering it a shrine: here Mr. Crowell was born! . . . Other streets running east from the square need not be mentioned at this time.

13

Back of the Hotel-Terminal Tower Buildings, the shabby little Cuyahoga River writhes northward. With a final squirm, it rounds a large bluff of white sand and enters the lake. This is not the time to admire the high level bridges over the river: or the skill with which engineers have blasted out, on the east bank, a cavern for an underground railway station so vast that several great buildings, such as the Post Office, the Union Depot, and the Terminal Tower, stand right on the top of it. Being in quest of yesterday, we leave it to you to muse upon this downtown nether world, replete with trackage for a fleet of trains, streets for auto traffic, and gleaming passageways, one of which comes up into the hotel itself. . . . Just before the river enters the lake, it runs through a covey of riff-raff buildings, one of which is an old hotel with an evil smell. But you are to remember this hotel, as it has an interesting part in our story.

Now let us go into the Florentine glory of the hotel lobby, take an over-stuffed chair, and dream awhile . . . the uproar of the traffic grows dim . . . the calendar slips backward . . . the raised letters of civilization disappear . . . the dense forests of the old Northwest Territory return, replacing the modern building . . . the little Cuyahoga looks much more important now. It is no longer degenerate from city contacts.

Here we are, back in primitive America! A dramatist would tell you these forests of oak, walnut, and butternut are just begging to be made into mantles and spinning wheels, bedsteads and chairs, wagons and barns: that this is a wonder-site for a future city! Out there on the hills are fields just right for oats and oil domes. In short, everything is all set for a Gold Tide, and the appearance of an American aristocracy with corn fed children. . . . It is no longer 1945; it is 1796 . . . the month is July . . . the day is the twenty-first. . . . Bring out the bell, the book, and the candle. Curtain!

\* \* \*

There on the summer-blue waters of Lake Erie is a stubby little vessel moving in like a wooden shoe with sails on it, making its way towards that white sand bluff, for a landing in the mouth of the Cuyahoga River. Anchors down for the Silver Swan! And while the boat is heaving-to, the scrip will quickly tell you of the captain and the crew!

The boat itself is rough-hewn, hacked out of the wilderness a year ago and launched in Lake Erie just above Niagara Falls, near the Village of Buffalo. For three months it has been "poking along, looking over the one hundred and fifty miles of wilderness shore-line from Buffalo to the Cuyahoga River."

The captain is that fair-sized hunk of violent young manhood just turned forty, General Moses Cleaveland, Yale graduate, class of 1786, and Barrister by the will of God. Canterbury, Connecticut, was his birthplace, January 29, 1754; the Revolutionary War, the source of his rank as "Brigadier General in the Militia." After student days in Yale, he practiced law for a time; then became a realtor when the State of Connecticut sold the Western Reserve. ("Realtor," Colonial for a Yale graduate selling real estate.) Along with the General are fifty more Roving Yankees, mostly from Connecticut. And the firm which they represent is The Connecticut Land Company.

\* \* \*

Mr. Crowell, in the Biographical Interviews, often spoke of the Western Reserve, and quite properly. That "gigantic real estate deal" captured the imagination of his forebears, the Connecticut Crowells and Parsons, and finally in the year 1853, occasioned the entry in the register of the Forest City House on Superior Street of "Henry Luther Crowell and wife." A thumb nail memo on the Western Reserve is therefore in order.

\* \* \*

At the close of the war in 1783, an empire-sized region of raw continent lay east of the Mississippi, which had in turn been owned by France, Great Britain, and in part, Quebec; "265,878 square miles of the best land you ever laid eyes on." By the Paris treaty, this tract was ceded to the United States. Two years later, Congress called it "The Northwest Territory." It is scandalously affirmed that one T. Jefferson proposed it be cut up into new states, and named as follows: "Assenipia, Cheronesius, Sylvania, Pelisipia, Illinoia, Polyptoamis, Washingtonia, Mesopotamia, and

Michigania." If this be true, aforesaid T. Jefferson could have rendered valuable service in naming Pullman sleepers.

Several conflicting claims at once arose as to which of the Thirteen States owned the Northwest Territory. The most vociferous claims were made by New York, Virginia, Massachusetts, and Connecticut. But the Connecticut Yankees outsmarted the others. In the year 1786, Connecticut briefed her equities: "She had a right to the new land by her charter of 1662, which gave her title to 'those lands limited east and west by the Sea.' (What sea? South Sea? Pacific Ocean?) So, in order to end all dispute, Connecticut with a notable beaux geste wished to cede all her rights and claims in the Northwest Territory to the Federal Government, except. . . ."

"Except!" There's the Ethiopian! Except a pleasant little patch of six thousand square miles of the best forest land in what is now eastern Ohio! The Nutmeg State Fathers felt it was only fair that her public spirit should be recognized in a little keepsake. This little keepsake they called "the Western Reserve," or "the Connecticut Reserve," all Connecticut had left over from her voluntary impoverishment. Like the gentleman from Tombstone, who affirmed ownership of Arizona, but was willing to settle for Phoenix.

The Western Reserve extended one hundred and twenty miles west of the Pennsylvania line, and lay north and south in the Horse Latitudes, forty-one and forty-two degrees. The same frugal Yankees, 1795-6, organized "The Connecticut Land Company," and purchased seven-eighths of the Western Reserve from the State, for the sum of one million two hundred thousand dollars. And the covered wagons started to roll westward.

\* \* \*

There was certainly no accounting for the men of Connecticut. One would think these post-Revolutionary Yankees could find, in the trackless solitudes on the west side of their own state, all they needed to slake their land thirst. But they did not, these restless men of New England! Though fixed enough in frugality and faith, they were marked by a boyish wanderlust that for a full

Hotel Cleveland and its Siamese Sister, the Terminal Tower Building. The Public Square is in the foreground; the shabby little Cuyahoga River, degenerate from city contacts, at the rear, happily out of view. These buildings center an area of six hundred acres where the City of Cleveland began. Within a yard-arms distance, there was once a street called "Sheriff," now Fourth, where Mr. Crowell was born.

Edifice, Second Presbyterian Church on Superior Street, to which the Luther Crowells belonged.

HENRY LUTHER CROWELL

Father of Henry Parsons Crowell

Rev. James Eells, D. D., second pastor of the Second Presbyterian Church of Cleveland (January 24, 1855—April 3, 1860). On December 16, 1869, he was recalled to the church, remaining pastor until June 22, 1873. (Copied from a print in the records of The Old Stone Church.)

Rev. Theron Holbrook Hawks, D. D., third pastor of the Second Presbyterian Church (April 21, 1861—April 26, 1868). He it was who "led Mr. Crowell to Christ." (Copied of an oil painting. Church of the Covenant, Cleveland.)

Joel Burton Parsons, (born 1883) brother of Mrs. Henry Luther Crowell. "He came down from Connecticut following the death of Luther to look after the three fatherless boys." (Photo supplied by his daughter, Miss Marion A. Parsons of Cleveland.)

William Henry Waite, who "took his nephew, Henry Parsons Crowell, away on the afternoon of Luther's death."

Frances Parsons (Mrs. William Henry Waite) "the beauty of the family": sister of Mr. Crowell's mother. So much did Frances and Mrs. Luther Crowell resemble each other as girls that, lacking a girlhood picture of his mother, Mr. Crowell constantly kept the above likeness on the library tables of Green Court and Winnetka homes.

GREYLOCK INSTITUTE

As rebuilt after the fire of
April 14, 1872, along the lines
of the Original building.

PRINCIPAL BENJAMIN FRANKLIN MILLS

HENRY PARSONS CROWELL

Student at Greylock Institute, age sixteen. From the collection
of Mr. Crowell's daughter, Mrs. Frederick Cowles Herrick of
Cleveland.

LILLIE AUGUSTA WICK
(In her teens)

"The little Wick girl" had become a very attractive young woman.
When Henry left Cleveland for California in the fall of 1877, they
were engaged.

century put their little wooden boats into every ocean, and their emigrant trains into every wilderness.

Hardly had the ink dried on the Treaty of Paris, 1783, before the Yankees were moving westward, swarming like locusts over the Alleghanies and the Blue Ridge Mountains. Little did they care what this meant to New England! For more than half a century, "the ox horns pointed west, until folks began to wonder if anybody would be left in New England."

A large number of these colonists were from Connecticut. "They were characterized by thrift, industry, and the manner in which they established public schools." Even the money received from the sale of the Western Reserve was set aside by the State of Connecticut for the support of public schools.

All of this explains the arrival in our six hundred acre amphitheatre, of the Silver Swan, General Moses Cleaveland, and his Fifty Yankees, July 21, 1796. This landing in our coliseum, you are to remember, is the beginning of the city of Cleveland. And you are also to note that the natural resources of this new country are so great that we have asked the orchestra to begin playing the Cash Register Symphony. Something certainly is going to come out of this!

# II

## CITY OF SILK AND MONEY

In which a City is founded, named after the General:
it drops the "a," and basks in a Midas Spot Light: likewise
the record of a young couple from Connecticut, named
Crowell, who settle in Cleveland.

Now it came to pass that Herbert Briggs, Master of the Thirteenth District School, replied, "Since thou hast read all the other volumes of our little library, here is one filled with excellent counsel." It was the Wisdom of a King, which like a white light on dangerous reefs, flashed a signal to every age: "If riches increase, set not your heart *upon them.* God hath spoken once; twice have I heard this: that power belongeth unto God." (*Sketch Book*)

# CITY OF SILK AND MONEY

THE Silver Swan is at anchor behind the Sand Hill, so the story may proceed. (What would the Yankees have thought had they envisioned the Main Avenue High Level Bridge soaring far above their landing place?) General Cleaveland considered the mouth of the Cuyahoga River "the best spot since Buffalo." A landing party erected a rude cabin on the east bank to receive the stores of the settlers. The adjacent forests were "surveyed for public buildings with a green reserved for a public square." (That's right—The Cleveland Public Square.) "The General then located wide streets in the forests, contiguous to the square, one of which was the Buffalo Road." (Later some poor soul changed it to "Euclid Avenue.") He then sold six lots adjacent to the square to the following first proprietors:

"Richard M. Stoddard, Job B. Stiles,
Joseph Landen, Nathan Chapman, Wareham
Shipherd, and Mr. Baum."

Thus if you please, began the City of Cleveland, in the Forests of Cuyahoga. But you say, what became of the "a"? Tut, tut! that's a mere nothing at all! An editor of the Cleveland Advertiser in the year 1830, found that "Cleaveland" was just a little long for the top form, so he dropped the "a."

\* \* \*

Some rude person affirmed that from the first, Cleveland has been a city of silk and money. There is more than a measure of truth in this. Take as an example the parcel of ground on which the Hotel Cleveland stands. On March 18, 1802, the Connecticut Land Company sold Samuel Huntington "practically all the land on which the Terminal Tower Building is located." Ten years

later, April 20, 1812, Huntington sold to Henry Edwards all
frontage on the south side of the square (264 by 66) "for a yoke
of oxen six years old and $10." Shortly thereafter, the Edwards
heirs sold "the easterly half, 132 by 66, for $300."

Let the bell of the cash register and the click of the comptometer
now commingle with the orchestra music! That's the way we
want it! Money! Money! Watch the price soar on the hotel site!
In the year 1929 there was a popcorn wagon on a wee bit of the
open space. It paid an annual rental of $300 per square foot. And
now that the giant Terminal Tower and Hotel Cleveland Buildings dignify the Sam Huntington lot, only an expert in Washington could suggest the value. Everything in our Six Hundred Acre
Coliseum is just right for one of those lush periods of money-
making. Oil millionaires! foundry millionaires! ship building millionaires! sundry millionaires! And one of them is to be a lad about
to arrive in Sheriff Street—Henry Parsons Crowell.

\* \* \*

We are ready now to continue our Drachma Drama. Let us
make it a fast-moving sequence, after the best manner of a news-
reel. Imagine your favorite "voice" reading the following date
lines while the pictures flash on.

*1800*: The little four-year-old settlement nudges into the wilderness and begins to grow.

*1805*: First post office is established, and the settlement made
a port of entry.

*1809*: It becomes a county seat!

*1811*: First library.

*1814*: Incorporated a village.

*1816*: First bank! (Film speeded a bit to show customers rushing in and out.)

*1818*: First newspaper! And, look folks, it really has something to headline—There comes the first steamboat ever
to arrive in Cleveland, "The Walk-In-The Water." It may
look like a funny little tub to you, with its smoker between
the masts; but it's a new era! The boat has made the journey
from Buffalo in two days! On its third trip it required four
days by reason of getting stuck on a sandbar at Erie; and one
of the passengers was the father of President Fairchild of
Oberlin!

*1820*: Population is now 150, and the First Presbyterian Church is organized.

*1824*: Cleveland builds and launches its first "home-made steamboat."

*1825*: Cleveland gets a great impetus! On July 4 ground is broken for the first great national highway west of the Ohio, and, same day, ground is broken for the great Canal of the Ohio.

*1830*: Population 1,076.

*1834*: First edifice of the First Presbyterian Church dedicated, February 26.

*1836*: "The City of Ohio," population 1,235, on the west bank of the Cuyahoga, incorporates March 3. "The City of Cleveland" on the east bank of the Cuyahoga is caught napping, but she incorporates two days later with a population of 5,282. These two "cities" for the next eighteen years, are to fight like a pair of tomcats over the Cuyahoga clothes line.

*1839*: The State of Ohio produces fourteen million bushels of oats.

*1840*: Cleveland's population 6,071.

*1842*: June 25. Peter Weddell opens the new Weddell House at what is the corner of Sixth and Superior. The Rockefeller Building now occupies part of the site. It has a bronze historical tablet on the corner which is worth your reading some day. This is the hotel we asked you to remember.

*1844*: June 4. Preliminary meeting in the Session Room of First Presbyterian Church, north side Public Square, to form the Second Presbyterian Church "on authority of the charter of 1837." Nobody is mad about anything. The records want you to be sure of this. Nevertheless, you are puzzled to find the new organization purchases the edifice of First Congregational Church, northwest corner Public Square, a few doors from the First Church. Price $3,200.

*1844*: September 3. Rev. Sherman B. Canfield arrives to become the first pastor of the Second Presbyterian Church.

*1850*: Population 17,034.

*1852*: The Second Presbyterian Church sells the old Congregational Church to the Second Baptist Church, buys a lot on Superior Street "east of the Public Square, the site of the present Crocker Building": erects and enters a new edifice.

*1853*: First Presbyterian Church razes its edifice to make way for a new and larger building.

*1853*: May 16. Henry Luther Crowell and bride, Anna Eliza (Parsons) arrive in Cleveland from Connecticut. They join the Second Presbyterian Church.

*1853*: William Avery and Eliza Davison Rockefeller and son, John Davison, fourteen, move to Cleveland from Richford, New York.

*1854*: Population 33,000! A great new era dawns! The City of Ohio, and the City of Cleveland consolidate, forming Greater Cleveland.

Business and society life are becoming notable. Dr. Lemuel Wick is president of the City Bank, Third and Superior. Later, this becomes the National City Bank. "Dr. Wick was educated to be a physician: never practiced: became a banker instead." Don't forget this name! You will soon meet it again. Cleveland now has a considerable social register of folks who have "done well"; yes, very well. Within a few years the list will be enlarged to include such others as the Colemans, the Coffins; Dr. Martin Luther Brooks; Dr. Henry Justus Herrick; Joel Burton Parsons, "wholesale grocer to the West," whose sister Anna Eliza married Luther Crowell; and William Henry Waite, rising young stock broker who married another Parsons girl, Frances, "the beauty of the family." We want you to know that the City of Cleveland, only half a century old, is a coming metropolis of good Americans, with gingerbread brick houses, and period furniture.

*1855*: Rev. James Eells, D.D. of Penn Yan, New York, accompanied by his wife, arrives January 24 to become the second pastor of the Second Presbyterian Church. He arrives just in time to welcome the first-born in the home of the Henry Luther Crowells, on Sheriff Street. . . .

# III

# BROADCLOTH BACKGROUND

Boyhood of Henry Parsons Crowell, and the appearance
of a Great Peril in the Luther Crowell Home.

The constant aplomb of Mr. Crowell indicates a Broadcloth Background. Among his forebears were American pioneers, judges, Yale students, army officers, early business and professional men. Added thereto were years of contacts with captains of industry, inventors, and artisans from Brooklyn to Saskatoon. He was the very sort of a man in whose living room you would expect to find oil paintings of ancestors. The most formative of all factors, however, was the unfeigned faith he had from a child. The family altars of his forebears, the Crowells and the Parsons, glow like air-beacons across the night clear back to Colonial Days. In his own time, Mr. Crowell's fellowships were with the outstanding of all denominations: men committed to evangelical fervor, trinitarian faith, and sound doctrine. All of the foregoing help explain his quiet power, sure touch, and unbroken equanimity. (*Sketch Book*)

# BROADCLOTH BACKGROUND

*1855*: January 27. A frigid Erie Fury whips across the little City of Cleveland; snow in great windrows over Public Square; the blanketed horse of a family physician stands in front of a house in the new residence section, near the Public Square. The city papers announce,

"Born: To Henry Luther and Anna Eliza Crowell at 14 Sheriff Street a son, Henry Parsons Crowell."

*1855*: August 12. Dedication of the new edifice of the First Presbyterian Church, Public Square.

*1857*: New edifice destroyed by fire.

*1858*: January 17. Dedication of the Old Stone Church, third edifice of the First Presbyterian Church. (This building was "gutted by fire January 5, 1884, rebuilt within the old walls, and dedicated October 19, 1884." The historic building on the Public Square is virtually the building of 1858. Therein, on a Sabbath of 1945, you may hear Toronto-born Robert Bissett Whyte espouse "the same solid trinitarian doctrines in the same fine diction" of his notable predecessors in the previous century.)

\* \* \*

HENCEFORTH this narrative to avoid confusion, will call Henry Luther Crowell, father of Henry Parsons Crowell, "Luther." Luther was born of good leather in West Hartford, Connecticut, 1824, his father before him, a propos de bottes, being a wholesale shoe merchant. It is regrettable that the Crowells were not much given to writing down what they saw and felt. But, at that, the meagre records disclose that Luther was "a very efficient young man with a brilliant mind, and a natural leader"; that he was a Presbyterian closely attached to his church. "He had no patience with unsound doctrine, and was deeply in love with the Lord Jesus Christ." There are strong intimations of dreams of Yale, which were not realized; and a deep interest in the far West. The Yale affections he passed down to Henry Parsons

Crowell, as well as the "lung trouble" which entirely defeated a college education. During boyhood days in West Hartford, Luther sought every available fact about Madison, Wisconsin, and the Western Reserve. One of these places was to be his future home.

In Presbyterian circles of Hartford, he met a young lady, Anna Eliza Parsons. Miss Parsons came of a notable family. Her father, Dennis Asahel Parsons (1801-1844) took great pride in speaking of his great-great-grandfather, Samuel Parsons, who was a "Leftenant in the King's Service." "Leftenant" was not the way Asahel spelled it, but he was too near the British to pronounce it properly. Anna's mother came of the John Meachams of Eufield, Connecticut; Anna Eliza was born at West Granville, Massachusetts, a village twenty-five miles northwest of Hartford, September 8, 1828, and was therefore four years Luther Crowell's junior.

Luther poured out his enthusiasms about the West to Miss Parsons; discussed the question whether he would settle in Madison or Cleveland. Anna was not greatly concerned *where* he decided to go, just so that, when he did go, she would go along as Mrs. Crowell. The courtship flowered into a pretty little wedding at Hartford, Connecticut, October 19, 1852. The following year, Luther having decided on Cleveland, the young couple made the journey in a "new four-horse stage," which was as bizarre in those days as a helicopter in 1945. Thus the old records of the Forest City House on Superior Street bear the entry May 16, 1853,

"Henry Luther Crowell and wife, Cleveland, Ohio."

\* \* \*

The young couple made their first home at 14 Sheriff Street. Let it be recorded, it was a Christian home. Bride and groom, each of them, had those adequate experiences of Christ, which were to protect them not only against the perils of wealth, but equip them for the unforeseen sorrows of the morrow. That home was in the world but not of it. It never surrendered to the shabby things that creep into homes of wealth. It became a center of Christian interests, and visiting churchmen in the pulpits of both First and Second Presbyterian Churches were welcome guests.

Luther Crowell "went into business" immediately upon arrival in Cleveland, forming a partnership with another young man,

John Seymour, in the establishment of a wholesale shoe house. A year and a half later, January 27, 1855, as noted in the date line at the beginning of this chapter, his first son, Henry Parsons Crowell was born.    *    *    *

The quality of this narrative will be enriched by more detail about the conditions in which the child, Henry Parsons Crowell, was to grow up: his home, his friends, his church, his city. So we select the month of June as well suited for making observations, having no taste for Cuyahoga winters. We will imagine the year to be 1859, which was a critical juncture in the lives of the Luther Crowells.

The little family of three is now living, June, 1859, just opposite the birthplace. The money tide has been flowing very nicely into the bank account of the young shoe merchant, thank you. You could see this with half an eye by casually visiting the new home at 19 Sheriff Street. There is a "nursery" on the second floor, and several "spare rooms." In the double parlor are dark, satiny tables with claw-feet in bronze; in the dining room, dainty objects of virtú scattered about. There are bits of early American glass, shelved in sunny windows, gleaming like jewels in red, blue, and amber.

The Crowell home has a notable Presbyterian flavor. Dr. James Eells, who welcomed Henry Parsons Crowell into the world, "came of an ancestry which had for two hundred years without a break furnished ministers for Presbyterian and Congregational Churches in New England. Dr. Eells was thirty-two when he settled in Cleveland, tall and graceful in figure, everybody's friend, affable, courteous." Luther Crowell and his pastor, Dr. Eells were of about the same age. They formed "a distinguished friendship," to be further enlarged by the friendship of Henry Parsons Crowell, and Dr. Eells' nephew, Howard P. Eells. In a certain dramatic fall a few years later, the Crowell and Eells boys were to take "a train load" of young Cleveland aristocrats back with them to Greylock Institute.    *    *    *

In this month of June, 1859, we will walk west along Superior Street, beginning where the Cleveland Hotel is today. Even in

'59, there is still an occasional Conestoga wagon, with its broad-tired wheels, fluffing westward over the unpaved street. "Not as many though as there were twenty years ago," old timers will tell you. Times are changing. In 1859, smart travel is by four-horse passenger coaches; east to Buffalo, west to Detroit. On Superior Street, you see Frank Cain hacks; grand phaetons, with curving leather dashboards; dog carts, and society on horseback.

A little over a block west of the square, you come to Seneca Street. There stands the Weddell House, on land part of which will later be occupied by the Rockefeller Building. The corner makes a fine place to watch the crowds this June day in 1859. The women wear very full skirts, and carry tiny parasols, closed. We assume they were always closed; for no wood cut we ever found portrays a lady with one of these cob-webby tops open. . . . There are "gents with stovepipe hats, holding on to them." (It was windy then, too.) . . . There are boys dressed like little Lord Fauntleroys. . . . Ah, good reader, so far as the prosperous were concerned, it was Mayfair Year for the Glass of Fashion.

Look now at the business houses of 1859. On the ground floor of the Weddell House, beginning at the corner is the firm "J. B. Davis, Alaska Diamond Co." Then "W. H. Kelley, Banker"; and "The Atlantic and Pacific Telephone Co!" Look north on Seneca Street. There is a sign for you—"Seymour and Crowell, Wholesale Shoes." The junior member of that firm is our Luther Crowell, father of the lad, Henry Parsons. The firm is so well founded, that as Mr. Crowell said several times in the Green Court Interviews, "It is still in existence." The firm later became "Crowell and Childs." Later still "O. A. Childs Company." By any standard you select to use, Luther Crowell, in this year 1859, is a coming man in Cleveland. He has a fine four-year-old boy; his wife is greatly admired; he owns the attractive home on Sheriff Street; and the bankers, to use a modern term, will tell you, "Luther Crowell is gilt-edged."

\* \* \*

But in this month of June, 1859, the sable clouds of sorrow arch above the Luther Crowell home; such sorrows as have no balm save in Him who overcame the world. Luther at thirty-five, for a long time has had a pale, anemic appearance. Lately he has been losing weight and his physician has been troubled by his hacking cough—"the way his cold hangs on." On this certain day in June, 1859, the doctor confers quietly with Luther and Anna. He finally announces with that gentleness none but a family physician can exhibit, "Luther has consumption!" He said it in a way that deceived no one.

It was like a death sentence. The Luther Crowell home, with all its pleasant advantages, passed under a shadow; that pathetic, and hopeless hopefulness of a home where the white plague marks a victim.

# IV

## DEATH COMES TO THE SHOE MERCHANT

In which the Great Peril constrains Luther Crowell to set guards against riches before his life is ended; Henry Parsons Crowell as a lad enters "an adequate experience of Jesus": and, by reason of his friend, Howard Eells, sets his heart on attending Greylock Institute.

"I do not have a clear memory of my father, for I was only nine years old when he died, leaving mother and her three little sons. Nor do I have a clear memory of Dr. Hawks. But I do remember that day, when heartbroken, I went into his vestry in the Second Presbyterian Church, and he brought me to Jesus. What Dr. Hawks said and did were adequate, for I have never had occasion to change my early views excepting as I grew in grace, prayer, and Bible reading." (*Mr. Crowell in the Green Court Interviews*)

# DEATH COMES TO THE SHOE
# MERCHANT

*1860*: February 11. Born to Charles Dutton and Annie Caroline (Bayard) Wick at 83 Euclid Avenue, a daughter, Lillie Augusta Wick.

*1860*: June 24. Born to William B. and Mary E. Coleman, at Ravenna, Ohio, a daughter, Susan Coffin Coleman.

*1861*: Born New Year's Day, in the Sheriff Street House, Edward Robey Crowell, "little brother of Henry Parsons!" The Luther Crowells move into a new home at 361 Superior Street. Anna Eliza Crowell, its wealthy young mistress, is notably devoted to her church: "Mother lived within half a block of the Second Presbyterian Church. She was interested, and earnest, and devoted to it." (Mr. Crowell, Green Court Interviews.)

*1861*: April 21. Rev. Theron Hawks, D. D. of West Springfield, Massachusetts, succeeds Dr. Eells as pastor of the Second Presbyterian Church. Dr. Hawks is "scholarly in tastes, a pleasing, effective speaker, a devoted pastor," and altogether committed to the faith once delivered. "Through his fiery evangelism two hundred were added to the church in the next seven years."

*1862*: November 23. The physician comes again to the home of the Luther Crowells: another baby brother for Henry Parsons, Charles Burton Crowell.

*1863*: Death of Charles Dutton Wick, father of Lillie Augusta. To meet the tragic need of the young widow and her baby daughter, Grandfather Dr. Lemuel Wick moves in at 283 Euclid.

*1865*: Charles Grandison Finney is a guest of Dr. Hawks. Finney observes the dangerous prosperity in the Second Church, and declares that "wealth must be held as a stewardship for God, or it will prove a curse." A powerful revival breaks out, and the fires of God glow throughout the homes of the church.

35

LUTHER CROWELL, "aware of his short day" became intensely conscious of the dangers of wealth. Did he not have three little boys who might be ruined by his prosperity? He had observed, first in his Connecticut home town, and now in Cleveland, that money kept for two or three generations, will either poison its possessors, or, impart a fine mellowness. He heard it affirmed in his church, and read it in his Bible, that when money is made without God, or is kept without God, the children are almost certain to become mean and vicious. But if "God is the Head of this House," an excellent poise would settle upon the members of such a home. Money can buy air and sunshine and azaleas; and *his* three little boys *might* need sunshine very greatly. In case of sickness, money can secure good doctors and nurses. Wealth makes for happy and healthy summers, and Georgia hams. There may be trips to Paris and London, and the family becomes trained and traveled.

Money can put sofas into living rooms, and the rise of civilization may be traced in the evolution of the sofa. You come by chapters down from the massy slab, on three legs, whereon King Alfred sat, to the four-legged beauty with twisted feet, and costly tapestry cover, portraying a parrot with twin cherries in its beak. Money secures silver plate by Lamerie, or china by Sevres. It hangs portraits on the walls, done by a Boston Copley, or a Narragansett Stewart. These portraits, hanging darkly, do something to you. Even the portrait of Aunt Hepsibah, with her high-waisted bodice, and balloon-topped sleeves, face as sharp as a shingler's hatchet—you were helped some way by the picture, even if none came from Hepsibah.

The children of these homes of advantage, especially the young females, take a fine butter-nut finish. The young females in turn, are in the market for similar young men. And so it goes, on and on! Unless! . . .

*Unless,* the home "forgets its God and begins to live to the flesh." Therefore, for the sake of three little boys, this home had to be centered in Christ. "Christ was the head." The tithe, which he had brought to the storehouse of God, was no longer adequate for Luther's new vision. Luther and Anna profoundly wished, therefore, to make sure the sacrifice was bound with cords, even to the horns of the altar.

\* \* \*

*1864*: November 20. The crisis of death darkens the Crowell home on Superior Street. Henry Parsons Crowell, nine, is frightened, unable to grasp the significance. In the afternoon when it was evident Luther would die, Uncle William Henry Waite, the one who married Frances Parsons, "the beauty of the family," took Harry away. When they returned at dusk, there was the sound of mourning in the house. Luther Crowell, his father, dead of tuberculosis at forty-three! It beat upon the boy's mind how devout his father had been; how successful; how good to his boys. When later Harry learned that his father had given him twenty-seven thousand dollars in cash, the money didn't seem his own at all. No, it was still his father's: better, it belonged to his Heavenly Father. He was under obligation to use it with wisdom; in fact, all money was a stewardship, a holy trust.

*1866*: Howard Eells, twelve, enters Greylock Institute, and begins to urge his friend, Henry Parsons Crowell, eleven, to matriculate there in 1867: "I also plan to go to Yale, Harry. Greylock Institute's best place to do preparatory work."

\* \* \*

Mercifully the future was veiled to Henry Parsons Crowell. He could not see that his brother Edward, now six, was to die of the same disease at twenty-eight; that the life of his brother, Charles, now four, was similarly to end at thirty-nine. Nor did he dream that conditions were already in his own body which marked him for death before the age of twenty—*but for the grace of God!*

\* \* \*

The sympathy of the Dr. Hawks' pastoral heart shone out in the next few days; his prayers, his presence in the bereaved home; his memorial sermon in the church, wherein without discounting Luther's success, he spoke of Luther's faith in Christ as the Pearl of great price; then the final commitment in the Woodland Cemetery.

As the family tarried about the newly-made grave, Dr. Hawks quietly comforted the little boys. When he came to Harry, the boy sobbed, "Dr. Hawks, could I see you tomorrow?"

To the evangelical heart of Dr. Hawks, the coming of the bereaved lad to his study was nought else than Providence. With anointed grace, Dr. Hawks talked to Harry of the Light of the World, prayed with him. And when the pair arose to their feet, the boy was on that Great Rock Foundation! "He never desired in all the years that followed to depart from the Lord." The beauty of his faith was presently reflected in his letters home. When he left the Pastor's study, there was a glory in his soul that all the world was to witness for the next three quarters of a century.

\* \* \*

Immediately after the death of Luther Crowell, Uncle Joel Burton Parsons of Hartford, Connecticut, moved into the Crowell home "to act as guardian for the three boys." A little later, he married and brought his wife to live there. Mr. Parsons was at this time thirty-four years of age; his wife a Cincinnati girl, somewhat younger. A warm fellowship developed between the couple and the three boys, particularly in the case of Harry. Some years later, Mr. Parsons was to have a leading part in Harry's going into the oatmeal business. The old records show that as late as 1873, the Parsons were still living with Mrs. Luther Crowell.

Mr. Crowell summarized conditions in the broken home during the Green Court Interviews: his father left his mother in good circumstances, and she carried on with the three little boys just as she thought her husband would have had it. To the boys, she held up high ideals of faith, obedience to the will of God; if it were in the will of God she wanted all her boys to receive a good education—Yale University if possible.

\* \* \*

"The School of the Believing Widow" exhibited its full powers in the hard years that followed; and the Presence of God abode upon the home of the growing boys. Blessed are the young Samuels who are lighted to their beds by the lamps of the sanctuary, and awakened by the sound of the morning hymn!

V

## SCHOOL DAYS IN GREYLOCK

Howard Eells persuades Harry Crowell to attend the
School at South Williamstown, Massachusetts: Author's
journey to the school site in the fall of 1944.

On October 18, 1944, a full account of the Greylock Journey was sent to Mr. Crowell. "I'm so glad you went," he wrote a few hours before his death. And I was glad, too. Of all the lovely pictures that hang on memory's wall, none are more hallowed than the time spent amid the fall glories of the Berkshire Mountains, at the ancient site of Greylock Institute. Here, more than anywhere else, young Crowell had confirmed in his life the things he heard as a lad in his Cleveland home, and from his pastor on Superior Street. (*Sketch Book*)

# SCHOOL DAYS IN GREYLOCK

HOWARD EELLS returned from Greylock Institute to Cleveland in the summer of 1867, determined "to make a Greylock man out of Harry Crowell." The boys were constantly together during the vacation days, and Howard frequently repeated his favorite theme: "You *must* go back with me to Greylock next fall, Harry. It's just the place to do your Yale prep work." Thereupon, with boyish enthusiasm, Eells would describe the Berkshire school.

"The building sits on a hill like a great noble palace, with high mountains all around. Every season of the year is wonderful. In October the maples turn red, and we boys go out gathering hickory and beechnuts, chestnuts and hognuts. As November passes, there's feasting; and the pond freezes over. Then comes toboggans, and bob sleds, and snow shoes, and skating to Emmett's Corners or right down to the village. In spring, the snow melts off the mountains, the storm windows are taken down, and the boys climb out on the cornice for a better view of Mt. Greylock. We certainly look funny in our white night gowns, running the cornice like ghosts, until a monitor comes! . . . Do you like to fish? Well, the streams around the school are filled with gay, speckled beauties. . . ."

"How are the sports at Greylock?" Harry would ask. "You know I like athletics."

This would bring Howard's enthusiasm to a climax: "We have the world's finest players, the immortal ball nine of Greylock. They knock the spots off Williams and Pittsfield: and football, too! There are tennis clubs, a fine gymnasium" . . .[1]

---

[1] Howard's panegyric is based upon an effusion excelling in the awkward beauty of a lad's poetry. It was printed in the Greylock Record of 1888, and is filed in the Berkshire Athenaeum.

Both of the lads were earnest Christians, marked by the fervor of the Finney revivals, so their conversation turned to the Congregational Church; to the devoted Christian teachers: and as a climax, to "the noble President, Mr. Mills." Eells won his case during the summer vacation, thus giving a notable date line for the book:

> *1867*: October. Henry Parsons Crowell matriculates as a student in Greylock Institute, Berkshire County, Massachusetts.

* * *

Mr. Crowell insisted that the scenes of his old school, Greylock, be visited. As to other places associated with his life, he thought it would be worth-while to go to Cedar Rapids or to Cheyenne. But when it came to his old school, "I *want* you to go to Greylock." Then he drew a map showing how to get there. Fortunate that the map was drawn, for Greylock ceased so long ago that it is scarcely a memory in Berkshire County.

The site of Greylock Institute is a hilltop on U. S. Highway Number Seven, fifteen miles north of Pittsfield or five miles south of Williamstown. No type of public transportation was available on Number Seven north of Pittsfield, so the six dollar round-trip taxi fare seemed reasonable. Albert Betters, taximan, was worth the tariff as a baedeker. The cab sped northward from Pittsfield along the very road Harry Crowell rode in a Tallyho seventy-seven years before. It was the seventeenth of October, with the roadside maples in flaming crimson, which prompted the query,

"When will it snow?"

"Any day now . . . see that house? Charlie Sabin was born there, the same Sabin that headed up the New York Guaranty Trust. He was a Greylock boy, helped make his way by selling candy to the students from a soap box. Charlie loved Berkshire County. Wanted to be buried on the old farm, but his first wife thought it was too plain. . . . He made a lot of money, but it didn't do him much good, and he didn't do much good with it." (We thought of another Greylock boy who made a lot of money and did a lot of good with it.)

The speeding taxi rounded Lake Pontoosuc, walled off to the west by Tower Mountain. . . . All too soon, the taximan said,

"This is as far as the O.P.A. will let me drive." It was far enough. We had arrived at the Greylock Hill. The taxi came to a stop in front of an ancient two story building, occupied by a grocery. Several other ancient houses were scattered about. This was South Williamstown! Thomas Steel, groceryman, was in perfect keeping with the by-passed village.

"This building," he said of his grocery, "used to be the hotel where Greylock boys spent their time. Right behind those shelves was an old fireplace, now bricked over, and just to the left of the fireplace was a picture one of the boys painted on the wall."

Sure enough, there, in ancient oil, behind the shelves, blackened and cracked with years, was a panel five-by-five, portraying a deer in the pines.

"See that hole?"

Steel put his finger on a perforation in the plaster through the deer's head.

"Charlie Sabin shot it one day to prove to the boys he was good with a pistol."

We made our way to the hilltop, fifty feet above the road, where the school building once stood. Nothing remains today but an old colonial house, just north of the site of the school building, grass-grown drives and some foundation scars. But the view which Harry Crowell loved is the same as it was years ago. To the east lay Hopper Valley, formed by Mt. Williams, Deer Ridge, and the lofty serenity of Greylock Mountain, which at 3,505 feet is Massachusett's highest summit. Not only the highest, but the best loved: in proof of which one has only to regard the shelf of books on Greylock Mountain to be found in the Public Library of New York City. Westward lie the Berlin Hills and Hancock Valley: in the distance the Vermont summits. No wonder Mr. Crowell said so often, "It was a beautiful place!"

\* \* \*

The taxi sped back to Pittsfield thru a lane of Autumn Gold that the research might be continued in the Berkshire Athenaeum. On the shelves of this building are one thousand volumes of the library of Oliver Wendell Holmes, presented in 1903 by Justice Holmes, "Because my father, Oliver Wendell Holmes and I held summer residence here for years; and because my grandfather, Rev. Abiel Holmes, was one of the original proprietors of the township of Pittsfield."

You would fall in love with the country yourself! Pittsfield is a fine, solid village of beautiful public buildings, and what a hotel! . . . I wrote to Deborah, "Some day soon, we're coming to Hotel Wendell for a vacation." . . . In the forgotten records of Greylock Institute, preserved in the Athenaeum, the research was completed. Therein were some photographs for this book, which we had never hoped to find.

\* \* \*

The photograph of the main building of Greylock Institute (See page 17) was produced from the treasure trove of things old by Miss Fannie G. Clark, Historical Librarian of the Berkshire Athenaeum. It is not the picture of the same building which young Harry Crowell knew. That building was destroyed by fire, and the one pictured in this book was built in 1872. However, the new building is so much a copy of the original, that but little difference may be noted. . . . In 1890, the school was discontinued: "I infer, without proof," writes Miss Clark, "because of a diminishing student body." From 1908, the buildings were occupied by the Idlewild Hotel. In 1930 "the landmark was demolished . . . and only the colonial dwelling where Mr. and Mrs. Charles A. Mills started housekeeping was left intact."

Do not be surprised, then, if country folk round about South Williamstown say to you, "I never heard of Greylock." In the Athenaeum records, however, you will find what you want concerning Greylock Institute:

> "Founded spring of 1842 by B. F. Mills and brother, J. A. Mills . . . students came from Albany by coach . . . enlarged 1853 . . . again 1862 . . . destroyed by fire 1872 . . . rebuilt same year . . . in 1888, (two years prior to discontinuance) a total of more than 1300 students had registered."
> The old catalogs, moreover, are filled with colorful notations . . . It was "the Select Family School for Boys . . . limited in number . . . the charge (in 1850) for board, washing, mending, use of library, fuel, bed, bedding, and C, $75.00 per term of half year . . . (later) $450.00 per year . . .

several rooms are furnished with stoves . . . to pupils occupying these rooms $6.00 extra is charged for the winter term
. . . an accurate account of daily recitations, delinquencies will
be transmitted to the parents . . . regular church attendance
required." In the catalog of 1878, the name of Edward Roby
Crowell is listed as a student in the classical department.

\* \* \*

The ancient records of Greylock are a trove that should challenge a Berkshire Walter Scott. But the chief interest of this school
of long ago, is the story of its founder, Benjamin Franklin Mills.
As a boy, Mills wanted to go to Yale: found his dreams were
broken off; then resolved to give his life to making education
easier for other boys. The following chapter will record briefly
the story of his devotion to this purpose. His life was of a kind
with that of Mark Hopkins. Some day, let us hope, Mills' biography will receive due study.

# VI

# WHAT WAS THAT ABOUT MARK HOPKINS?

The romance of a capitalized disappointment . . .
Harry Crowell as a student . . . his health fails—just like
that of his father.

Those adequate enthusiasms through which men live are generally imparted by a teacher. *"Thou* wilt light my candle," sang the Poet of Zion. Some have described this process of spiritual energizing as "imparting a ferment": and its philosophy is simple, indeed. It begins when the man-to-be-trained admires his instructor: presto! The work is done. "Affection is a coal that must be cool'd: Else, suffer'd, it will set the heart on fire." Thereafter, the teacher, through whom our disparate parts became a living whole, is praised upon every remembrance. Mention the name of Le Baron Russell Briggs of Harvard to Robert Benchley or Edward Weeks! Or speak of Herbert Briggs to the Boys of the Old Thirteenth! Likewise, the affections of the Master of Green Court for Benjamin Franklin Mills of Greylock never cooled. (*Sketch Book*)

# WHAT WAS THAT ABOUT MARK HOPKINS?

BENJAMIN FRANKLIN MILLS, founder of Greylock Institute, was born March 13, 1816, at South Williamstown, Massachusetts, where his grandfather was an early settler. His father, Reed Mills, grew up in the little mountain village, and married Abagail Comstock, a young woman of German descent, who lived on a nearby farm. Mills was farm-born in that New England era when the very atmosphere he breathed was surcharged with deep religious convictions, and a reverence for college education. This explains the amazing fact familiar to all who know the back country of New England; unpretentious mountain villages, and impoverished farms are the birthplaces for a great company of top-rank American statesmen, clergymen, authors, scientists, teachers, and men of affairs.

This emphasis upon sound doctrine, moral probity, and a trained mind were so continuously held before young Mills that he could not remember just when the dream of a college education began. His purposes, at the age of sixteen, were further confirmed by the brilliant career of another man, fourteen years his senior, Mark Hopkins of Williams College. Hopkins at thirty had made a name for himself as physician, scholar, and minister. At the age of thirty-four he became president of Williams College. The school was always, more or less, forced to operate with inadequate equipment. But the "beneficent influence of Hopkins over the student body, by reason of his great learning, moral strength, and symmetry of character," caused someone to observe in later years, "A university is a log with a boy on one end, and Mark Hopkins on the other." Mills saw much of Hopkins, since his farm home was but four miles from Williams College.

But Mills' dreams of college were utterly defeated. Like Joseph, however, his very defeat became the occasion of his greatest achievement. To secure the funds needed for college, he left the farm to clerk in a shoe store. His unusual abilities caused the owner of the store to make young Mills a partner in the business; then through mismanagement, the owner, three years later, failed and left Mills heavily indebted. It was a debt of honor: the young man gave himself to its settlement and was enabled to pay in full. But by the time the debt was paid, he was twenty-five, and college doors seemed closed. His dreams were broken off; he must go through life without a formal education.

Thereupon, a crusader's purpose captured his heart: "If I cannot have an education myself, I am going to help other boys to get one." Singular indeed, that no novelist or biographer has evaluated the story of Benjamin Franklin Mills!

In keeping with his purpose, he secured near his home a tract of farm and mountain land of a little over one hundred acres. A small structure sat on the central hilltop of this one hundred acres which could serve as a school building. In 1842, at the age of twenty-six, he sent out the announcement of "the opening of Greylock Institute at South Williamstown." Two students responded! In the next four years, the attendance never exceeded twenty-five.

But the sheer excellence of "his corporate zeal in an unincorporated school" was reported so widely that, in 1872, the building had grown into what Howard Eells called "a grand, noble palace." It had paid all its bills in full! Boys from the best families of the entire Eastern area of America were in attendance. At fifty-six, Mills considered his purposes accomplished and prepared to retire.

But on April 14, 1872, a disastrous fire destroyed the entire physical equipment of Greylock. No one but Mills himself was interested enough to rebuild. He reconfirmed his purpose, "I want boys to get what I couldn't." With rare courage, he financed a new building at $80,000 secured by his own notes. He refused either to solicit or receive a penny's help from anyone. He was once more successful, "paid out in full, and the institution continued as long as its life lasted; i.e. until the death of President Mills." [1]

\* \* \*

As in the case of his neighbor, President Hopkins, the real achievement of President Mills was the power he exerted over boys by reason of his moral strength, symmetry of character, and the personal interest he gave to each of them. He often said, "To me, every boy is a prayerful study, and I constantly seek the help of the Lord in dealing with them. Every boy is a member of my home."

If that has the sound of out-moded orthodoxy, we must make the most of it. He was an "old-time Congregationalist" holding membership, first in the Williamstown Church, later as a charter member in the South Williamstown Congregational Church. His faith had no tolerance for any form of unbelief. To him Jesus was born of a virgin; was Himself the very person of God; His blood alone the ground of salvation. These things he taught in the Sunday school and then drove home in the classes at the Institute. A contemporary of Mills thus speaks of his classroom labors:

> "He taught them the goodness of knowledge.
> He taught them the goodness of God."

He was a quiet man with a disconcerting habit of just listening to you. You told him your plans, your wishes. He listened in friendly silence. Finally, somewhat puzzled, you said, "What would *you* do, Mr. Mills?" He told you! You did it. No one ever tried to deny that in his dealing with men, Mills was an autocrat; but such a lovable one! He never insisted on imposing his own will. You asked him to do it.

Young Crowell admired him without reserve. His own father (Luther) was gone; President Mills took his place. To Harry Crowell, it was like heaven just to be with President Mills. And the President often looked affectionately into the face of the boy and said,

"Take your time, Harry. Be sure to find the will of God."

[1] These annals cannot follow the subsequent career of Mills, save to remark that his vigor and integrity caused his election as a Democratic Senator of Massachusetts in 1856, and in 1870, "Democrats and Republicans alike sent him to the Lower House of Congress."

When you look at the photograph of Mr. Crowell at eighty-seven, and it seems to say, "Take your time; find the will of God," you are simply listening to a continuance of the ideals of a certain good teacher, Benjamin Franklin Mills.

\* \* \*

Thus Greylock became the home of Harry Crowell as he was preparing for Yale from the ages of twelve to seventeen. When he and Howard Eells returned to Cleveland in the vacation of 1868, they persuaded Henry Hussey to attend Greylock the next fall. In the vacation of 1869, Crowell, Eells, and Hussey lined up five more boys. And when they entrained in Cleveland, in the fall of 1870, they had so enthusiastically portrayed Greylock to Cleveland lads that it was necessary to charter an entire Pullman sleeper to get them to the Pittsfield Tallyhos.

\* \* \*

If this biography were to be of a size with Lockheart's *Life of Scott,* much material of liveliest interest is available concerning Greylock days. This part of the annal, however, is concluded with bits of detail concerning Harry's progress in his studies. As to his grades, a reproduction of the Quarterly Report of March 25, 1870, is herein printed, as well as a letter, dated July 15, 1867, signed by George F. Mills, brother of President Mills. The quarterly report shows good standing in attendance, and "perfect recitations," and grades his general behavior as "No. I." George Mills' letter is of interest also . . . "Harry's gentlemanly bearing and obedient spirit . . . winning the confidence and esteem of his teachers . . . a very nice boy, and these we like to have with us."

Harry's letters to his mother, of which a sample is submitted, show the same great care in composition and writing that marked his career as a business man:

South Williamstown
May 17th,/67.

My Dear Mother:

The leaves are coming out very nicely here. How have they got along with the stores next to you? I spoke "The Kentucky Hunter" last Wednesday. It is warmer here in the middle of the day but about the same in the mornings and evenings. I like my roommate very much. I got my clock fixed very nicely and it keeps splendid time. Howdie gave me that sheet of paper and so I wrote you on it to let you see what kind of paper they have here. My finger improved very nicely after you left and is quite well now. I brush my teeth every morning. I went over and played Base Ball the other day and when we were playing a boy named Frank fell from a beam in the barn and sprained his hand very badly. Mr. Charles Mills is President of the Greylock Base Ball Club. I am in the third nine: my position is Short Stop. I have not heard from Aunt Fannie yet. I wrote to Aunt Jane the other day. Tell Charlie Keith to answer my letter as soon as he can. I would like to hear from the other boys very much. I have only received two letters and those are from you. I am in Mr. Charlie Mills' class at Sunday School. I am not a bit home sick now. I hope that Warren and the girls are well. You must tell me all the news in Cleveland. You forgot to give me some stamps when I came away and I wish that you would send me some. It is 9 o'clock and I must go to bed. Love to all.

Your affectionate son,
Harry P. Crowell [1]

All in all, Harry's school days are the conventional record of a normal, American boy.

\*   \*   \*

In the Green Court Interviews, Mr. Crowell said, "I was never a brilliant student. I was athletically inclined. Thoroughly enjoyed the gym. Had gym suits tailor-made. (Rather! look again at the exquisite tailoring of the scholar in the previous chapter!) I was good at baseball, a leader in athletics, and pretty well developed. Greylock was a beautiful Christian school and meant everything to me. The teachers were such earnest Christians, especially President Mills. He has been a great influence over my life for seventy-five years. . . . I was never sick at the beginning. But gradually my health failed. I was taken out when I was seventeen!"

\*   \*   \*

Taken out when he was seventeen! Never to go further in school! To Yale or anywhere else! In his last two years at Grey-

---

[1] In Mr. Crowell's youth, he was often called "Harry," and often signed himself "Harry."

lock, his "cold hung on"; just as it did with his father, Luther. His color changed, his weight fell dangerously low. On April 14, 1872, he tearfully watched "the great, noble palace" burn to the ground. The boys were dismissed, and the Cleveland group went home. "Be prepared to return next fall; we will resume school, and will be able to take care of you," was the text on the bulletin given to the lads.

But Harry Crowell was not to return in the fall of 1872, or any other fall. The Cleveland physician examined him critically. Then he said to Anna Eliza, "Harry will have to stop school or die. He has lung trouble . . . just like his father."

# VII

## THE MINISTRY OF ADVERSITY

He enters a ten-year period of broken health, but makes a vow at the very beginning which is to panoply his entire life.

Thereupon, the boy's dreams became tear-faded threads. Oftentimes in the lulls of trade, he gazed without seeing through the Seneca Street windows of the shoe store. Where would he be ten years from now? Clerking in a shoe store? Perhaps, ten years from now, he wouldn't be working at all—. His mind went to the grassy plot in Woodland Cemetery where his young father was buried.

These melancholy meditations were frequent and involuntary. They made him feel like a trapped animal. A critical ten years lay ahead of him. He had not the slightest idea as to the outcome.

But the God of all grace knew. Those ten years were to permanently subdue a man's will to the will of God. In the future, that man was to endow Christian institutions, put Moody Bible Institute on a sure foundation, and he had to be tempered so he could be trusted with millions. (*Sketch Book*)

# THE MINISTRY OF ADVERSITY

EELLS and Crowell continued their Cleveland fellowships during the summer of 1872. But in Crowell's heart there was a sense of defeat which Eells' optimism had no power to allay. In the fall, Howard Eells was to begin his first year in Yale University, and, following the Greylock pattern, he was to be the forerunner for his younger friend, Harry Crowell. Often, during vacation days, Eells with the easy optimism of good health said, "You'll be all right, Harry. A year out of school, private instruction, and you can go back with me to Yale in 1873."

But there was to be no private instruction. On this point the doctor was firm. "Harry is a very sick boy. His only hope is to drop out of school entirely. Perhaps it would be good for him to do some sort of work." It was natural, therefore, for Harry in the fall of 1872, to go to work for the shoe firm, Crowell and Childs, where his father had been senior partner. Fall and winter passed with some degree of pleasure. He enjoyed the shoe business. In the Green Court Interviews, Mr. Crowell chuckled, "I was supposed to take it easy, but I worked as hard as any of the clerks."

Harry Crowell's interest in the Bible deepened. His disappointment launched that close attention to the Word which continued unbroken for nearly three quarters of a century. In the Green Court Interviews he said:

"I was reading the Bible sufficiently in 1873 to realize the emphasis God put on the number seven . . . Seven years! Perhaps I might get well in seven years! I saw, too, that my gratitude to God must be expressed in tithing."

So he brought to the Second Presbyterian Church week by week, a tenth of his income. Thus, beginning to tithe on three figures, he subsequently found it easy to continue to tithe when his income rose to seven figures.

Then, too, he delighted in the Boys' Bible Class taught by Dr. Martin Luther Brooks. This sturdy old physician made him think of President Mills. It was a joy to hear the Doctor's solid expositions of faith. Dr. Brooks' earnest words on personal devotion and honor; unquestioning belief and stern orthodoxy further emphasized what President Mills had taught.

But there was one person in the Second Presbyterian Church whom he greatly missed summer and fall, 1873. "The little Wick girl," now twelve, had left Cleveland in January, accompanied by her mother, to continue her studies in Germany. There she was to remain three years, two in a school at Stuttgart, Germany, and one traveling over the Continent. In the party also was her grandfather, Dr. Lemuel Wick.

\* \* \*

The most influential event in the two years of Harry's life as a shoe clerk was a meeting held in the Second Presbyterian Church in the spring of 1873. Pastor Eells had invited a young business man named D. L. Moody "to bring a message." Moody had become widely known as an evangelist, and had planned to be in Great Britain in 1873, holding meetings in a number of cities. Liverpool churches had promised to advance him money for traveling expenses; but week after week passing with no word from Liverpool, Moody accepted Dr. Eells' invitation. During the service, Harry did not take his eyes from the dynamic Moody.

In the address, Moody said his heart had been on fire to get to England to win ten thousand souls for Christ. He liked to think big things for God. The Lord deserved it. Whether it was money, or evangelism, or what, one should dream great things for God! Then he told how Henry Varley had said to him the year before in a Dublin haymow:

"The world has yet to see what God can do with and for and through and in a man who is fully and wholly consecrated to Him.

"Ah, friends, that was the word of God to my soul! The world has yet to see! With and for and through and in! A man! Varley meant *any* man! Varley didn't say he had to be educated, or brilliant, or anything else! Just, *a man!* Well, with the Holy Spirit in me, I'll be *one* of those men! And now that's why I want to dream great things for God; to get back to Great Britain and win ten thousand souls!"

\* \* \*

Young Crowell could not hold his tears back:

"Moody's words were the words of the Lord to me. I saw now that the wrecking of my school plans didn't really matter. God didn't need his men educated, or brilliant, or anything else! All God needed was just a man! Well by the grace of God, I would be God's man! To be sure, I would never preach like Moody. But I could make money and help support the labors of men like Moody. Then I resolved, 'Oh God, if you will allow me to make money to be used in Your service I will keep my name out of it so You will have the glory.' "

He was so powerfully affected, so fearful of breaking down that he slipped out of the service to walk along the lake side. For a long time he walked beside the waters, saying over and over to himself, "God shall have the glory! God shall have all the glory!" [1]

\* \* \*

It is difficult to regard these matters unmoved. That day there arose in the heart of young Mr. Crowell, the resolution which finally made it safe for him to be trusted with millions. Adversity thus became the matrix in which his enabling idealism was born.

---

[1] Mr. Crowell smiled in the memory of the incident: "I never heard Moody again. Didn't shake hands with him. Never saw him again." (*Green Court Interviews*)

# VIII

## HE FINDS A PROMISE

His interest is attracted to the frequency with which the number seven is used in the Scriptures; he curiously begins to wonder if he is to recover his health in seven years; then he finds a remarkable text which he takes as a promise to himself.

"He shall deliver thee in six troubles: yea, in seven there shall no evil touch thee" (*Job 5:19*).

# HE FINDS A PROMISE

DURING the months following Moody's Cleveland visit, Harry's health declined rapidly,[1] but his increase "in wisdom and stature and in favour" was equally evident. Not that he had ever lacked in these graces since the day "he took Christ" in Dr. Hawks' study, but the fiery trial seemed greatly to refine and strengthen him. He gave more time than ever to Bible study. His letters at this period show a depth of purpose which characterized the rest of his life. In a note to a friend, he writes:

"I pray you may enter more fully the Paradise of God's love. Oh, for a deeper, clearer view of Him who is the Creator and Inspirer of all. Let us dwell longer at the feet of Jesus, that we may lead many souls to the Spring of Everlasting Life."

The memorabilia also reveals a surprising grasp on Christian doctrine. Professional religionists, "men in the God-business," were often misled by Crowell's reserve, and were inclined to be patronizing toward him; "Mr. Crowell is an ardent layman, but untrained. He doesn't understand." He understood, no mistake. In the interviews, he spoke of a certain discreet modernist whose public utterances were carefully fashioned so as to avoid giving alarm; "For three years, now, this man's subject matter has lacked the savor of life." Yet Mr. Crowell always treated the man in question with courtesy and thoughtful consideration; he was even a house guest in Green Court. But this man never dreamed that Mr. Crowell had noted his deficiency, and had taken his measure.

It was during the fiery trial that Harry received assurances of deliverance. By August, 1874, he was in such a miserable state that he was obliged to give up secular work, and spend his time "resting." His attention to the Word, however, continued.

[1] A considerable part of this period was spent in bed under the care of Dr. Wier Mitchell.

One feature, particularly, attracted his interest; how frequently the Bible referred to the number seven. The Spirit specified seven men of honest report; the wicked prophet built seven altars, and gained the ear of God: seven cubits was the width of the door; seven weeks and Messiah should be cut off; seven baskets-full! seven golden candlesticks! "He became aware of the importance God attached to the number seven."

One night, with Cuyahoga summer in the air, he read a passage in Job, "He shall deliver thee in six troubles: yea, in seven there shall no evil touch thee." He was so startled, he closed the Book. He felt it was the word of God for him; for him, Henry Parsons Crowell! A light of assurance, brighter than midday filled his heart; "In seven there shall no evil touch thee." Of the meaning he did not fully know; but he was sure the Lord was comforting him. He was not to die at an early age! He would live! Yes, he would live to a good age, and make a lot of wealth for the work of the church. . . . And when this wealth was gained, it would never be his; he was to be merely a steward . . . he would never let himself get in the way of the glory of God . . . all would be well . . . all he had to do was to wait and see the salvation of the Lord.

\* \* \*

His condition became so critical that his doctors held a consultation, then made a surprising recommendation: "Harry Crowell has to live out-of-doors the *next seven years!* or else!"

When he heard these words, he turned away quickly and hastened to his room; he was afraid of breaking down. So, that was it! "In seven there shall no evil touch thee!" The Lord was to heal him in seven years out-of-doors! How swiftly, he thought, God answered his need! . . .

The next problem was, where should he go? Certain Cleveland friends who had returned from a western trip immediately urged him to go to Colorado. "Denver is the very place for you; cool summer nights; open winters with abundance of sunshine." They were enthusiastic about it: "It's a coming city. The Rocky Mountains stand off to the West, with their deep-blue shoulders, and snowcapped summits."

Everything fitted together. In seven years of out-of-doors he was to be delivered; "in seven no evil shall touch thee." It seemed that God wanted him to begin the seven years at Denver. By September, he could be on his way. How wonderfully God's answers came!

We leave it to the earth-bound of pulpit or professor's chair to label such experiences "childish," and to dismiss them with civil leer. For our part, we have no heart for such presumption; nay, we must even watch respectfully while men seeking His will, "open the Book at random." The Eternal of Days continuously speaks to his chosen in ways mysterious, and by songs in the night.

# IX

## SEVEN YEAR QUEST

He journeys far in quest of health; seven years out-of-doors, and he is delivered from disease; thereupon, at the moment of his healing, he is offered the little Quaker Mill in Ravenna.

"Seven years in search of health! And health was found! The hand of God was clearly in it all. He had moved me right along, every inch of the way in those seven years. He took me out of the first farm through a tornado, and out of the second by a hot wind. And now that my health was restored, He was opening the way for me to secure the Quaker Mill. I felt compelled to go to my room to thank Him for all of His blessings." (*H. P. C. in the Green Court Interviews*)

# SEVEN YEAR QUEST

## FIRST YEAR: FALL OF 1874—FALL OF 1875

IN SEPTEMBER, 1874, three years after he was forced to discontinue his education at Greylock, Harry Crowell began his determined quest for health. In late September, "alone," as he several times remarked, he boarded the train in Cleveland on his way to Denver. The word "alone" indicated poignant memories, perhaps misgivings, therefore,

"Did you have any doubt as to your ultimate recovery, Mr. Crowell?"

"No, I felt assurance in my heart I would get well. But, I was only nineteen. I suppose I was lonesome."

Chicago's vigor in repairing the ravages of the disastrous fire of October, 1871, greatly interested him as he walked through the business section. He reached the station of the Chicago and North Western Railroad; "a temporary terminal," built to replace the one at Kinzie and Wells, which had been destroyed by the fire. This temporary terminal which was to meet his eye for several years to come, stood near Canal and Kinzie, on the west bank of the North Branch of the Chicago River. Meanwhile "the great new Wells Street Station" was being erected; and as a matter of interest for young Chicagoans, the Wells Street Station was located where the gigantic Merchandise Mart stands today. The station at Canal and Madison which you see in 1945, was opened in 1911. The various stations of the Chicago and North Western Railroad had a refreshing interest to Mr. Crowell during his entire lifetime. Each one had its peculiar memories. They "reminded him frequently of God's goodness. Often he would recall the boy of nineteen, alone, starting from the temporary terminal, in quest of health. And when he remembered His blessings, he felt thankful." [1]

[1] This reconstruction of yesterday was provided by Frances V. Koval, Publicity Manager, Chicago and North Western Railroad.

As the train moved westward, Harry gazed from the window upon the new agricultural frontiers of Illinois and Iowa. Fall splendors were upon the fertile fields. Darkness had fallen when the train reached Cedar Rapids; midnight at Omaha. The lad resumed his vigil at daybreak as the train passed through the little gray hills of western Nebraska . . . the wilder frontiers of Wyoming roused renewed interest; and finally the lusty village of Cheyenne.

Cheyenne had dreams in her eyes! "It was on the Main Line of the U. S. A.!" The new Denver Pacific brought the Southland through Cheyenne by way of Kansas City and Denver; the Union Pacific brought people from Chicago and the East. Cheyenne, being a mile high, was esteemed by English cattlemen as "the best country they had ever seen for Herefords."

At Cheyenne, he boarded the Denver Pacific for the one hundred and six mile ride to Colorado's capital. He liked the trip immensely. Something about the West made him feel buoyant; made him forget. . . . It was good to see country that wasn't fenced in . . . A few miles out of Denver on the down-slope, he was startled to see a herd of dainty little animals with tufted tails, bounding along with the train. "Antelopes," they told him, "and shot some from the train for meat."

Near La Salle in Colorado, the train came to a jolting stop. A great herd of buffalos, like a flow of hairy, black lava, poured across the track in front of the locomotive. "It was fully ten minutes before the train could proceed."

Towards evening, the train reached Denver. He had read much concerning the city: "Nearly a mile high; population, about six thousand. Everybody called it 'The Queen City of the Plains.' " He had read about the mining, the virgin farm lands, the production of hides, wool, and tallow. Yes, he even knew about its one good hotel, "The Inter-ocean." As he unpacked his grips in his room, he could not help noticing how much better he felt than he did back in Cleveland; he was even lighthearted, just as he was in the early days at Greylock. His thanksgiving, after he had extinguished the oil lamp, was full and rejoicing.

Next morning he noted the strangely old fashioned dining

room with its big, red-squared tablecloth. There he was surprised to meet George Worthington, another boy who had lived in Cleveland! "Of all things! It's a small world." George, also, was on a quest for health. Here began a significant friendship. For the next three years the lads were to spend much time together, living on ranches, trailing through cattle lands on horseback, engaged in winter sports in the foothills.

Neither of them ever forgot a colorful event a few nights later. Half a dozen Navajo chiefs in full costume sat down in the quaint old dining room to confer with government representatives on reservation issues. "It was very impressive," Harry wrote home. (Outstanding events to the end of his life were always "very impressive.")

After nine months of out-of-door life, springtime came to the Rockies, and the boys were homesick. They turned eastward again. On the train to Chicago, they made an important decision; next fall, they would meet and go to California. California was in the air; everybody talking about it. "Goodbye! California next year!"

\* \* \*

When Harry Crowell greeted his friends in the Second Presbyterian Church, "they were all pleased with the progress he was making." In the vestibule he saw a young lady; he could no longer say "the little Wick girl." How grown-up she appeared! And how attractive with several years of European travel! This was the first time he had seen her since the summer of three years ago. He could not get his mind off the change such a short time had made.

\* \* \*

Well, one year had passed! "He was sure the hand of God had been upon him for good."

## SECOND YEAR: FALL OF 1875—FALL OF 1876

In September, 1875, Worthington and Crowell departed again for the West . . . a few hours in Chicago, noting the progress;

departure from the "temporary station" of the C. and N. W. . . .
Cedar Rapids, Omaha, Cheyenne. From here, the limitless
stretch of western deserts with their sage-fragrance, held their
attention for two days and nights. How beautiful the pageantry of
fall sunrise and sundown on rose-tinted mountains . . . finally, the High Sierras . . . down the west slopes . . . scores
of windmills running full tilt in the Sacramento Valley . . . the
train ferry near Vallejo . . . passenger ferry at Oakland . . .
then San Francisco, the lusty young city of twenty thousand, beside the Golden Gate . . . Fall glories bathed the scene . . .
they liked the Bay and Tamalpais on the Marin side . . . then
a tramp steamer to San Diego.

\* \* \*

Interest never ceased! California was all they thought it would
be . . . San Diego Bay with its lobelia-blue waters, and jelly-
fish floating about like opal globes . . . Point Loma stretching
Pacific-wise like the finger of God . . . The City of San Diego
itself, little more than a Mexican village of two thousand, but
"very impressive." It took several weeks for them to get enough
of the fragrant, gray-green deserts behind San Diego.

In San Diego, they purchased two saddle horses, and equipped
them for cross country travel. By easy stages they rode through
Escondido, across the gaunt mountains to Fall Brook, Temecula,
and Riverside. From Riverside they went through San Bernardino,
and over the pass in San Bernardino Mountains to the Mojave
Desert . . . Palmdale, Tehacapi, Bakersfield, Fresno, Merced.
They found the dusty roads east of Merced very hot in the afternoon. One October morning "we stopped at a little place where
there was a stage coach station, with a watering trough. It was
very hot—130 degrees. After the horses drank, we remained in
the saddle awhile. Of a sudden my horse's legs folded up—he
went to sleep, and down he went! Of course he wasn't a stylish
horse." (And the Master of Green Court chuckled at the memory
of it.)

They entered Yosemite and made a circuit about the floor of
the Valley. "It was very impressive"; so much so, the boys decided to return in 1877, fully equipped to scale Half Dome!

**Greylock Institute,**
(BERKSHIRE COUNTY MASS.)

*BENJ F MILLS, A. M., Principal.*

South Williamstown, July 15..... 1867

Mrs. Crowell

Dear Madam—

I enclose Harry's report for the first quarter of the present term. It gives me great pleasure to give you a favorable report of Harry's progress and deportment. He is doing nicely in his studies, and by his gentlemanly bearing and obedient spirit is winning the confidence and esteem of his teachers. He seems to be a very nice boy, and these we like to have with us. He enjoys good health and appears uniformly cheerful and happy.

Yours with respect,
George F Mills

Harry's Quarterly
Report,

March 25, 1870

**Greylock Institute,**
South Williamstown.
BERKSHIRE COUNTY, MASS.

QUARTERLY REPORT
—OF—

Master Harry P. Crowell.

Commencing Jan. 13— ending Mar. 23—

| | |
|---|---|
| Number of Recitations. | 191 |
| No. of Perfect. | 191 |
| Number of Imperfect. | 0 |
| Number of Rhetorical Exercises. | 7 |
| Number Fulfilled. | 0 |
| No Number Unfulfilled. | 7 |
| Number of times Tardy. | 0 |
| Number of Days Absent. | 0 |
| GENERAL BEHAVIOR. No. 1 | 5 |

No. 1 denotes a careful ob-
No. 2 denotes a neglect in the observance of all Rules of the Family and School room.
No. 3 indicates a failure in the observance of Rules
a marked remissness in this respect.

South Williamstown, Mar. 23— 1870

Benj. F. Mills,
PRINCIPAL.

Letter from George F. Mills, July 15, 1867, noting "Harry's gentlemanly bearing and obedient spirit."

THE QUAKER SPECIAL

A spectacular advertising venture, no doubt suggested to H. P. C. by his
Percheron Special. (From an oil painting in the Cedar Rapids offices.)

THE QUAKER SPECIAL REPEATED

Photo taken at Paterson, New Jersey, June 11, 1897, by Frank Banto of the
Quaker Oats Company.

Back to San Francisco in time for Harry to celebrate his twenty-first birthday, January 27 . . . Then by ferry to the Marin side . . . Petaluma; and across the mountains to Napa . . . There they left their horses in a livery stable and proceeded by stage across the rugged triple peak of Mt. St. Helena, where seven years later Robert Louis Stevenson was to write *The Silverade Squatters* . . . through the mountains to Willow; Red Bluff, Redding, and Shasta.

They spent a long time in the spring of 1876, exploring the mountains and fishing for trout in the upper waters of the Sacramento River. "It was very impressive. All you needed for bait was a strip of red flannel." One cannot consider the primitive character of California as it was at that time, without feeling the state-wide excursion was quite an adventure for two eastern city boys. No ribbon-smooth highways! No elite wayside motels! They were not far behind the pioneers!

\* \* \*

In the midst of their California journey, summer of 1876, they decided to attend the Centennial Exposition in Fairmont Park, Philadelphia. . . . They received undying memories of Memorial and Horticultural Halls, and the beautiful Parthenon Building. They also visited the Spring Garden Street home of the little Wick girl. . . . Late summer they returned to California, and Harry realized two years had passed! Every month brought such evidence of improvement that the boy knew he was not following a cunningly devised fable! "In seven troubles no evil shall touch thee!"

## THIRD YEAR: FALL OF 1876—FALL OF 1877

Fall and winter, 1876 and 1877, were spent in California's colorful valleys, glowing like a string of jewels between San Francisco and Los Angeles; Santa Clara, Salinas, Santa Maria, Santa Barbara. By the middle of May, 1877, they had equipped for scaling Half Dome in Yosemite Valley. Stout clotheslines, a bag of rugged spikes, and a short-hafted sledge apiece, were the chief scaling aids. It makes one dizzy to think of such simple means for conquering the cloud-piercing slopes of the great rock. . . . As they rode through the bee pastures along the Merced River, the

Maricopa Flower Carpet was in full glory. No Persian rug could vie with it. . . . The boys listened to the muffled roar of the waterfalls, leaping at a bound for hundreds of feet, fluttering in the wind like a filmy pennant. They gazed upon the mile-high eminences along the river, and came to Mirror Lake, nature's reflecting pool for Half Dome. . . .

\* \* \*

On the wind-swept summit of Half Dome, they gazed for a long time at the vast assembly of granite titans, beginning with Glacier Point on the south side, hanging dizzily over its three thousand-foot drop. They looked at El Cajon on the north side with its sheer slope to the valley floor.

In the hotel that night, the mountaineers heard the boys' account of their venture. They would not believe the tale until the next day they found the ropes and spikes, like a spider filament soaring cloudward, just as Crowell and Worthington had left them.

In the early summer of 1877, the boys separated, George remaining in California, and Harry starting east to Atlantic City. He had several things in mind in connection with this trip. In the first place, ever since he had listened to Greylock students talking of Atlantic cruising, he had made up his mind to some day try it himself. The chief reason for this eastern trip, however, were considerations rising from the notable improvement in his health. He decided to confer with Dr. Weir Mitchell in Philadelphia, and to determine his exact physical condition. If this proved satisfactory, he had made certain decisions concerning Miss Lillie Wick!

\* \* \*

At Atlantic City he looked up John Tully, a salty old fisherman, and chartered his sloop. The little boat had a fair coat of paint, was fore-and-aft rigged, with one mast and a fixed bowsprit.

Day after day, they coasted New Jersey, sometimes tacking through openings in sand reefs to visit seaside villages. . . . They sailed into the broad water of Delaware Bay, made a brief visit in Wilmington . . . then they coasted Chester, with its fine, tree-covered hills!

At Philadelphia, Harry hurried to the office of Dr. Mitchell . . . "Well, my boy, I am greatly pleased with the progress you are making. But, remember! You are to remain out-of-doors three years longer!" The boy's heart leaped with joy: "I thank Thee, Oh God! I'm going to get well! And when I get well, I'm going to be able to serve Thee as I have hoped!"

"The doctor was pleased!" Harry could now go to Cleveland and tell Miss Wick something he had dreamed upon every day in the California pilgrimage. Salty old John said when the boy boarded the little sloop, "Well, you must have heard good news!" "I certainly did!" said the lad.

\* \* \*

The return trip to Atlantic City was leisurely. Tully knew just where the best eel holes were located. They took oysters from the beds, not caring about the "r-less" month: they fished from the boat side. Tully's conversations were mostly boat-talk. By the time Harry said, "Goodbye, John," at Atlantic City, he had a lifetime knowledge of "sloops and cutters, fore-and-aft rigging, boom and gaff main sail, center boards and square sterns."

"You know," Mr. Crowell remarked at Green Court, "I'm still interested in ships." Rather! His intimate correspondence discloses that in World War II his influence went right into the drafting department of U. S. fighting vessels.

\* \* \*

In Cleveland, he hurried immediately to 455 Euclid Avenue. When Miss Wick, now seventeen, received him in the living room, it was hard to maintain any reserve. Lillie was so radiant! . . . Before the visit ended, he found she held the same ideas he had so long cherished. By the time he left again for the West, they were engaged.

## FOURTH YEAR: FALL OF 1877—FALL OF 1878

From Cleveland, Harry hurried to the far West to join George Worthington. They toured California until the spring of 1878, which ended their travels together. Worthington had recovered sufficiently to take his place in the business world. Harry, confident of his own recovery, began to cast about in his mind as to what business he should take up. *He had a powerful incentive now!* Some day he would be setting up his own home.

One day a chance acquaintance spoke glowingly of Fargo, North Dakota:

> "There was something most attractive about the open country; you left the forests of Minnesota and came into natural farm land. Five years ago, it was only an Indian Reservation. The Indian title was extinguished. A town was laid out and named after Bill Fargo, of the Northern Pacific Railroad. The town has only eight hundred inhabitants, but the vast area all around was just right for farm and stock ranches. The Great Dalyrmple Farm proved Fargo to be an empire in the making."

He decided to visit Fargo. But first, there were complications in Cleveland that made it seem advisable to go there. His engagement to Miss Wick had given her mother great sorrow. Mrs. Wick felt it was disastrous to even contemplate marrying a lad in such poor health. "With a crushed heart, and out of deference to her mother's grief," she had therefore broken the engagement. Undoubtedly Harry's purpose in returning to Cleveland was not to plead his case, but simply to let Lillie and Mrs. Wick see for themselves that he was recovering his health.

Harry left Cleveland for Fargo April 29, 1878. He leased a room in a Fargo hotel, and for several weeks rode horseback along the Red River, or fished for pickerel in the Minnesota Lake country. One day he felt convinced that since he must live out-of-doors awhile longer, he would be happier if he had something to do. "He laid it before the Lord." Then he said to a Fargo real estate man, "What have you to sell?"

"Two sections," replied the man, "Exceptionally good. Never been farmed. Want to buy them?"

"How much?" said Harry—and the deal was closed.

\* \* \*

The sections lay twelve miles south of Fargo. Harry immediately bought a horse and buggy so he could "commute back and forth." He then busied himself in stocking the farm, securing horses and mules, erecting a large barn. Then he superintended the planting of one section to wheat.

During the Green Court Interviews, he reviewed the outcome of his first venture in farming.

One evening after reaping, I started to drive back to Fargo. As I drove, I was looking at the wheat shocks scattered over the plains, when suddenly I saw the black funnel of a tornado rushing towards the farm. I drove rapidly towards Fargo, watching the tornado and figured it would just about hit the barn. The next morning I returned expecting to find the barn in ruins. It was entirely undamaged. I thought, "How did it escape?" There was a slough thirty-five feet wide and eight feet deep alongside the barn. Could a slough deflect a tornado? No, I thought, God must have changed the direction of the tornado. It followed the slough two miles, turned at a left angle, and destroyed every building on a beautiful farm. All the shocked wheat was lifted up, carried east over the Red River five miles away. In the tops of the trees, along the river, clothing was hanging which had been on the farm.

Almost immediately the real estate man came to me and said, "Would you like to sell your farm? A man from Erie, Pennsylvania would like to buy such a farm."

I figured a good profit: "Cash?"

"Yes."

My line of argument ran this way: The Lord preserved the buildings and the property. Now He sends a man to buy, and pay cash. Does it not seem that here is an indication that the Lord does not want me on this farm? The deal was closed.

Before leaving Fargo, I said to the real estate man, "What other property have you?"

"I have a very exceptional tract of land west and south of Wahpeton; seventeen thousand acres in South Dakota."

\* \* \*

Harry took an option on the tract, then returned to Cleveland to finance it. He walked into the office of the bank.

"How did you like Fargo?" the banker asked.

"Fine. I bought a farm and sold it."

"Note?"

"No—cash. Now I want to finance the purchase of another farm. It has seventeen thousand acres."

The banker whistled softly. Folks for the next sixty years would have a way of whistling softly at the Crowell deals. The banker talked it over with Uncle William Henry Waite. The men laughed gleefully over the invalid. "Does pretty well for a sick man," said Uncle William.

"Doesn't look sick to me, nor act sick," replied the banker. "You know, I think it is safe to back Harry in something big."

Uncle William was a horse fancier. His particular hobby was Percherons. He said to Harry, "Why don't you develop some good Percherons on your farm? All the farmers around there need Percherons. I'll tell you what I'll do. If you wish, I'll go through Ohio with you next spring and buy a herd."

## FIFTH YEAR: FALL OF 1878—FALL OF 1879

In September, 1878, Harry returned to Fargo, and closed the deal for the seventeen thousand acres in South Dakota. As he rode about the wide spread of his new purchase of twenty-five square miles, he frequently recalled what his uncle had suggested about Percherons. The more he thought about it, the better the suggestion seemed. Therefore, he wrote a letter:

"Dear Uncle William: I will be in Cleveland at the turn of the year, and will avail myself of your kind offer to secure the Percherons."

\* \* \*

With all this talk about Percherons, some of our readers are no doubt thinking, "What is a Percheron?" Well, a Percheron is a horse. But that answer is not particularly enlightening since there are at least four breeds of horses—draft, harness, saddle, and pony. Each of the four breeds in turn has several types. For instance, the drafts have Belgian, Shire, Clydesdale, Suffolk, and—*Percheron!*

Now you have it! A Percheron is a draft horse, and a very handsome chap at that. He is the fellow with his tail in ribbons, and his mane plastered down like a peek-a-boo blond; the heavy limbed giant that is led prancing in front of the grandstand at the Vigo County Fair. He looks as if he were always ready to bite. We do not think he will, but it is best not to take a chance.

The Percheron got his name from the old French district of La Perche, where he was born. He is therefore a Frenchman. Earlier in his family history, there were often Flemish marriages, with an occasional Arabian romance, so that the colts would not become ungainly. And say! while you do not expect the Percheron to be a racer, he can keep up a heavy chump! chump! trot for hours. His admirers say he is the aristocrat of work horses. Look at his feet! small if you please. Look at his ribs! round and prosperous. Look at his street suit! Nice smooth gray; sometimes black, or bay. And look at his head! Appears as if Emerson's had got on John L. Lewis' shoulders. Why bless my heart, if you should compare the Percheron to a *cow,* he is an equine Hereford! He was the very kind of a horse for which the frontier farmers were looking and the answer to a stage driver's prayer. He was big enough and willing enough to pull the mortgages off everything around the place.

\* \* \*

In the spring of 1879 Harry Crowell and his Uncle William Waite went over Central Ohio purchasing the stock. "We bought three hundred Percheron mares and a brilliant stallion, and sent them to Cleveland. There we made up a train, and shipped them to Fargo."

## SIXTH YEAR: FALL OF 1879—FALL OF 1880

By the middle of September, the Percheron train moved westward from Cleveland, a sort of pioneer for the Quaker Special which toured the Pacific Coast in 1892. What Crowell learned in shipping three hundred Percherons to the Dakotas in 1879, was later applied to the sensational fifteen car, two caboose Quaker advertising special that rolled across the West, into Portland, and along the coast.

\* \* \*

Old timers in Fargo still talk about the Pullman Horse Car Train, and the Red River Percheron Parade. The animals were detrained at Fargo, then herded to the ranch in South Dakota. Farmers came miles to see this army of big Calibans, thumping along the Red River, as they proceeded to Harry's new farm.

The balance of 1879 was devoted to extensive preparations;

building of barns, assembling of machinery, enlisting help, and organizing crews.

"With every day in this labor, I felt my condition improving. I thought I was well. But I made up my mind to follow the doctor's orders."

## SEVENTH YEAR: FALL OF 1880—FALL OF 1881

Mr. Crowell watched the gardener at Green Court, mowing the California Rye Grass lawn. Finally, he continued the story:

When the spring of 1880 came, I secured an excellent man as foreman, who also was a good farmer. We planted twenty-five hundred acres of the seventeen thousand to wheat. The prospects were that the crop would be twenty-five bushels to the acre. Everybody said, "Great wheat." It looked that way until the milk was flowing into the head to form grain. Then a three-day hot wind. The crop shriveled into eleven instead of twenty-five bushels to the acre.

My line of reason ran this way: A tornado headed me off in my first venture, a dry spell in the second. Is God moving me a second time from farming? If He were, it was agreeable to me, for I was turning against farming anyhow. I felt I would rather get into a business where if I made a mistake, I could correct it.[1]

In the first farm, a man came along at once and bought the twelve hundred and eighty acres. Suddenly, as before, another man came who wanted the seventeen thousand acres and the horses. He was a business man from Minneapolis, and a politician. He must buy a farm. The three hundred mares first interested him.

The farm was sold to him, part cash. In the purchase price, there were some buildings in Minneapolis that were renting. Immediately after the sale, I started back to Cleveland. I reasoned day by day, does the Lord want me to stay out-of-doors any longer? The seven years are up. At no time during the seven years did the doctors change their point of view. They said "You must." And I agreed with them. Of one thing I was confident: God was guiding. I felt that I was now in good health again, but I would just wait awhile and see what God

[1] Dr. Thornton, *History of the Quaker Oats Company*, questioned the soundness of such a conclusion. He felt that Mr. Crowell encountered problems in the business world just as trying as in farming. But Mr. Crowell never agreed: "I still prefer corporation problems to tornadoes and dry spells."

would do next. I knew He would soon show me what He wanted.

Within thirty days of the sale of the farm, a man came to my uncle, Joel Burton Parsons, a Cleveland wholesale grocer, and said, "I bought a mill, the Quaker Mill at Ravenna. I doubt if it will make a success. I offer it to Harry Crowell."

When I heard about this, I immediately thought: This is probably what God has planned for me. I had been seven years in search of health, and health was found. It was apparent that I no longer was obliged to live out-of-doors: I was ready for indoor life and work. I could not help reviewing the whole affair in my mind, and when I did, the hand of God was evident in every part of it. As I grew better and became well, God evidently did not want me to be a farmer. He took me out of one farm by a tornado, and out of the second by a hot wind. And now that the seven years were finished, He was opening the way for me to secure the Quaker Mill. I felt compelled to go to my room. There, for a long time, I thanked Him for all His blessings.

# X

## "ALL THINGS FOR GOOD!"

Just as Mr. Crowell has fully regained his health, the
little Quaker Mill enters the scene like an Industrial Cin-
derella: but we can't let him go riding off with her,
coach-and-four, until we appraise her dowry.

By fall 1881, our Biographical Subject has achieved that excellence which comes through the fire, the forge, and the anvil. It was adversity which led him as a boy to resolve, "Oh, God, if Thou wilt allow me to make money, I will keep my name out of it, so Thou wilt have the glory." And continued adversity brought him into a large place.

At this point in our story, great riches are to be put into his keeping. It is very dramatic. Mr. Crowell always insisted it was of God: God led him every step of the way. And when we behold the little Quaker Mill appearing at just the proper moment, we have no interest in questioning the Providence which Mr. Crowell so earnestly affirmed. (*Sketch Book*)

# *"ALL THINGS FOR GOOD!"*

**I**F THE Quaker Mill at Ravenna had been merely another little gray grinder in a rustic village, there would be no need of any further record than to say, "Mr. Crowell bought it." But that little mill had such importance that it may be thought of as saying,

> "My natural advantages made me indispensable in combining and consolidating the leadership, clientele, property, and manufacturing technique necessary to produce the Quaker Oats Company.
> *"I gave you Henry Parsons Crowell, and I gave you the Quaker Oats Company."* [1]

It would therefore be a violation of the laws of suspense to let Mr. Crowell buy the mill in this chapter.

The Quaker Mill in 1881 centered a number of conditions just about to combine with economic importance. We will not overdraw Mr. Crowell to the point of assuming he comprehended the industrial possibilities. He thought the venture was a good one; but his most ardent fancy never intimated it was *that* good. The only valid comment is to affirm Mr. Crowell was the man of the hour, shaped by the faith which began in Dr. Hawks' study, and seasoned in seven years of trial. He was ready, having that sense of stewardship which enables Providence to put great wealth into a man's hands, and enables the man to possess it in safety.

\* \* \*

Three important circumstances will now be considered; three integers about to twist into the unbreakable quality of a threefold card. The first was the surprising advent, at a late hour in human

[1] The very last detail in the two years' research for this biography was a visit to Ravenna, October 23, 1944. The little mill seemed to glow with historic importance. That very evening, the phone in the Cleveland Hotel rang, and Mr. Crowell's sudden death was reported.

history, of a new member in the cereal grain family—Miss Avina
Sativa. The second was the appearance of a group of men in the
United States, Canada, and Great Britain, with a genius wedded
to flour-making. The third was the coming of new methods in the
ancient art of corn milling, whereby burrstones were to be stored
away with coal oil lamps.

The place where the cording of these three strands could easily
be initiated was the Quaker Mill at Ravenna; and the man for
performing the exploit could be the new owner of the mill.

It has never been the purpose of this book to deal with the history of the Quaker Oats Company any further than is necessary to
bring out the likeness of Mr. Crowell. *The History of the Quaker
Oats Company* has been written, and so well written, by Harrison
John Thornton, that there is no need of another treatise. What
Bennett and Elton did for the annals of corn milling, Dr. Thornton has achieved for the Quaker Oats Company. With incredible
patience, he assembled a multitude of dry facts; then he carded,
colored, and wove them into a splendid document. There are
many references in the work revealing that Mr. Crowell held the
leading human interest for Dr. Thornton; for instance at the very
beginning:

> "Without the benefit of Mr. Crowell's clear recollection and
> balanced judgment, this task must have been infinitely more
> difficult . . . His life spans almost the entire sweep of the
> subject . . . contact with his serene and genial disposition has
> been one of the joys of the undertaking."

Gladly, therefore the labor is divided with Dr. Thornton. Let
him show you the mills; we exhibit the miller. The dying roar of
runner stone on bed stone; the emerging purr of steel rolls; the
fan-fare of State oat production in the Big Ten Hit Parade; the
condensed stories of yesterday's cornmill giants will be used somewhat; but used frankly as an artist's daub against which the
Crowell profile may be seen to better advantage. The strands of
our threefold cord are about to be woven; then swiftly interwoven; not to attract interest to the strands, but that an epaulet
may be fashioned for our hero's shoulder. Stand by! As the strands
are corded—"Avina Sativa," "The Passing of Burrstones," and

"Here Comes an Old Miller!" The decoration being completed, we will bestow it upon "The Maestro of the Quaker Oats Symphony," right in the chapter where it is proper to announce that he bought the Quaker Mill.

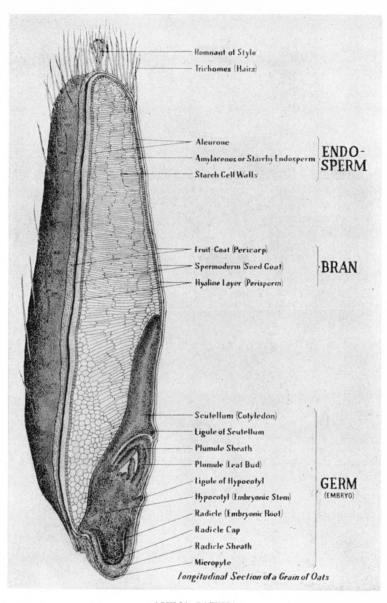

Remnant of Style
Trichomes (*Hairs*)

Aleurone
Amylaceous or Starchy Endosperm
Starch Cell Walls

} ENDO-
SPERM

Fruit-Coat (*Pericarp*)
Spermoderm (*Seed Coat*)
Hyaline Layer (*Perisperm*)

} BRAN

Scutellum (*Cotyledon*)
Ligule of Scutellum
Plumule Sheath
Plumule (*Leaf Bud*)
Ligule of Hypocotyl
Hypocotyl (*Embryonic Stem*)
Radicle (*Embryonic Root*)
Radicle Cap
Radicle Sheath
Micropyle

} GERM
(EMBRYO)

*Longitudinal Section of a Grain of Oats*

AVINA SATIVA

"The Beauty of the Cereal Grain Family. She just had everything." (Drawing of a corn of oats by Dr. A. L. Winton, Co-author, *The Structure and Composition of Foods.*)

THE FOUR STAGES OF CORN MILLING. FOUR SMALL CUTS BELOW
FROM BENNETT AND ELTON, *The History of Corn Milling.*

I. Handstone Era, Abraham to Pharaoh. Picture of the "Bullan Stones of Ireland," where eight colleens could work and visit while getting dinner.

III. The Quern Era, from the time of Christ to 1875 A.D.

II. Saddlestone Era, Pharaoh to 200 B.C. This is "the maid behind the mill."

When the Quern Age was in Flower. "The never-failing brook, the busy mill, the decent church that topped the neighboring hill."

IV. The Modern Mill, with steel rolls, etc. 1875 to date. (Quaker Plant, Saskatoon, Canada)

# XI

## AVINA SATIVA

In which a new member appears in the Gramen Family,
and is swiftly acclaimed by the world.

"Wherefore, if God so clothe the grass of the field, which today is, and tomorrow is cast into the oven, shall he not much more clothe you, O ye of little faith?" (*Matt. 6:30*).

# AVINA SATIVA

AVINA SATIVA is indeed a newcomer in the Family of Cereal Grains, and to judge by the encomiums of her friends, she is the beauty of the family. The 1945 Oat millers of America affirm, "She is the outstanding leader of all common (inexpensive!) food. Keen attention is focussed on her." It is good business on the part of the several makers of Oaties and Groaties to keep attention focussed. Currently, they have brought in Betty Vitamin B-1, like a celebrity at a war-bond sale; and her Dick-ka-Dicky-Do is,

"Thi-a-min! Thi-a-min! Oatmeal the Thi-a-min Queen!"

But oatmeal got along very well long before the public became vitamin-conscious; and she will still be in the breakfast bowl long after the blurbs for Thiamin have passed away with the praise of cod liver oil. You might say, so to speak, that Avina Sativa is immortal in the Breakfast Table Revú, like ham and eggs.

Can you spare a little time—if it's made profitable to you? Pull up a chair, then, and hear a brief account of Avina Sativa.

Avina Sativa is defined in your New International as "a cereal grass, or the grain, or seed thereof." The word "grass" at first thought suggests the green herbage upon which the cattle of the field graze; or, the matted blades, billiard table green, requiring weekly treatment with a lawn mower. But a few years' labor on the swards of Cherry Blossom Lane widens one's ideas of grass. He comes to know there are many kinds of grasses: Blue from Kentucky for a velvet carpet; Oregon Bent, which can prosper under a Pepper Tree; California Rye, the staple for a winter lawn in Augusta. Furthermore, certain grasses become known as enemies; Bermuda, esteemed in Maricopa, but loathed in Santa Clara; Creeping, which writhes out like a gray devil across the fifth green. . . .

The roll call of members in the Grass Family makes it appropriate to remark that all groups in nature are incredibly diversified, often numbering one thousand members.

Take palms for instance. The coral shafted Cocos Plumosa of San Gabriel, the aristocratic Royal of the Everglades, the dainty Traveler of Miami are only a Scotch fringe for the Phoenicaceae Family. There are over one thousand kinds of palms! Likewise, grasses. There are Sedges, and Rushes and Barn Grass; Beach and Bear, Witch and Arctic; Porcupine, Pony, Yellow Top and Wallabi—grasses that stink, and grasses that smell like Araby; Johnson Grass, to spoil the day for an Arizona Zanjerro; and if you ask him, he'll tell you what a So and So Johnson was for ever importing that stuff; Job's Tears, which puts necklaces on Woolworth's counters; and Buffalo Grass for buttoning down Nebraska dust; Sand Burrs, to plague barefoot boys; Bitter, Sour Sweet, and Spice . . . Why go further with a Who's Who of the Gramen family? There are, as with palms, more than one thousand kinds of grasses! This widens appreciation of what the Son of man wanted us to understand of the Father's Providence who did "so clothe the grass of the field." And one of the ten hundred kinds of grasses is Avina Sativa, to which the shorter name of "Oats" is given.

Oats, themselves, number more than fifty types: Downy, for poor soil and dry hills; Yellow, for light meadow-land; Short Oats for mountain tops; Avina Fatua for California's Easter gown; Animal, in South Europe, whose twisting awns squirm like a weasel; bristle pointed Avina Strigosa . . . Avina Forsaku, on ravine bottoms of the Sahara, for hungry camels . . . But as before advised, the beauty of the Gramen Family is Avina Sativa.

If you go down to Iowa's little Athens, Cedar Rapids, you will find a giant stand of mills covering fourteen acres, established primarily for the business of grooming Avina Sativa for the world's porridge bowl. For that's exactly the business of The Quaker Oats Company.

\*     \*     \*

Oats appeared rather late in history. They certainly were not in Joseph's Nile granaries. Years later when Pliny first saw oats, he thought they were "wheat with the measles." Some think oats originated in San Juan Fernandez, that eighteen mile Erin off the coast of Chile. It always has been an isle of dreams, with valleys full of strawberries, peaches, and turnips; lately we've heard it was there that Robinson Crusoe had his first dish of oatmeal mush. We leave to the Evolutionist the assignment of discussing oats in the Bronze Age. We know nothing of it.

Just when oats emigrated to America, no one knows; but they suddenly appear as if by magic in Colonial acres. "In 1602, Bartholomew Gosnold, exploring the waistline of Massachusetts and New Hampshire found an island between Martha's Vineyard and New Bedford and planted oats." In early Colonial days, you could find oats in the fields around Saugus. (Number One Highway north of Boston.) Casual references like the above increase; oats became the high octane for New England filling stations; "oated my horse at Button Willows."

By 1660, oats had gone south to the Land of Cotton, and George Washington sowed an acre or so at Mount Vernon, "to see if they could withstand the winter." Actually, oats love cold weather like a Swedish skating star; what they cannot endure at all is a Summer in Miami.

By 1849, oats started west to grow up with the country, and assumed an important part in the agricultural conquest of the frontier. "Fences crept into the western silence to cut the untamed spaces into patchwork," says Dr. Thornton very prettily. And behind many of those fences, you could see oat patches. The sections given over to oats began to increase amazingly. You can see this in Iowa's oat ledger. In 1849, for instance, the State produced less than two million bushels. In 1879, the total was above fifty million bushels.

Time fails for reviewing the annual hit parade of the Ten Big Oater States, save to post 1906 as an example. That year the order was Iowa, Illinois, Wisconsin, Nebraska, Minnesota, Indiana, Ohio, South Dakota, Michigan, North Dakota; producing a grand national total of nine hundred and sixty-five million bushels, valued at three hundred and six million dollars. In 1930, the grand total jumped to one billion, five hundred million bushels. 1944?

Well, oats are holding their own, despite the fact the gasoline is in the field. What horses quit eating, men appropriate.[1]

Up to the year of Mr. Crowell's birth, however, oats "were still horse-food." What little was used for human beings came in glass jars at the drug store, like flax seed for poultices. The English scornfully remarked that "the Scotch were robbing the ponies."

But the English always were dour about oats. Early in the package period of the Quaker Oats Company, the small British consignment did not increase. Crowell called the foreign representative home, "What is the trouble?" "Well, what we do sell goes to Royalty," he reported. "And they feed it to the dogs." In American comics, oats were always good for a laugh. The Cosmopolitan Magazine as late as 1910, according to Thornton, cartooned a Yankee farmer, who ate oats for breakfast, later drank from a horse trough, then stood at a hitching post while his wife went over him with a curry comb.

But despite all this banter, when Joel Burton Parsons proposed that his nephew, Mr. Crowell, purchase the Quaker Mill, the Ugly Duckling oats was about to rise above her persiflage era, and become runner-up for first place in the Cereal Beauty Show. Her photograph, published herewith, makes it clear that she just had everything—Vitamin B-1, Thiamin which, as everyone ought to know by now, is "easily digestible food energy." Furthermore, Avina Sativa had "available iron, phosphorus, and protein for body building!" Also, Riboflavin and Calcium! And if the Quaker Scientists continue to find new blandishments, who can foretell what will be reported by 1950?

Suffice to say, when the little Quaker Mill was up for sale in 1881, Avina was ready for the world, and the Mill had certain natural advantages for helping bring her to her own. All that was needed was that some very competent young man—like Mr. Crowell—buy the mill and become her business manager.

[1] If you must know, why not write to the Department of Agriculture? The secretaries sent such an interesting assortment of Oat Pamphlets to Cedar-Palms that the writing of this biography came nearly getting oat-logged.

# XII

## THE PASSING OF BURRSTONES

In which the tardy progress of corn milling is traced through its three primitive stages; how none of these were fast enough for Avina Sativa; and how, when she did arrive, presto! windmills blew off the landscape like dandelion heads, and the giant factories appeared.

The writing of a book like this does strange things to the author. For instance, much reading about the glutinous glory of Quaker Oats moved me to suggest to Deborah, "Why can't *we* have some oatmeal mush?" . . . Never once did I consider becoming a miller; but in writing the Life of H. P. C. I was obliged to become one—theoretically. It was necessary to look up "oat middlings and shorts," and now my conversation is as dusty as an elevator. I can tell less informed souls that middlings are coarser wheat mixed with fine bran. It's what you have left after you bolt out fine flour and coarse bran.

"Bolt?" you say. So did I. And that's how I came to be a miller. A bolter is a glorified kitchen flour sifter. That's a good word: use it—

"Time and nature will bolt out the truth of things."

Then, there are "shorts." What are they? Well, they are the parts of mill grain next finer than bran, mixed with factory sweepings, with very little floury particles remaining. Now you can better understand your Chestertons and Shaws,

"All she got of life, poor dear, was just the *shorts.*"

(*Sketch Book*)

# THE PASSING OF BURRSTONES

THE term for the preparation of the seeds of cereal grasses as food is "corn milling." This needs underscoring for many think the word "corn" refers exclusively to maize, or Indian corn. "Corn" is applied to almost any small, hard particle, all the way from "a corn of powder," to the seeds of various grains: rye, wheat, barley, maize, and oats. The term "corn milling" then is a collective, and serves to designate methods past, present and future for grinding grain.

In the year 1898, two Englishmen, Richard Bennett and John Elton, began the publication of a treatise, which ended up in four volumes. They called it *The History of Corn Milling*. Bennett was a Liverpool grain-jobber of means, who was captivated by the colorful windmills of antiquity which abounded near his home. As a result, he began to purchase, through personal search and world-wide advertising, ancient flour-making instruments, until his own baronial residence resembled the British Museum. One feature greatly impressed Bennett; namely, that the humble, inexpensive implements for bread-making had outlived the pyramids, though their ancient makers had no such ambitions. It appeared that flour milling devices had more of a survival quotient than philosophy on granite.

Bennett's ardor finally moved him "to make literary amends for two centuries of neglect of mills and milling." He therefore enlisted Elton, who had a cunning pen and a flair for research. Elton, enjoying Bennett's haven of paid leisure, went right to the bottom of the matter. He neglected nothing that was relevant, even quoting vast sections from *The Domesday Book* of William, the Conqueror, because these pages referred to windmills, fish ponds, plowgates, and soke. He garnished his chapters with dainty side lights from international literature:

> "The cronach stills the dowie heart,
> The jurran stills the bairnie;
> But the music for the hungry waine
> Is the grinding of the quernie." [1]

The resultant labor of Elton not only made amends for two hundred years of neglect of corn milling, but for six milleniums! The work is a clever literary treasure worthy of a place with Walton's *Compleat Angler*. When the obliging Mr. Robert Rea, of the San Francisco Public Library, sent *The History of Corn Milling* to Cedar-Palms, the lights burned through the night. Three hundred fascinating wood cuts! Tracking the pleasant sound of grinding back to Abraham and forward to Cedar Rapids!

No one need ever publish another book on corn milling unless he says, "A footnote to Bennett and Elton." Beautiful is no word for it. You rise from the four volumes, your heart gay with windmill sails, and your ears echoing to the music of ancient breadmakers:

> "The never failing brook, the busy mill,
> The decent church that topped the neighboring hill."

\* \* \*

Nothing limped more painfully out of antiquity into modern stream-lining than the technique of corn milling—unless it was public and private transportation. It was only yesterday that the hoof-beats of overland stages, the sails of ocean boats were replaced by the shrill "b-a-w" of limited sirens, and the nasal blasts of ocean liners. It was only this morning that you looked up into the blue to see the giant airplanes which have shriveled our globe into a sixty-hour world.

Let us make a closer study of the painfully slow progress of bread-making, inasmuch as the Quaker Oats Company, and others in the same field, could never appear until hand manual methods were antiquated.

The illustrations on the special plate roughly date the three eras in corn milling. When it comes to chronological exactitude, any reasonable person will be satisfied with loose-fitting assignments.

---

[1] You ought to know that the author of this Shortnin' Bread classic was Glasgow-born John Jamieson, 1759-1838.

The first period might be called "The Handstone Era" from History's Dawn to Pharaoh, wherein the bread-maker held a small boulder and brayed the grain to flour on another rock. This work was done almost entirely by the women, at large personal cost—skinned knuckles and aching muscles; laboring as did Sarah when she was commanded, Genesis 18:6, "Make ready quickly three measures of fine meal, and knead it, and make cakes upon the hearth." Angels ate that bread and liked it; and myriads from that day to this have esteemed mother's loaves the bread of heaven.

\* \* \*

The second period might be called "The Saddlestone Era," roughly from Pharaoh to a few years before Christ. In general, the operator (a woman again) sat *behind the mill;* that is, behind the higher side of a stone which had a saddle-shaped trough in it. She ground the grain by moving to and fro a stone shaped like a rolling pin. This she grasped firmly in her two hands, crouching as she worked. It was harsh labor, and left the operators deformed in hand and forearm. It is the saddlestones to which Exodus 11:5 refers, "the maidservant that is *behind* the mill." When you look at the cut you will see she is indeed, "behind the mill."

\* \* \*

The third might be called "The Quern Era" which overlapped with the Saddlestone, "and continued until yesterday morning." At the beginning, the quern was made of two stones; a lower, or bed stone, which was stationary, and an upper, or runner stone which rotated. The lower stone was shaped like an hour glass, and the runner fitted over it, and revolved about it. The runner had a handle on it, and required two persons to operate. Once again, this was a woman's task. The quern is referred to in Matthew 24:41, "Two grinding at the mill." The Lord did not say "Two *women*"; but the translator was so familiar with the sight of women operators, that he just put in the word "women."

From here on the quern was modified and progressively powered. The bed stone flattened out, along with the runner stone, which was driven successively by water, wind, slaves, animals, tides, and steam. Had the quern endured a while longer, it would, alas, have hitched electricity to the runner stone, like Samson to a horse sweep.

Nevertheless, the Queen Age was the picturesque era of flour-making, giving us the giant replicas of Dutch Windmills for Golden Gate Park, and thousands of ancient relics in wood, brick, and stone. These mills once sat with busy wheels beside their charming wiers, and stimulated a veritable fountain of poetic thought. We have yet to find any poetry on the modern successors, such as the giant at Cedar Rapids. Many readers have seen these charming old windmills; and some are old enough to have seen them in operation.

\* \* \*

But the quern and the Quern Age, though they endured unbelievably, had to pass. If Avina Sativa were to be properly handled in vast quantities, other methods were long overdue. The Burr-stone must be relegated to museums, with Conestoga Wagons. A group of Modern Millers appeared, contemporaneously with Avina Sativa; and these millers were equipped with a modern technique, and adequate personal ability.

## XIII

## "HERE COMES AN OLD MILLER!"

In which you see the good old miller replaced by the modern go-getter; you view a vast market being created; you see how a little Mill "centers history's unconscious focus"; and you remember again that Mr. Crowell is being urged to buy it.

"I see the wealthy miller yet.
His double chin, his portly size:
And who that knew him could forget
The busy wrinkles round his eyes?
The slow, wise smile that round about
His dusty forehead drily curled,
Seemed half within and half without.
And full of dealings with the world."
                    Tennyson, *The Miller's Daughter.*

# *"HERE COMES AN OLD MILLER!"*

PEOPLE in yesterday's world sang an old folk song concerning the miller:

> "As the mill goes round
> He's gaining on his ground."

Yes, he's gaining on his ground all right. He's gaining on his ground, if you can call six millenniums of antiquated devices "gaining." But never mind, Old Miller, you're at the turn of the road! Those steel rolls at Philadelphia, crushing oats, half-cooked oats—will change the whole picture. Those steel rolls will drive out windmills, and make way for Valhalla Factories.

\* \* \*

There has always been something reassuring about a corn miller. He is a fine, solid, lay figure as wholesome as a blacksmith. No one, save a hard-pressed mystery hack could dream of a miller doubling as a bandit, black-mailer, or faro-dealer. One thinks of him, "his grey eyes lit up with summer lightnings of the soul, so healthy, sound and clean and whole; his memory scarce can make me sad."

If Boreham had not laid his quills aside, he could write a shelf of books on corn millers. Hope *somebody* does it! But the special burden of this chapter is to sketch with etcher's lines, somewhat of that group which lived just at the dawn of commercialized mush. Had it not been for them, Mr. Crowell's exploit in oats would never have taken place. These corn millers of the last half of the nineteenth century provided the genius, energy, experience, inventions, clientele, and resources necessary to produce the Oatmeal Business.

Wherever we begin this review, some one will be displeased— so, let's start with a doctor. It's a singular thing that modern

Akron, Ohio, owes its industrial stature to a pair of physicians. One was Dr. Benjamin Franklin Goodrich (1840-1885) who made Akron rubber-conscious, and gave us some fine auto tires. The other was Dr. Eleakim Crosby (1779-1854) who looked like Phillips Brooks, and never seemed to be able to decide whether he was a business man or a physician.

Dr. Crosby was born in Litchfield, Connecticut; read medicine in Buffalo and settled in Simcoe, Canada. When he enlisted in the war of 1812 as a surgeon, Canada confiscated all his property. In 1820, he moved to Middlebury (East Akron) and in the intervals of practice, "toyed with corn milling." He really had quite a stride for a frontier day. He bought up sufficient farm land "to secure the rights appertaining to river banks, so as to divert water from the Cuyahoga River through his lands." He tamed the little river into a race-bed right down Main Street, around the hills and through the woods. "And there it flows today, under streets and great buildings . . . a life artery in a great city." [1]

Dr. Crosby built the Old Stone Mill in 1832, a five-story stone structure. The town which sprang up around it was first called "Cascade," then—"Akron!" Crosby's mill "led to an epidemic in mill building."

The Old Stone Mill was sold to Commins and Allen in 1867, taken over by the Akron Milling Company in 1884, and finally became "the oldest unit within the Quaker Oats Company." You will now search for it in vain. On the very day of Mr. Crowell's death, October 23, 1944, I asked Mr. George Curtis Fretz, Manager, Akron Quaker Oats, "Just where was the Old Stone Mill?"

Mr. Fretz, like all of his Quaker colleagues, is affable and courteous. He is a Doylestown, Ohio, boy, graduate of the local high school, with a year of business training in the Actual Business College of Akron. Forty years ago, at the age of nineteen, he "went on with the American Cereal Company (now Quaker Oats) and has been with it ever since." When I asked the above question, he walked to his office window overlooking the rear of the building. "Right there," he said, "where the corner of this building stands." I walked out to that corner, Mill and South Canal Streets, and

[1] Carl D. Sheppard, *A Centennial History of Akron*, (1925).

dreamed of a pioneer day over a hundred years ago, when in all truth, Dr. Eleakim Crosby began to lay the foundations of the Quaker Oats Company.

\* \* \*

We now put a skirl of bag pipes into these annals, for the Campbells are comin'. If there is any culpability in fixing oatmeal upon North America a warrant should be drawn on the Scotchmen. First, John Stuart, Ontario settler about 1850: exporter to Great Britain of apples, cheese, and *oatmeal!* In 1860 he bought an old saw mill near London, Ontario, at Ingersoll, and started oat milling. This became his "North Star Mill," with a single run of burrstone, and a daily capacity of twenty-five barrels.[1]

Robert Stuart, John's son, had dreams in his eyes, and such a passion for the West, that he imparted it to his father. The two came to Cedar Rapids in the Kerosene Age, 1873, and built "The North Star Oat Meal Company."

Now see what came out of that! On the fourth of February, 1944, I returned to the Cedar Rapids Plant for the third inspection. Mrs. Irene Werner, who had been assigned as a personal guide by Mr. Arthur Poe, conducted me through acres of complicated Mandrake machinery, which was automatically boxing, sealing, water-proofing, weighing. These machines did everything except talk to visitors, and their roaring output required several freight *trains* each day. Dried eggs, dried soup were also going out of this plant in Jovian batches, sealed in water-proof cartons, billed to the boys overseas. All this was accompanied by frequent dull "booms!" as food was shot from guns (The Puffy Family). It is an overwhelming work shop, the world's largest cereal mill. (See illustration.)

The grandsons of John Stuart, John and Robert Douglas Stuart, have succeeded Mr. Crowell in the administration of the Quaker Oats Company, and may be seen, if you are fortunate, in the lofty offices in Chicago's Board of Trade Building.

George Douglas, likewise, Scotland-born, was successively stone mason, and culvert builder for the C. B. & Q. Railroad. He bought into the Cedar Rapids concern about 1870. He was described as

[1] Nothing of the mill remains today. While resident in London, I browsed about Ingersoll, feather-questing for a bit of fiction, *Sugar Bush.*

"tall and powerful, a Presbyterian, wearing a plug hat and frock coat." We doubt, however, if he retained his kilts and sporran. He looked like Abraham Lincoln, and talked like Harry Lauder. From where we stand today, it seems as if in the firm of Douglas and Stuart, the first named put up the shrewdness, the latter the skills that made the Cedar Rapids giant.

It is a memorable experience to visit the Cedar Rapids Mill. It is not only a big mill, but it gets proper handling all the way from Arthur Poe, manager, to the last man or woman of the more than thirteen hundred employees. Arthur Poe you may remember as the flashing quarter back who did such a lot for Princeton just at the turn of the century, when Princeton obviously needed it. If you cannot remember or understand all you see in the great mill, (and you will not) then Mr. Emil J. Petranik, plant superintendent, will answer your letters. There's a fine docket of patient replies from him, here in Cedar-Palms. Mr. Crowell said, "You will like the Quaker boys at Cedar Rapids." He should have said, "You will like the Quaker boys, period." Time fails to tell of Scotch George Cormack, John and Alexander Forrest, with the saving grace of an occasional Irishman like Andrew Johnson, who pioneered the way.

\* \* \*

Just one more name associated with the oatmeal pioneers—Ferdinand S. Schumacher, Hamburg-born, March 30, 1822. "Keen, deep set eyes; a tiny, wiry German; large head, with a smooth upper lip"; a white clipped beard, and a voice like Adolph's . . . so nervous, that after an hour with him you enjoyed a calmer person, much as if you took a tabby cat on your lap after trying to cosset a Sierra Chipmunk. In 1840 he settled on a farm near Cleveland, then moved to Akron about 1851.[1]

In Akron, Schumacher began selling notions, then groceries. While in the grocery store, he often thought of a certain commodity which he had dispensed over the counter in Hamburg—cracked oats. He therefore rigged up a device for cutting oats into minute cubes. These oat cubes he peddled over the counter. We will have to admit that these oats were somewhat of a hazard. If

---

[1] *A Centennial History of Akron*: a notable collection of source material, lumber-yard style.

a housewife failed to cook them for two hours, there were complications . . . but we will also have to record, right there A STAR WAS BORN.

Schumacher's oats took hold rapidly. About the year 1854, he secured an old woolen mill, remodeled it, named it "the German Mill," and started producing twenty barrels a day. Early in the industry he sold his products from a push cart.

Year by year Schumacher's business mushroomed. In 1881, at the time the Quaker Mill at Ravenna was being offered for sale, Schumacher's famous Jumbo Mill at Akron was scientifically cutting and rolling toothsome "Rolled Avina," and "Delectable Farina"; and Schumacher was easily the foremost miller in the world.

\* \* \*

Right here, we make an entry of apparently small weight, an industrial accident so to speak, which put the thin edge of the wedge into the Schumacher enterprise, and secured to the little Quaker Mill a priceless heritage. In 1875, William Heston, a Schumacher employee, patented a device for cutting oats. We blush for Heston, unable to forget how he looked over the shoulders of one Asmus J. Ehrrichsen who was also making a cutter. We cannot forget how Heston rushed to get a patent. This he assigned to Schumacher "on conditions"; of which the next chapter will speak in detail.

The Heston patent came at the beginning of a new era in the methods of corn milling. This industry, which had for centuries been satisfied with antiquity, now entered a period during which revolutionary devices appeared in spring profusion. As an example, George H. Cormack, of Rockford, Illinois, produced at least sixteen valuable inventions and improvements, and thus deserves the title of "the Edison of Corn Milling."

In 1876, Ferdinand Schumacher went to Philadelphia to see the Exposition. (Think of it! Young Harry Crowell was there, too!) At the Exposition, Schumacher saw a device that literally "rolled him off his feet,"

"Rolled Oats! that is, oats partially cooked, then rolled under heavy pressure!"

Esteemed Reader, the details presented in these three chapters are entitled to the time required. No one with a relish for key facts would prune out a line. These chapters, as Hillis was accustomed to remark with fine inelegance, "made a juncture big with destiny!" All of which, in a peculiar way, pertains to the life of Mr. Crowell.

Oats have arrived! Burrstones displaced! A race of capable millers and inventors appear! The millers have gained separate clienteles, which, if fused, would sum up to a multitude! There are vast resources! Startling new methods! It is the dawn of Big Business in the world's strongest nation! And the Quaker Mill at Ravenna, by reason of a priceless birthright, has a star role in The Oatmeal Epic.

The episode with which this chapter closes was just made for an exposition mural—Joel Burton Parsons offering to his nephew, Henry Parsons Crowell, the Quaker Mill at Ravenna!

# XIV

## THE MILL AND THE GIRL

Why particularize this? He *is* going to buy that little Quaker Mill, and he *is* going to marry that little Wick girl!

Well, Mr. Crowell, we've been watching that "little Wick girl" moving into your affections for seventeen years. We knew what was going to happen all along, Mr. Crowell, and it was just what we wanted. We'll manage to weather the disapproval of dour souls, who feel your biography should "stick strictly to business." For our tastes, there is no better window for viewing a man's real self than his love-life. Who could write of Spurgeon without Susannah? Or of Moody, without Emma Charlotte? And who could write of you, Mr. Crowell, without Lillie Augusta? Without seeing your letters to each other as you were fighting back to health? Or witnessing your grief when after three years as your wife she departed this life? Well, Mr. Crowell, one gets a much better idea as to the kind of a man you were on learning that you carried certain of Lillie's little love trinkets to the end of your life, than by watching you fill the American skyline with great factories! (*Sketch Book*)

# THE MILL AND THE GIRL

THE evident Providence of God in Washington's life was so great that there were times when Henry Cabot Lodge could no longer write. "Three times Washington's death seemed inevitable, but God. . . ." Likewise it is impossible to repress the same feelings when Mr. Crowell, habitually as taciturn over his affairs as William the Silent, lets you know near the end of his life just what happened. His account permits you to witness spell-bound how the will of the Cleveland boy was tried by fire until he could say, "My will is mine to make it Thine." You then see him seven years in the furnace, and realize that the furnace was the source of his perennial calm; "what time I am afraid, I will trust in Thee!" You mark the rise of a determination to get wealth, and you see that determination bathed in heaven by a resolve that God should have the glory!

As we learn all this, it quickens our pulses upon remembering that is why the Book commends Biography: "Meditate upon the heroes, whose faith follow, considering the outcome of their lives! Jesus Christ the same, yesterday and today and forever!" Yes, it is the *faith* of our heroes that blesses us! And by reason of much thinking upon Mr. Crowell, we find ourselves beginning to say in the presence of our own problems, "Take your time! Take your time! Find what the will of God is!"

\* \* \*

Now a word about the strategic advantage enjoyed by the Quaker Mill. Remember William Heston in the previous chapter working for Schumacher? Mr. Heston, who looked over a Swede's shoulder as he was designing an oat cutter, then rushed out and "got a patent on one of his own?" Well, Heston assigned this patent to Schumacher "on condition"; on condition that he,

Heston, could use it in any mill in which he was interested. In 1877, Heston, Henry D. Seymour, and two others went over to Ravenna, organized the Quaker Milling Company, and built the Quaker Mill. So—the Quaker Mill had a right to use the oat cutter! This windfall may be put to Heston's credit.

Then too, the word "Quaker" was itself a million dollar asset, as good a name as was ever applied to any trade article or corporation. Heston said he "thought the word 'Quaker' up out of his own head." Seymour affirmed the name was his idea. Mr. Crowell in the interviews was of the opinion the credit for "Quaker" belonged to Seymour. Mr. Crowell's opinion seems correct, when we recall how fluent Heston was in borrowing the ideas of others. But the name Quaker was so good, a number of firms tried to appropriate the same. In every case they were either frightened off, or ordered off by civil law.

However, Heston's cleverness gained him nothing. In two years, the business sagged so badly it was sold to Warren Corning. Corning put it in charge of two of his relatives. After another two years, Corning came to Joel Burton Parsons and said, "They're not going to make a success of it. I offer it to Henry Crowell." Don't forget now, that little mill, though in the red, still has adequate invisible assets in a good name worth riches, and the right to use oat cutters. All these matters have a pick-up which vies with the best in fiction. Oats have arrived! Burrstones have passed! The notable millers are ready! And the little mill at Ravenna, with her priceless name and her right to use a modern oat cutter, can bestow upon her owner Double A One Priority for the honor of leading the Oatmeal Symphony.

\* \* \*

Mr. Crowell, in the Green Court Interviews, smiled at the memory: "It was very impressive. The seven years had passed, and I was well. I realized God had led me every step of the way. I realized, here is a business where one can make mistakes and correct them; a much better business than farming."

"How about the Ferdinand Schumachers, Mr. Crowell?"

"Well I could deal with men like Mr. Schumacher much better than with Dakota cyclones. I thought, should I not have a partner?

THE OLD STONE MILL
Akron, Ohio
(Reproduction from old photo.)

DR. CROSBY

DR. ELIAKIM CROSBY
Who looked like Phillips Brooks, and built the
Old Stone Mill, 1832.

"The Old Stone Mill on a busy day."

Schumacker's Empire Barley Mills
Akron, Ohio, 1863

Robert Stuart

George H. Cormack
"The Edison of the
Oatmeal Milling"

Ferdinand S. Schumacker

North Star Mill, Cedar Rapids,
Iowa. Built by John Stuart
and son, Robert, 1873.

Mrs. H. P. Crowell
(Age 22)

Mr. Crowell
(Age 27)

"They were married June 29, 1882."

Charles Dutton and Annie
Caroline (Bayard) Wick

Annie Bayard Crowell (Mrs.
Frederick C. Herrick) aged
ten, and "the little grandmother," Mrs. C. D. Wick.

Dr. Martin Luther Brooks,
Sunday school teacher of
Henry Crowell's class and
grandfather of Dr. Frederick
C. Herrick.

The Stillman Hotel, where Lillie Augusta Crowell died January 10, 1885, aged
twenty-five.

Why not take Jim Andrews? He is in a wholesale firm dealing with cloth; no prospects. He'll be glad to join me."

James Hanson Andrews was in the Crowell family so to speak. His sister, Mrs. Joel Burton Parsons, was Crowell's "Aunt Amelia." Andrews, one year Crowell's junior, turned out to be a top-shelf figure in the oatmeal business. Crowell was the dreamer, Andrews the doer; the name of Andrews is written high in the history of Akron. But over in Ravenna, they do not like Andrews to this day; he was a "driver" of some sort or other.

"I also thought," said Mr. Crowell, "since Ravenna is only thirty-five miles from Cleveland, I could be close to mother. I could spend week-ends with mother."

\* \* \*

We smile guardedly and say sotto vocé, "So, you wanted to be near your *mother,* Mr. Crowell? Well, how about the little Wick girl, Mr. Crowell?"

In my desk at Cedar-Palms, there is a tiny seventeen link gold chain, five inches long, a clasp at one end to attach it to a watch and a golden ball at the other. The ball is five-eighths of an inch in diameter, with a Tiffany-set garnet. You look at this little trinket thinking, "This is holy ground." The cherished trinket was attached to Lillie's watch. If no one is looking, you press it warmly in memory of the girl just blossoming into womanhood, who had loved Mr. Crowell from so early an age, she could not remember when it began. You press it again with deeper feelings when you find that for over sixty years, Mr. Crowell carried it in his vest pocket. A few days before his death, he placed it in the Chicago vault with his most valuable papers.

\* \* \*

On that November day in 1881, Lillie Augusta was decidedly no longer "the little Wick girl." She stood before him radiant and twenty-one. To natural grace had been added the culture of two years of art and voice study in Stuttgart, Germany; one year of European travel, additional study in a private school in Cleveland; and extended study of the harp and voice training in Philadelphia. That golden harp, whose strings once responded to her fingers, may be seen today at the top of the curved stair at

2211 Harcourt Drive in Cleveland. You look through the glass doors at wild-bird pattern China sets, which she painted; you see her art works framed and hanging on the walls. You probably never will see her hand writing; those letters she wrote to "Harry." But if you did, the careful writing and diction would augment your estimate of her. . . . Oh, she was an altogether lovely young lady, this Miss Lillie Wick!

Your pleasurable anticipations of what is about to happen as she stood before him, "radiant and twenty-one," will be increased by more detail concerning the broken engagement (Chapter IX). When Mrs. Charles D. Wick, Lillie's mother, first learned, some time in the fall of 1877, the "precious secret" her anguish was pitiful. Through tears and entreaties she succeeded in finally persuading Lillie to break the engagement; she feared Harry would never recover his health.

This cannot be held against Mrs. Wick, "the Little Grandmother," as she was affectionately called in later years. Her own life had been an Odyssey of sorrow. Hers were fears which proceed from mother-love; and it was the deference accorded to mother-love that moved Lillie to comply.

The record of the trying years which followed the broken engagement is well preserved in Lillie's letters. One thing you note upon examining them is that her love for Harry began when she was very young. Mrs. Herrick considerately made available "Mother's precious letters." These letters were all undated. When they were returned to Mrs. Herrick, with slips attached giving the approximate dates, she wrote: "I knew the fight for health lasted seven years, but I hadn't realized the length of their love affair, nor my Mother's youth when it began." Mr. Crowell evaded a definite reply on this point during the interviews. He would not say more than, *"We grew up together.* Lillie was a wonderful Christian girl."

Sometimes in the testing years Lillie's letters gave way to despair:

> "Dear Harry: It seems as though you and I are to travel a thorny path to heaven. . . . If such is the Lord's will, I submit."

But, when Harry made his brief visit in Cleveland, April, 1878, the effect was like magic. Lillie wrote to a friend a few days later, "When Mother and I saw Harry's improved condition, hope revived." On May 4, 1878, she sent a letter to Dr. Weir Mitchell, taking him into her confidence completely:

> "When we were engaged, Mr. Crowell being then so delicate, Mama feared his recovery to perfect health impossible, and the idea of her dying and leaving her fatherless and only child with an invalid husband drove her to despair. Knowing the trouble she had passed through, and with the desire to lighten this last burden, I sacrificed the fondest hope of my life and broke the engagement. . . . Mr. Crowell returned to Cleveland, April 21, with so decided an improvement in every respect that both Mama and I are greatly encouraged . . . hope revived! . . . . Do you think Mr. Crowell's health will ever permit our hope to be realized? . . .
>
> Lillie Augusta Wick"

Lillie's letter elicited from Dr. Mitchell a reply that is as heart warming as if it came in the morning mail:

> "My dear young Lady: A girl so true and devoted as you, and who can make such a sacrifice, deserves that a doctor should come in like the third volume of a novel, and make the paths straight. Let me advise you. Tell Mr. Crowell I think he will get well at the cost of two or three years on a farm . . . tell him I must see him then . . . then it will be time enough to talk of a renewed engagement. . . ."

Correspondence following the broken engagement continued, though not in great volume. Harry's western letters to Lillie are fine specimens of solicitous interest and confident faith. Concerning an accident from which Lillie narrowly escaped, he wrote:

May 1879

> "Another kind letter from little Mama informs me of your rapid recovery. Gratitude fills my heart that God has been with you and kept you from permanent injury . . . I am sure you will be well by fall. I can report good news in regard to myself: improvement constantly. So for the love you bear me, do not allow a single thought of me to mar your happiness. And believe me, ever lovingly and faithfully yours,
>
> Harry."

But on this good November day of 1881, the storms were past, the winter over and gone! The young man who stood before Lillie was, as Scott would state it, "free from those rowdy habits into which some plunge in the intervals of relaxation; marked by an instinctive delicacy which make one recoil from the low and vulgar."

Harry had kept the dawn of espousals like a royal robe, never to be worn in cheap contacts, reserved for regal affairs! For a time to come! For a heroine of distinctive features, whom he for years had loved! He had outgrown the sallowness of ill health.

There he stood, the new owner of the Quaker Mill, sound! Completely restored! Dr. Mitchell himself would have said, *"The* time has come!"

How good God was!

\* \* \*

They were married June 29, 1882, by Dr. Charles S. Pomeroy of the Second Presbyterian Church, at the home of Lillie's aunt, Mrs. Charles S. Bissell, 1082 Euclid Avenue. Her own mother, very ill, was under treatment with Drs. Mitchell and Pepper in Philadelphia. The young couple moved at once to Ravenna. In 1883 they moved back to Cleveland, temporarily residing in the home of Mother Crowell. On the third day of May, 1883, their daughter, Annie Bayard Crowell, was born. For convenience, they took an apartment in the Stillman Hotel, which up to thirty years ago stood on the north side of Euclid near Erie. And there, January 10, 1885, "a day sable with grief and heartbreak," the young mother died in her twenty-fifth year, and within three weeks of her husband's thirtieth birthday.

\* \* \*

Annie Bayard Crowell integrates the story most charmingly. The records of the Old Stone Church thus take note:

> "Crowell, Annie Bayard, daughter of Mrs. Lillie Wick Crowell with Mrs. Annie Caroline Wick as Godmother . . . baptized May 11, 1887 by Rev. Hiram C. Hayden."

On July 22, 1908, the young Cleveland surgeon, Dr. Frederick Cowles Herrick (1872-1943), who had followed her to Paris, married her there in the American Chapel.

Now, see how interestingly Dr. Herrick fits into the story! Dr. Martin Luther Brooks, who taught the Sunday school class which Mr. Crowell attended as a boy, had a daughter, Mary Hanna Brooks, who married Dr. Henry Justus Herrick. Dr. and Mrs. Herrick in turn were the parents of Dr. Frederick Cowles Herrick! Thus Mr. Crowell as a lad was a pupil of the man whose grandson was to marry Mr. Crowell's daughter!

Mrs. Herrick in temperament is much like her father, H. P. C. Four times, she and Dr. Herrick presented to Mr. Crowell "the grandfather's heritage";

> October 25, 1911, Henry Crowell Herrick, now Lieutenant, United States Naval Reserve, in the Navy Air Arm.
>
> August 2, 1913, Frederick Cowles Herrick, Jr., now doing personnel work at the Devereux School, Devon, Penn.
>
> January 26, 1918, Bayard Brooks Herrick, now First Lieutenant (Army of the United States) serving overseas in the 100th Cavalry Reconnaissance Troop.
>
> March 22, 1920, Anne Frances Herrick, now a teacher in the Malvern School, Shaker Heights, Cleveland.

The progress and interests of the four Herrick grandchildren, and the two Crowell grandchildren, of whom we will speak later, were favorite topics with Mr. Crowell.

\* \* \*

Mr. Crowell's reserve upon the subject of his first marriage is not hard to understand. One day while talking with Mrs. Herrick, he accidentally took the little chain from his pocket, then replaced it. . . . When Mrs. Herrick was eighteen, her father paid her a brief visit, gave her all of her mother's jewelry and said, "They're your mother's; you shall have them." . . . A short sentence out of yesterday's records, like one of Beecher's vest pocket rubies, sums up the life of "the little Wick girl," as it bore upon the life of Mr. Crowell:

> "The inspiration of her loyalty and devotion was the great reason for Mr. Crowell's early successes."

## XV

## MAESTRO OF THE QUAKER OATS SYMPHONY

Herein, we go back to the economics classroom; we refresh our memories on such topics as Entrepreneurs and Agents of Production; we go still further, and consider big men, and a man big enough to lead them.

And now, in the evening of your life, Mr. Crowell, the Quaker Oats Company elects you Honorary Chairman of the Board!

Well, it was none of your doing, was it? You always aimed in everything you did to give God the glory.

No, it was not at all of your doing. But the action of the Board warmed your heart, didn't it, Mr. Crowell? It reminded you of a certain eternal truth—"He that humbleth himself shall be exalted!" (*Sketch Book*)

MRS. FREDERICK COWLES HERRICK
"much like her father, H. P. C. . . ."

QUAKER OATS, CEDAR RAPIDS, IOWA

# MAESTRO OF THE QUAKER OATS SYMPHONY

A N INSTITUTION is born when "a coordinating agent" combines "the agents of production." The all-language, blue ribbon word for the co-ordinating agent is the French "entrepreneur." For the agents of production, alas, we will have to get along with plain English. A worth-while analysis of any institution must be conscious of the merits of both entrepreneur, and, agents of production, or the analysis will be one-sided.

These pages wish to be equally fair towards the merits of the several strands which, interwoven, produced the Quaker Oats Company; and, the merits of the one who interwove them. That is why separate chapters have been devoted to Avina Sativa; to the new race of corn millers; and, to the advent of proper tools for modern corn milling. Nothing could be done by anyone without the foregoing; and nothing could be done with the three factors apart from an entrepreneur. The entrepreneur, in the case of the Quaker Oats Company, was to be Henry Parsons Crowell.

\* \* \*

This is a good time for a close-up of the new owner of the Quaker Mill, as he stands in place ready to lift the baton for the Oatmeal Symphony. You should keep in mind that being twenty-six, his character is fixed. That "rule of thirty" may rouse indignation; but it is too formidable to be held in contempt. A man at thirty is just about what he is going to be to the end of the play. He may develop, he may grow. But his development and growth will be an unfolding of what he is. That is why the Good Record puts such an underscore upon "the days of thy youth."

Straightway we are compelled to face Crowell's lack of formal education. Sickness stopped his academic training at a point not greatly exceeding junior year of high school. But, without deprecating education, let us be frank about the matter. Every competent man is self-educated, his real progress resulting, without benefit of classrooms, from those lonely and desultory hours in which he reads some choice book, studies his chosen work, closely observes the passing scene; or sometimes, from a bitter apprenticeship to adversity.

If a man cannot go to Yale, he is not necessarily foredoomed to defeat; and if he does go to Yale, his success is not thereby underwritten. In either case, "the lonely and desultory hours are the formatives." To a casual observer, a man during these hours is to all appearances like a vessel without pilot or rudder. In reality, however, natural inclination is at the helm. And natural inclination, if disciplined to the will of God, always makes the port. You remember young Crowell's Yale dreams were broken, and you think of him fighting seven years for health. You feel sorry for him. Don't! And do not feel sorry for yourself if you are in similar circumstances. The sons of God seem always to serve their apprenticeship in Egypt.

\* \* \*

If the agents of production happen to be men, men of parts, the entrepreneur must have a peculiar character. He must know exactly what ought to be done, he must rigidly set himself to see that it is done—but oh, he must be so gentlemanly about it! To keep the hinnies hitched, he has to be very patient. Even Balaam found it worth while to listen until the Donkey Song was finished.

Now, look at our autocrat at twenty-six. His eyes are mild blue, hair black and meticulously groomed, with a final little up-sweep on the right-hand part. This is done by holding down a finger beside the brush. Nose aquiline; forehead, untroubled; nicely arched, black eyebrows. He has a very heavy, black mustache, wears a faultless piece of tailoring, wing collar and bow tie. He is five feet seven and one half inches, weighs 150, and speaks in a voice winsomely dry and calm. When he looks you in the eye, even though you are opposed to him, you detect no venom in him. Do not look at him too closely if you have decided to oppose him;

his kindliness will disarm you. In a tight session, he is quieter than ever. No one in sixty years ever saw him leap to his feet and shout, "Do this, or else!"

If you remember Benjamin Franklin Mills, you think, Crowell is Mills all over. "Take your time! (Mills continues to say in young Mr. Crowell). Take your time! Find the will of God! Know what ought to be done. When folks who do not agree with you wish to talk, let them. Be quiet while they talk. After they've talked themselves out, they'll ask you what you think ought to be done. Be prepared to tell them. They'll do it!"

At twenty-six he is just what he will continue to be until almost ninety; an Autocrat Bound in Buckram. In the years that follow, you are to watch him dealing with eminent divines who wish to change the character of M.B.I. It is still a Bible institute. He deals with hot-minded capitalists who want to make bituminous stoves. Perfection still centers on oil. Back-pasture breeders feel that in cattle raising you have to worry along with four grades. Wyoming Hereford has two. Old-timers sing the virtues of "the old open barrel, in the cor-ner, groc-ry store." Quaker uses pretty packages. In all such matters, no one but an amiable autocrat could have held the course. Therefore, after a hundred tries to capture Mr. Crowell in a phrase, none has such quality as *Breakfast Table Autocrat*. (Thank you, Mr. Holmes!) That's what he was, and that's how he did it! We will stand to this until Luther's tiles have slipped to the ground. His oatmeal technique, which we now portray, was applied with equal excellence to everything from Hereford cattle to Bible institutes.

\* \* \*

Jim Andrews went into the production side in the Quaker Mill, Crowell took up the administrative. My readers are to remember, this is not a history of Quaker Oats, it is a biography of Mr. Crowell. . . . At the very outset, as a result of his lifelong habit of thinking things through in the light of the will of God, he had formed very definite ideas about conducting the oatmeal business. From the memorabilia of H. P. C. we quote verbatim his own conclusions as he wrote them down on some sheets of paper:

## POLICY OF THE A. C. (AMERICAN CEREAL) COMPANY OF OHIO

That we should make better oatmeal and cereals of all kinds than had ever been manufactured.

That no matter what the cost, we would abandon systems and methods and scrap machinery whenever changes could be made for the improvement of quality, or the lessening of the cost.

That we must not be dependent for volume or profit upon any one cereal, or country, or section of country; but to have our business so broadly distributed that panics or commercial disturbances or depressed times would not seriously cripple us or prevent our paying regular dividends.

That our selling organization should consist of men who were honest, intelligent, of good character and who were natural merchants and willing to render the very best of service to the customers. Our purpose was not only to give to the customers the very best of cereals, but to render to the jobbers and retailer a service that could not be equaled.

We were to scatter and diversify our business in all parts of the world, and do educational and constructive work so as to awaken an interest and create a demand for cereals where none existed. To this end, we would have no understandings, working arrangements or agreements with our competitors, but always keep ourselves in position to make any price that might be necessary to meet competition, should we want or need the business.

(In short)

My policy has been to make better oatmeal and cereal of all kinds than has ever been manufactured; to combine such companies as are interested, and willing, into a chartered company with capital stock, having full control over all its units. This chartered company will scrap machinery, or even the mills of constituent members as improvement necessitates. The general company should displace old names with a single trade name, and seek a world market. To this end, it must do educational work, and create an oat demand where none existed. It is only by such a broad distribution and central management that we can avoid the perils of panic, competition, or disaster to some one plant or other.

The Akron Milling Company, of which the Quaker Mill was a member, became very apprehensive of ruthless competition. Therefore, in 1885, they succeeded in getting twenty mills together in a voluntary oatmeal millers association. This was in part a result of Crowell's urgent advice, but he did not say "voluntary"; he said "organic." The twenty millers were afraid of organic union; they were sure a gentleman's agreement was just as good. But the gentleman's agreement soon expired. They invited Ferdinand Schumacher of the Jumbo Mill to come in with them. But "the little Dutchman" yelled, "Nein! Nein! Tausandmal nein! For why should I need *you* in *my* business?"

But by November, 1886, competition waxed so vicious that Schumacher "was scared. Worried and suspicious of everybody, he sat down with twelve other millers in Davenport, Iowa, and formed the Consolidated Oatmeal Company." Crowell said quietly before they formed the company—"Watch carefully. What we want is one trade name, central authority, capital stock. Watch that we do not form a pooler." But, they *did* form a semi-pooler, and made Crowell president. "And as before, it did not work." Just about this time, corn-shock Websters who wanted to move to Washington, saw in "Poolers" heaven's answer to their prayer for a big fat straw man. They thereupon made it much nicer for people to have poison oak than to be part of a pooler. Mr. Crowell smiled dryly at this turn, but said nothing. It was working out fine. He had no need for riding herd on the timid millers; circumstances were doing it for him.

\* \* \*

On the night of March 6, 1886, Schumacher's Jumbo Mill was completely destroyed by fire, leaving him in financial ruin. For the first time, Schumacher was ready to listen. All he had left was a valuable clientele. In April, when the Akron Milling Company approached him again, he was reasonable. With singular generosity the new company was called "the Schumacher Milling Company." By this time, Schumacher had come to dislike Crowell. To Schumacher, Crowell "was just an Emporkömmeling!" (upstart). So he "played his cards in such a way that Crowell was not elected to *any* office in the Schumacher Milling Company."

In June, 1891, a number of rival companies wanting to "get in," a new company was organized, the American Cereal Company. By this time the millers were "getting the size of Schumacher, the little fellow," so they put Crowell back as president of the new organization.

Not even yet, however, were the millers willing to follow Crowell's wishes in full. Crowell had no use for "holding companies," but the American Cereal Company, over his protest, was made a holding company. "It was a shaky setup."

\* \* \*

About this time "a division arose in the company." Schumacher's dislike for Crowell became violent. When Crowell began a campaign against "the old oatmeal barrel in the cor-ner groc-ry store," tensions between the two tightened like a saddle cinch. Crowell said, "The barrel is open to anything; we should package and advertise our goods." Schumacher roared, "Crowell is crazy, already yet! The grocers don't want packages, and the peoples don't want it neither. This advertisings is silly business! We'll *save* our money; let our *competitors* advertise."

In 1897 Schumacher succeeded in voting out Crowell's friend, Robert Stuart; and in 1898, he succeeded in throwing out Crowell.

\* \* \*

Mr. Crowell, in the Green Court Interviews, smiled at the memory. "I knew Mr. Schumacher's policies would not work, but I just kept still. It was not long before the directors of the American Cereal Company conferred with Myron Herrick and James Parmeley. They said, 'We can no longer run under Schumacher.' Herrick was a banker, Parmeley a realtor. They sent for me. So, in company with my mother, I went back to Cleveland and conferred with them. They raised the finances necessary to buy Schumacher out, and put me back as president. Schumacher at this point dropped out of the picture."

\* \* \*

On September 20, 1901, the millers went still further in following Crowell's advice; they organized the Quaker Oats Company under the laws of New Jersey. However, there were still too many voluntary features which Crowell did not approve. In 1907, they decided to let Crowell have his way all along the line, so they organized and chartered the Quaker Oats Company, *to have and to hold*. This company was to have one trade name, complete control over all the units, even to tearing a mill down if that seemed advisable. They had central authority, packaged goods, and a world-wide outlook.

This at last was just what Mr. Crowell had urged beginning in 1882. Twenty-five years of taking his time, patient waiting! No one familiar with the facts will wish to question that the element which put the Quaker Oats Company out in front was the patient, gentle, but relentless determination of Henry Parsons Crowell. This same technique he applied to all his life interests—Breakfast Table Autocrat!

Yet, so kindly was his procedure that few sensed how inflexible he was when once his mind was made up.

Theodore Roosevelt, who "never felt bully about trusts," lowered his lance and charged full tilt at the Quaker Oats Company. Crowell was the front. He took his time. Thought it through. Calmly testified. Federal attorneys blunted their spears against Crowell's tranquility and imperturbable statements. June 1, 1920, the Government moved to dismiss its own suit.

\* \* \*

News analysts in their scripts-for-Hollywood thus instruct directors: "As I begin to speak, let the orchestra play march-type music, with fan-fare effect, similar to the opening of the March of Time." It is a good device.

Music, please! Time marches on! Watch our autocrat lead his ensemble in such a way that a world market is built; the world's breakfast habits are changed! A Quaker Oats package is put on the shelves and in the kitchens of the globe!

(Fan-fare Crescendo) And today, 1945, The Quaker Oats Company has scattered over the world, twelve great plants, a dozen minor establishments, more than sixty elevators in the United States, and twenty in Canada. These units, with the Quaker-operated munitions plant in Grand Island, Nebraska, total one hundred and one, a quarter of a billion dollar enterprise, with business standards as high as the Quaker whose name it bears.

But Mr. Crowell did not do it all, and these pages have not once said so. The enterprise had to have men of parts in the beginning, succeeded by their sons, grandsons, and men-trained-in-the-plants, a notable company. Neither could this notable company have done it all. *They* had to have H. P. Crowell "to establish and maintain efficient relations between the agents of production."

\* \* \*

In his eighty-seventh year, 1942, Mr. Crowell reached a decision he had long contemplated. To all outward appearances, his eye had not dimmed, nor his strength abated. But—it was wisdom to retire from leadership before he, unaware of a change, was found to be holding power without the ability to use it. God had been very good to him. He had been young, was now old, but he had been blessed in all things. He gazed with clouded eyes from his lofty window in the Board of Trade Building. Yes, it was time to retire. He rang for a secretary . . . dictated. . . .

\* \* \*

In one folder of Mr. Crowell's correspondence, obviously cherished above the rest, was a letter:

Chicago, May 22, 1942
*General Advice*

At a meeting of the Board of Directors held today, the following changes in the official organization of the Company were made:

After a lifetime of intimate official service to the Quaker Oats Company, and its predecessors, Mr. Henry Crowell retires as Chairman of the Board. Mr. Crowell began his activities in the cereal business in the Quaker Mill Company, Ravenna, Ohio, in 1881. [Sixty-one years.] His participation has been continuous from that time except for a break of one year, due to a change in administration in 1898. With such an experience, it is impossible to measure the beneficial influence of Mr. Crowell's leadership and character on the Quaker Oats Company. We all wish for him still many years of health and enjoyment. The Board of Directors has expressed its appreciation and regard *by appointing Mr. Crowell Honorary Chairman of the Board.* [Italics mine] . . .

Robert E. Coon, Secretary

Mrs. Henry Luther Crowell
(age cir. 50)
H. P. C. said, "I thought if I bought the mill,
I could be near mother."

"The little Quaker Mill at Ravenna, Ohio, could say, 'I gave Henry Parsons
Crowell. And I gave you the Quaker Oats Company.' "

James Hansen Andrews
(age cir. 70)
Partner in the Quaker Mills

Plant at Cedar Rapids

Upper plant at
Akron, Ohio

Lower plant at
Akron, Ohio

Plant at Peterborough, Canada

THE BIG THREE OF THE QUAKER OATS COMPANY DIVISIONS

For Men

For Animals

SOME QUAKER PRODUCTS

John Stuart, Chairman Board of Directors, Quaker Oats Company and Arthur Poe, Superintendent, Cedar Rapids Division. Mr. Stuart is presenting Mr. Poe (March 1, 1944) with a Quaker Button, upon the occasion of his completing forty years with the company.

R. Douglas Stuart
President

George Curtis Fretz
Superintendent, Akron
Division

OFFICIALS, QUAKER OATS COMPANY

# XVI

## A STOVE TO COOK YOUR OATS

The tale of a Swede with a little tin stove, a young hardware clerk in a store where the Cleveland Hotel is located, and the beginning of the world's greatest factory for oil burning stoves.

"Mr. Crowell, despite his exceptional modesty, was a man of great personal charm, and his keen mind, clear judgment, and wise counsel, which served so long as a guiding spirit to the other executives of Perfection Stove Company, will not only be felt as a great business loss by them, but in his death they will have also lost a friend, whose high sense of honor, cheerful disposition, and wholehearted co-operation have endeared him to them throughout their long years of association with him." (*Perfection Reporter,* November, 1944)

# A STOVE TO COOK YOUR OATS

THE wide apostolate of D. L. Moody required England, Ireland, Scotland, Wales, the United States, and the Dominion of Canada as a biographical background. But there was a gentle eminence in Northfield, Massachusetts, which so dominated his life that his biography could fittingly be titled "Round Top." This little hill overlooks his birthplace, and the home in which he lived the last twenty-five years of his life. It is the shrine of Northfield Seminary, and on its summit, awaiting resurrection morn, lie the bodies of Moody and his beloved Emma.

Similarly, the life of Mr. Crowell might well have been titled "Public Square," after Cleveland's city-center park. He was born within a stone's throw of the Public Square; there he played as a boy; near-by he worked in a wholesale shoe store. It centered the lives of his friends and acquaintances; and into the Terminal Building at the end, came his body for interment in Lake View Cemetery. The Public Square was the symbol of Cleveland to him. It seemed fitting that so much of the interpretation of his life should have been dreamed out in Hotel Cleveland—on the Public Square!

Incidentally, here's a protest against the attempt to change the name "Public Square" to "Monumental Park!" We have never had any respect for palimpsest perpetrators; men so callous, or indolent, or both, as to write what they wanted to say over ancient records. No matter how worthy their message, that was not the place to put it. We would as soon submit to renaming the Boston Common "Little-Brown Square," as to remain silent when "Public Square" is labelled "Monumental Park." It is an historic blackout of the colorful beginnings wherein Moses Cleaveland "surveyed for public buildings, with a green reserved for a public square."

Since Mr. Crowell's life revolved so largely about the Cleveland Public Square, it is not a matter of surprise that here in book-center, we return to it. . . .

It is the year 1882, as nearly as may be figured, and the scene is a hardware store located right where the Cleveland Hotel stands today! A tinsmith with a marked Swedish accent walked into the hardware store with a paper-wrapped bundle under his arm. Unwrapping his parcel, he displayed to the store owner a contraption he had designed himself, and built in his own home. Alas, no one in the City of Silk and Money seems to remember the man had a name! So the Swede not only received a mere pittance for his genius, but even his name is forgotten!

His device was a crude, small chimney-stove, hardly more than a glorified lamp, but with a larger oil reservoir, and a bigger wick than a lamp. He had a top frame riveted on, which was to hold cooking utensils over the heat.

"Vould you like, please, to buy my lamp-stove?"

The store owner not only bought it, but gave the workman an order for more. This and subsequent orders were placed with the tiny foundry of Taylor and Boggis. "It was not long before the hardware trade generally knew of this new device." In the hardware store there was a clerk, Francis Edson Drury, born 1850, in Pittsfield, Michigan, near Ann Arbor, and educated in the public schools of Adrian. He came to Cleveland in 1870 "and secured a job as a small salaried clerk in the hardware store."

No one was more fascinated with the lamp stove than Drury. "His mind leaped to the possibilities it offered. The more he thought about it, the greater the opportunity seemed to him." Drury felt he just had to get into the enterprise, so he "associated himself" (big words for "put in a little cash") with the foundry.

But merely to make (unpatented) stoves for someone else, did not satisfy Drury. He therefore conferred with Taylor:

"Let's make oil stoves and sell them ourselves," he suggested. Then he "painted the great future of the business."

"Let's let well enough alone," Taylor snapped. "We are making money enough out of the business as it is. Why risk what we are making now by taking chances in the business itself?"

This closed the matter—so far as Taylor and Boggis Foundry Company were concerned. But not for Drury. Right at this point Henry Parsons Crowell entered the scene. One day in 1888, when Mr. Crowell was calling on Miss Susan Coffin Coleman, he mentioned that Charles Crowell, his brother, on account of broken health, was giving up his business, the Cleveland Desk Company, and going West for his health. "It was necessary to find someone to take Charlie's place."

Promptly Miss Coleman, of whom the next chapter will have much to say, replied, "I know the very one for you. He is an enterprising young man, and penniless; but he could make money if he had a chance." Thereupon, she arranged a meeting between Mr. Crowell and Mr. Drury.

Drury earnestly pictured the possibilities of the oil stove business as he saw it. Thereupon, as Mr. Crowell's daughter writes, "Father supplied the necessary capital, and in 1888, together with Mr. Drury, organized the Cleveland Foundry Company. I have dim recollections of Father and another man frequently talking together in the living room of the Stillman Hotel apartment. In later years, Mr. Drury used to tell me how I interfered with their business conferences by crawling all over them."[1]

In the year 1887, Mr. F. E. Drury and Mr. H. P. Crowell entered into a contract to provide funds with which to organize a company, for the purpose of doing a general foundry business. They started to operate in the old buildings of the Buckeye Stove Works at Platt Avenue, corner of the Cleveland & Pittsburgh Railroad. Incorporation papers were taken out early in the year 1888 under the name Buckeye Foundry Company, but only a few months afterward the name was changed to the Cleveland Foundry Company. (Records, E. A. Dodd)

The Swede with a tin stove, a penniless young hardware clerk, and the giant plants of Perfection prophetically fogged in above

[1] Letter, March 9, 1945, of Mrs. Herrick. The history of the beginnings of the Perfection Stove Company has some rather vague zones; but help in lighting them up came from the research of Florence M. Gifford, Head, General Reference Division, Cleveland Public Library; the historic summaries compiled by Edwin A. Dodd, Secretary, and Clyde A. Thompson, Assistant Advertising Manager of the Perfection Stove Company; Rev. Guy H. Volpitta, Pastor, Woodland Hills Union Church, Cleveland; Margaret Stinson, Secretary to Dr. Whyte, The Old Stone Church; and Helen H. Raymond, Secretary to Dr. Bird, The Church of the Covenant.

them, would make a far likelier mural for the walls of the Terminal Station than "conventionals" which try to deliver their messages through startling gears and thick-limbed Calibans. That event marked the beginning of the world's largest exclusive manufacturers of oil-burning stoves, whose products are in millions of homes, and whose profits, so far as Drury was concerned, went by the millions into a number of things from theatrical tinsels to the support of colleges. In later life, Mr. Drury made his winter home in Augusta, just to be near his friend, Mr. Crowell, and "died there April 3, 1932, Chief Patron of the Play House, (Cleveland, Ohio) heavy supporter, Cleveland Orchestra, and general philanthropist" (*Cleveland Plain Dealer*).

The Cleveland Foundry addressed itself to making oil stoves. In 1890, it offered on the market its first product, a lamp type stove made in one, two, and three burner sizes, sold under the resounding trade names of "Puritan, Triumph, and Defiance." It is impossible to say why the name "Defiance" was selected, unless the Foundry had in mind that whatever one did, the stoves smoked.

Mr. Dodd writes in a whimsical vein, "They cooked, it is true, and that was something in those days, when the idea of cooking with oil was still decidedly in the experimental stage. They also smoked, on little or no provocation. And when they smoked, they smelled. They even smelled when they did not smoke."

And thus, when the year 1901 arrived, the Cleveland Foundry was running out "a happy assembly line of stoves." But the year 1901 was Anno Mirabulus for the company, as we shall see.

\* \* \*

It is now timely to dovetail into the record a thumbnail sketch of another of Cleveland's Money Makers, "John D. of the Standard Oil Company." In Chapter Two, "City of Silk and Money," it was noted, under the year 1853: "William Avery and Eliza Davison Rockefeller and son John Davison, fourteen, move to Cleveland from New York."

"John D." was born in Richford, New York, July 8, 1839. He was educated briefly, in Cleveland's public schools, and "could hardly wait to accept a position as clerk in a forwarding and commission house." In 1858, at nineteen, he formed his own commission house, Clark and Rockefeller. In 1862 under the firm name of Rockefeller, Andrews and Clark, he began to refine oil. In 1865, he built the Standard Oil Works in Cleveland; formed the Standard Oil Company in 1870, the Standard Oil Trusts in 1882. Money flowed into his bank accounts like Mokelumne floods in May. So much accrued that by 1921, he had given away over $500,000,000. It would be better to write that out, Five Hundred Million Dollars! But John D., we fear, had much in common with the James family; at least the U. S. Government thought so. Though it dismissed its anti-trust suit against Quaker Oats, it dissolved Standard Oil in 1892.

The point of interest in this story, however, was a troublesome problem encountered in Rockefeller's oil refining. Under the imperfect cracking processes at the turn of the century "a considerable portion of every barrel of petroleum became kerosene. Thus Rockefeller was accumulating a lake of coal oil, with no market for it." Something had to be done. It was.

In the good year above-mentioned, 1901, the Standard Oil Company had three thousand salesmen, a lake of coal oil no one wanted, and—a bright idea. They approached the Cleveland Foundry with a suggestion: "Would you mind if our three thousand salesmen undertook the sale of your stoves?" Would they mind! Of course we are not tempted to interpret Standard's idea as originating in the milk of human kindness, any more than we will think of World War Number Two being resolved by the warming ideals of brotherhood. Crowell and Rockefeller never met personally; all transactions were carried on with Drury at the front, Crowell, in true form, in the background.

Naturally, the Cleveland Foundry Company began to prosper. Out of this grew the Cleveland Factory Company and the Cleveland Metal Products Company, the latter organized in 1910. Under date of January 2, 1917, a merger was effected between the Cleveland Foundry Company and the Cleveland Factory Company, with the Cleveland Metal Products Company, under the name of the latter company. On October 6, 1925, the name of the latter was changed to Perfection Stove Company to better connect the name with their nationally-advertised products, namely, Perfection Oil Cook Stoves, Ovens, Cabinets, Heaters, Water Heaters, etc.

Mechanical Engineers were engaged to improve the operation of the various devices. They cured the stoves of physical faults of combustion and added a number of devices that people never dreamed could be operated by the "little plain sister" of Standard Oil—coal oil! (E. A. Dodd)

\* \* \*

No part of the long research was more delightful than the contacts with the Perfection Stove Company, and the inspection of the giant factories in Cleveland. There are two plants, occupying over twenty-seven acres of land, on which there are buildings with a total of 965,805 square feet of floor space, and a normal pay roll of 1800 men and women. There are also seven district offices in the United States.

The name "Mr. Crowell" was an open Sesame; he was beloved throughout the enterprise. President Chadwick spoke of Mr. Crowell's unfailing kindness, his wise counsel which more than anything else accounted for the success of Perfection. He spoke of Crowell's clear vision, patience, lovable personality—and, *"no mistake* about it, his inflexible autocracy in administration."

One likes to hear this large Vermonter, President Chadwick, talk. His own life story is good material for some biographer; for his life also, is "a specimen of the richness and continuity of American life." It has many of the dramatic patterns that Americans love to contemplate; New England farm boy, backwoods schools, night study, university! Up he goes! Salesman, sales manager, gang boss foreman . . . President! On the way up, he took time out to build a pretty fair six-cylindered automobile which you will remember by the name "Chadwick"; furthermore, he took time out to put his general economic impressions into book form, *Balanced Employment*. He will tell you in a deprecatory way he has been with Perfection only a short time, "around thirty years." But when he gets back to the subject of Mr. Crowell, there's no deprecation. "I'm not much of a churchman," he

MAIN PLANT OF THE PERFECTION STOVE COMPANY

Mr. Crowell at thirty-three, when the Cleveland Foundry
was built.

The Cleveland Foundry

Original factory
force of thirty-six

Francis Edson Drury

Secondary Plant, Perfection Stove Company

## FOUR PEACE TIME PRODUCTS OF THE
## PERFECTION STOVE COMPANY

Perfection Oil Burning Table
Top Range →

Superflex Oil Burning 24-
hour Winter Air Condition-
← ing Furnace

Puritan Kerosene Burning
Water Heater →

← Ivanhoe Heater

## FOUR WAR TIME PRODUCTS
(Mainly for Corsairs and Helldivers)

Jeffersonville
Quartermaster
Field Stove →

Cabin and
Windshield
← Assemblies

Airacobra
Cabin Door →

Model 400
← Engine Heater

# OFFICERS OF THE PERFECTION STOVE COMPANY

Lee Sherman Chadwick, President

George L. Harrison, Vice-president and director of manufacturing.

Edwin A. Dodd, Vice-president and treasurer.

John C. Wallace, Vice-president and director of sales.

Donald S. Smith, Vice-president and assistant treasurer.

Clyde Thompson, Assistant Advertising Agent.

The Vassar Student
(1878-1882)
(Loaned from the Vassar Archives)

The Young Wife
1890

Mother and Son
1898

"My five year old son"

SUSAN COLEMAN CROWELL

says apologetically, "but I can go for Mr. Crowell's type of Christianity."

Leading officers came and went "to meet Mr. Crowell's biographer." Many letters have passed since then, which have gone far beyond the character of mere business correspondence. But everything bears the evidence of the esteem in which Perfection held Mr. Crowell. Immediately after Mr. Crowell's death, "The Perfection Reporter" thus memorialized its leader:

> "Despite his many other interests, Mr. Crowell's indomitable courage enabled the Company to grow to its present industrial stature . . . his exceptional modesty, personal charm, keen mind, clear judgment, wise counsel have endeared him to all of us throughout the long years."

Those who came close to Mr. Crowell, on the other hand, realized that none of his industrial enterprises was more esteemed than The Perfection Stove Company. Perfection to him was eloquent of the Old Home Town, and the Public Square; and of the days when as a young business man he was coming to his own.

# PART TWO
## CHRISTIAN STATESMAN
## 1898 – 1944

BOARD OF TRADE BUILDING, CHICAGO

You can stand in La Salle Street, look up to a certain lofty floor level, and see the windows of Mr. Crowell's office. You will recall with amazement that there, with a diligence worthy of his fiery forties, he continued to serve his generation until he was within a few weeks of his nintieth birthday.

# XVII

## SUSAN OF OLD RAVENNA

In which, after the several years of bereavement, following the death of Lillie Augusta Wick, Mr. Crowell weds Susan Coffin Coleman, who enriches and complements his mature years.

When the reserve with which Mr. Crowell shielded his personal affairs is penetrated, you note how in each of the two phases of his life, Christian Business Man, and Christian Statesman, there was a notable woman. Lillie Augusta Wick was the morning star for his young manhood, inspiring him in his fight for health, and in his early business success. And Susan Coffin Coleman, with equal significance, blessed his mature years. Upon catching the vision of living his life so as always to please his Lord, he conducted his secular interests as one under sacred orders; and his dreams were shared and cherished by Susan as if they were her very own. (*Sketch Book*)

# SUSAN OF OLD RAVENNA

THE warm winds and gentle rains of April, 1888, moved across Portage County, Ohio, and the citizens of "Old Ravenna," as they affectionately called their little mill town, felt as if a burden had been lifted. For ninety consecutive days, they had experienced snowstorms and bitter cold; and the stream which turned the mill had been solidly frozen for so long that the path over the weir seemed a permanent feature.[1]

But now, at April-end, pussy willows, whose treasure can never be entered by tropical people, graced the vases on Ravenna center tables, and, the Murfeys on Main Street had a very attractive visitor!

It was perfectly natural for Miss Susan Coffin Coleman, just returned from a year of special study in Germany, to leave her Cleveland home, though she had been there but a few days, and hasten to Ravenna. Did not the Portage County Records carry this entry—"Born to Mr. and Mrs. William B. Coleman, in Ravenna, June 24, 1860, a daughter, Susan Coffin Coleman"? And was it not equally natural for Miss Coleman to be a house guest in the Murfey home? Just across the street from her birthplace, another little girl was born, Rose Richardson. Susan and Rose grew up together. And Rose Richardson was Mrs. Ned Murfey!

[1] Ravenna is somewhat accustomed to hard winters. Under date of February 20, 1945, Rev. Earl R. Henderson, Pastor of the Ravenna Methodist Church, a greatly esteemed help in research, wrote, "I went down to the Old Mill, or where it used to be. It was a real effort to get there, for here in Ravenna, we have had the greatest snow for many a year . . . the little stream that revolved the Old Mill was frozen over. We walked right across it. There is a line which reads, 'The Birth Place of ?'—but ice and snow so covered the rest, I was not able to decipher it. It was a most lovely sight, and you would have been delighted. The man who built it must have had a love of beauty as well as of power. There is an old structure still standing bearing the words 'Quaker Oats'. . . ."

Even as it is impossible to interpret Charles Haddon Spurgeon apart from Susannah, so it is impossible to understand the hiding of power in Mr. Crowell's mature years without taking into account Susan Coleman. No one illustrates better than she Goethe's untranslatable line, "Das Evig—weibliche Zieht Uns Hinan!" Therefore, it is time well spent to devote an entire chapter to her, who for thirty-four years was Mr. Crowell's constant companion, friend, counsellor, sharing joyfully his every vision as Christian Statesman.

For a long time, adequate information concerning Susan's early life could not be had. At last certain persons were located who from personal memory furnished the coveted data—Miss Cornelia M. Raymond of Vassar; Mrs. Rose Murfey of Chicago; and Mrs. Mary Andrews of Washington, D. C. Prof. C. E. Chapman calls such persons, "History's first line documents, living witnesses." Chiefly through the three above-named, Susan's early story is excellently restored, and the following is a mosaic largely fashioned from the testimony of these three women, "richly advanced in years."

\* \* \*

If any interest attaches to Genealogy's Dusty Shelf, open Steven's *Nantucket.* There you may trace the paternal side of Susan's ancestry. William B. Coleman, her father, had a perennial love for the little island, Nantucket, and the little sister island, Martha's Vineyard. We have no quarrel with any who cherish these tiny Massachusetts areas; they are beauty marks put by the hand of God on the face of the New World. Old Tom Macy made "a powerful good bargain, when he bought Nantucket from the Indians for one hundred and fifty dollars and two beaver hats." In early Colonial days, Nantucker Harbor sheltered one hundred and fifty whalers, and a population which lived to the cry, "Thar she blows!" The romance of that period has passed into story books; the old fishing vessels are gone; the harbor today is filled with white sails and the "put-put" of outboard motors. But we cherish Nantucket just the same; like it a little better when we find that Will Coleman was born there, and later, as a young man, settled in Old Ravenna, married Miss Mary E.

Humphrey, lived on Main Street, and was the father of Susan Coffin Coleman and Frank H. Coleman.

Susan also loved Nantucket. In her Vassar days, she made special research on the island, gathering materials for a major thesis. Her paper is in possession of her son, Henry Coleman Crowell. You may read for yourself her colorful paragraphs depicting Nantucket's old-fashioned ways and charming scenes, together with the words of commendation pencilled in the margins of the thesis by her teacher.

When Susan was about ten years of age, the family moved from Ravenna to Cleveland. She never forgot about old Fluff, the family cat: "He didn't care for Cleveland, and as soon as ever he got loose, he returned to Ravenna, thirty miles away, on foot."

The first mention of the W. B. Colemans in the Cleveland city directories is in the issue of 1874, which shows them living at Whitman and Randall, "in a brick house, painted, and outstanding in that neighborhood." In her childhood, Susan attended the Kentucky Public School of Cleveland and there received her first impulses to go to Vassar. Several of her classmates were about to matriculate in Vassar and "talked of it all the time." Susan's father was favorably inclined. "Vassar was a stylish college. It was expensive; but, though he was not exactly a wealthy man, yet he had prospered in the coal business, and was well able to send Susan." Susan's mother, described as smart and clever, was also naturally in favor of Vassar. In 1878, therefore, Susan, eighteen years of age, matriculated at Vassar, "a splendid pagan, though animated by high ideals."

For the subjoined part of the record, we are indebted to Miss Cornelia M. Raymond, whose father, Dr. John Howard Raymond, brilliant philosopher and Hebraist (1814-1888) organized Vassar College. Miss Raymond has retired as Director of Vassar's Bureau of Publication, but is still working on the early records. Her personal recollections are of high value. She writes:

"I remember coming to Vassar as a little girl at the opening of the college, with my father, President Raymond. Oh, there are advantages in growing old at Vassar! And one is these memories!"

She also knew of Susan, and where memory did not yield a complete account, Miss Raymond searched the old records until she found what was desired. Not only so, but she loaned from the files the college-girl photo of Susan which graces these pages. Susan graduated from Vassar in the class of 1882. Miss Raymond graduated in 1883. Miss Raymond comments:

> "I have no clear memory of Miss Coleman, but her personality may be known by the testimony of her classmates who were still living at the time of her death in 1922. She was a very good student. We marked on the scale of 5, that being the highest, and she was generally 4 or 4½. While at Vassar, she was admired for her wonderful beauty, her vivacity, and fine penetrating mind. Later, her logical mind was given to the study of the Bible, and her wealth to the spread of the gospel. [That word "later" is most significant; for the testimony of those who knew Susan emphasizes a remarkable change.]

Another acquaintance of Susan's writes:

> "She became an Episcopalian at Vassar, but it didn't go very deep. She was simply a nominal Christian, a splendid pagan though animated by high ideals. It was almost impossible for her college friends to realize how this conventional society girl flowered into the saintly hostess of Green Court."

Entries in Susan's Vassar Good Times Book reflect nothing of her mature passion for the kingdom of God and His righteousness. Her enthusiasms went completely to dramatics, the social round, and literary activities. Her general popularity brought her the honor of selection in the famous "Daisy Chain." [1]

Following graduation, Susan taught mathematics and Latin in the Liggett School of Detroit, Michigan, 2555 Burns Avenue. The Bursar of the Liggett School writes that the old records show "Susan Coffin Coleman, A. B. Vassar, as an esteemed member of the faculty 1882-1884." After teaching for several years, Susan

---

[1] "We still have a Daisy Chain at Vassar, but the old glory has departed. The Senior girls made wreaths of daisies (a daisy chain), which were placed, after graduation, near the Class Tree. . . . Twenty-six Sophomore girls were selected by the Senior committee to carry the chain. . . . These were naturally the attractive, popular girls, the socially brilliant. The newspaper world played this up, until it was headline interest in the world of fashion, and a Daisy Chain Girl had her photograph published as a matter of national news."

spent some time in her Cleveland home, followed by a year of special study in Germany, 1887-1888. It was upon her return to the United States in the early spring of 1888, that she hastened down to Old Ravenna for a visit with Rose Murfey.

This visit had a surprising denouement, and Mrs. Murfey never forgot her part in it.

> She had never seen Susan, just back from Europe, so charming; like Spring herself . . . a splendid worldling balanced by a high sense of honor, and though she was twenty-eight, she retained the vivacious and clever traits of the teens, and you could not resent it.

Right here the lines begin to interweave. Ned Murfey, Rose's husband, was one of the young men Henry Parsons Crowell had attached to his newly acquired Quaker Mill. The young Murfeys held a deep affection toward their chief; one of their children was named "Harry Parsons Murfey." [1] Mr. Crowell, a very lonely young man since the death of Lillie, often dropped into the Murfey home for a visit.

And one of these visits was on a spring evening of that April, 1888! Mrs. Murfey, an elderly woman living near Chicago, still warms to the memory of it all; delights to retell the outcome; rejoices in her part.

> "Was it not spring? Was it not her home? Was not Susan her dearest friend? And—was it not love at first sight!"

*     *     *

The courtship proceeded with alacrity. Sarah Rush, for years an Irish domestic in the Crowell home, carries a trove of memories of:

> what my mistress told me. But mind you, are you sure it's all right with Mr. Crowell for me to talk? [Then she warms to her subject in charming Erin accent.] I came to Mr. Crowell in August, 1916, from Bel-fast. My sister Annie Rush died in 1932, June. She came to Mr. Crowell in 1898, when Coleman was just a baby. Mr. Crowell put up with me. He's fine, but I'm queer. Mind you! Nothing of this in the book without Mr. Crowell okays it.

[1] Mr. H. P. Murfey, of the Chicago Quaker Oats staff, in turn has a son, "Harry Parsons Murfey, Jr."

Right after he met Susan, he said, "would you go drivin'?" They hardly got started before Mr. Crowell said, "Whoa, Susan!" The mistress told me, "Here I was at his side, and I thought, Sure, and what kind of a young man is *this!*" Then Mr. Crowell said, "Not you, the horse. I knew the horse before I knew you." [Sarah now speaks of her mistress, long since deceased.]

"Ah, but she was tall like a queen! A really beautiful woman, grayish kind of eyes. Whenever you see a stout person who is untidy, it isn't necessary! Mrs. Crowell, even in the mor-ning, was so neat like a row of pins. When she took so sick she sent a telegram, 'Harry, I need you.' "

\* \* \*

On Tuesday evening, July 10, 1888, Mr. Crowell and Miss Coleman were united in marriage at the Coleman home, 124 Whitman Avenue, Cleveland. Her parents attended the St. John's Protestant Episcopal Church. Therefore, "the ceremony was read by the Rev. Henry D. Aves, of the fashionable west side church."

For a time, Mr. and Mrs. Crowell lived with the Murfeys in Ravenna. When the general offices of the oat millers association were established in Chicago, they moved to Chicago in the fall of 1888, living for a short time at 134 Pine Street, later at 82 Astor Street. In 1898, an important year for Mr. and Mrs. Crowell, we find them living at 167 Rush Street.

In 1892 they united by letter with the Fourth Presbyterian Church. For several years, they were simply "church members of the thoroughly conventional sort." The testimony of Mrs. Andrews of Washington, D. C., perfects the narrative at this point. Mrs. Andrews, born Mary Warren Fentress, the daughter of an attorney in Bollivar, Tennessee, married Sidney F. Andrews, a brilliant Chicago corporation attorney. Her husband, now deceased, has some excellent Christian institutions in Dixie Land, memorial to him. Mrs. Andrews writes:

"Susan came to Chicago a real worldling, a brilliant, high-minded attractive woman, but a worldling. Then in 1898, Dr. W. R. Newell began to teach a Bible class in their Rush Street residence. Susan was soundly converted. A more real right about face I never saw. For a time she continued in Chicago society, and I have often seen her in our waning [sic!] social occasions, slip her arm lovingly through that of another woman, and with tears in her eyes ask, 'Are you a Christian?' She was in love with Christ! After sitting in Dr. Newell's classes, her home, her hospitality, her household were at the Lord's bidding, and used entirely for Him."

The analysis of the Newell Bible Classes, which exercised an equally powerful influence on Mr. Crowell, is reserved for study in the next chapter. But the memorabilia of Susan's life testifies to a remarkable transformation as a result of these classes. In the "Record of the Class of 1882," Vassar College, is a letter from Susan dated June, 1902, and captioned "Twenty Years After":

"I wish I could go back the 10th of June, but I see no chance of it. I should love to meet with the girls again, and see the many, many changes in the college, as well as in each of us. As to the items for class history, I feel that I must send a word; for during the past four years, God has been very gracious to me and mine. . . . Since then, my whole life and nature have been changed. My husband, too, has had the same happy experience. This may seem slightly out of order for a class history, but after all, it is the only item of great interest I have ever had to tell.

It may make an agreeable variety, for most of us make much of the things of this life which pass away and omit the greater and better things of eternity . . .

So I am heading in the opposite direction from the old college times; but I am happy and assured that at last I have the firm Rock Foundation under my feet. I'll put a kodak picture of my five-year old boy in this. He, too, is a joy.

Susan Coleman Crowell"

Mrs. Henry Coleman Crowell ("Perry") likewise adds valuable testimony as to the change in Susan:

"To hear her say in later years, that she would like to stand on every street corner and ask everyone about his soul's salvation, and show him the Way, was as great a contrast to the society Susan of earlier days as could be possible . . . the change was unbelievable. I knew my husband's mother for only three brief years before her death. She was a brilliant, vivacious woman, and could talk on any subject. As a hostess, she was without peer, leading in the most interesting conversations, and always drawing *all* her guests into them without partiality. I always think of her with an open Bible, and I never knew her to talk of the things of the Lord without tears coming to her eyes, so deep was her love for Him."

\* \* \*

Immediately following her deeper experience, "Susan with a heart on fire for God," associated herself with two other young matrons in the Fourth Presbyterian Church, Mrs. William Borden (mother of "Borden of Yale") and Mrs. Sidney F. Andrews. They formed Bible classes for women, which, taking the surname initials of the three women, became famous as "The A-B-C Bible Classes of Chicago." The classes exerted a profound evangelical influence throughout Chicago, and the fruits are still in evidence.

\* \* \*

Nine years after the marriage of Mr. Crowell and Miss Coleman, their son Henry Coleman Crowell was born in the Astor Street residence, April 13, 1897. It should be remembered that Coleman Crowell was born in the general period of his mother's deeper experience, and his life is powerfully marked by her earnest prayers.

Coleman matriculated in Yale 1917, and in his second year transferred to the Scheffield Scientific School. He graduated from Yale, June, 1921, with the degree Ph. B. Today he is Executive Vice President of Moody Bible Institute, "thereby succeeding in what he esteems his father's chief work." In particular, it is Coleman Crowell's interest to manage the technical side of the great radio stations, WMBI and WDLM, and to have oversight of the legal aspects of the school. Tom Smith of the Moody Board writes: "I thank God for Henry Parsons Crowell's son, Coleman." He might well have added, "And I thank God for Susan Crowell, who in a peculiar way dedicated her son to this work."

\* \* \*

This record shall not be so abbreviated as to omit certain matters of deep interest to Henry Parsons Crowell. On July 7, 1919, Henry Coleman Crowell and Miss Lucy Perry Kimball were engaged. Thereupon, Mr. Crowell took "Perry" for a walk.

In a business-like way, he said, "Please tell me how you young people met, and all the details leading up to your decision to marry." The young lady complied as best she could. Then Mr. Crowell said with a smile: "Susan and I prayed for Coleman; prayed every step of the way, and I just wanted to see how the Lord answered our prayer."

Evidently Mr. Crowell was well pleased, for in the years that followed, it was a familiar thing to see him continuing that first walk with Coleman's wife. Mr. Coleman Crowell and Miss Perry Kimball [1] were married in Evanston, June 24, 1920.

Mr. and Mrs. Coleman Crowell enriched Mr. Crowell's heritage with two grandchildren:

> July 13, 1926, Mary Coleman Crowell
> May 3, 1928, John Kimball Crowell

How deeply Mr. Crowell's affections were centered in his six grandchildren may be seen in a letter to Mrs. Rose Murfey, in whose home he first met Susan:

> "My little granddaughter just approaching seventeen is wonderfully mature, reaching high marks in her classes . . . she is charming . . . I am confident she has a brilliant future before her. . . ."

\* \* \*

In 1897-1898 "when Ferdinand Schumacher threw Crowell out," Mr. and Mrs. Crowell moved to Cleveland for a few months, occupying T. P. Handy's city home. In the fall of 1898, they returned to Chicago, and took residence at 167 Rush Street. Soon thereafter, Dr. Newell's Bible classes began. . . .

In 1901, as the result of a disastrous fire in the Rush Street home, the Crowells moved to Winnetka, and six months later, purchased the residence at Seven Seventy Humboldt Drive.

This was a dignified city-home, occupying two and one-half acres. The property is at street level with Humboldt Drive until the house has a place to stand; then it drops swiftly into a ravine area where a spacious formal garden, beautiful with summer

---

[1] The help rendered by "Perry" (Mrs. Coleman Crowell) in providing source material for this book was too extensive for detailed acknowledgment. She was indefatigable in unearthing old documents, photographs, etc. As an example, she found the notes of Mr. Crowell's Saddle and Sirloin Club speech.

structures and shrubbery, is located. The whole estate is en-nobled by stately trees. Half a mile away, another tract of an acre and a half was purchased, upon which berries and vegetables were grown for the household. The entire four acres in the two areas have been supervised for over forty years by the Eng-lish-born gardener, Edward Boulter. "Boulter is so zealous," said Mr. Crowell, "that he will not let a dead twig on the trees go un-challenged."

Though Seven Seventy Humboldt was indeed a castle with a pleasant seat, it was never Number One Home to either Susan or her husband. It was more of a summer lodge to be occupied each year about May 1, and joyfully departed from in November. The year really began for the Crowells when, with the entire staff of servants, they entrained for Green Court in Augusta. You can discern this in Susan's letters. She whimsically speaks of hav-ing a good view of the lake, "but you can't see it because the trees have grown up." She writes of having a garden and keeping a cow:

> "But when strawberries are ripe, the cow is dry: and when the cow produces, there are no strawberries. It was a great relief to my husband when I announced I was going to give up farming! Soon I'll be back in my garden at Augusta . . . among my azaleas . . ."

Green Court was really home! And that is where we like to think of Susan, among her exotic azaleas and engaged in her Georgia Bible classes.

\* \* \*

Susan was Mr. Crowell's frequent companion on his busi-ness trips over America, and several times to Europe. On the continental trips, she purchased choice linens, china and silver service. Deborah (who knoweth) said, "I never saw such evi-dence of exquisite taste."

She became semi-invalid toward 1920 by reason of a heart ail-ment, and thereafter remained at home. But her Christian testi-mony continued to the end. In June, 1922, Mr. Crowell reluctantly left the Winnetka residence, departing on a business trip with deep misgivings. Shortly after he left, as Sarah Rush tells the story, Susan felt the end was near, and wired, "Harry, I need you!" Heartbroken, Mr. Crowell rushed home, sat waiting beside his beloved one; talked of the precious things they had found together. On June 17, 1922, within a few days of their thirty-fourth wedding anniversary, as Mr. Crowell said in the Green Court Interviews, "She went to be with her Lord . . . she was a beautiful character."

\* \* \*

No, you cannot understand the Christian achievements of Henry Parsons Crowell without a knowledge of Susan. She it was, "under her Lord," who inspired him to walk in humble service and world-wide beneficence. During the Green Court Interviews, I suggested,

"But, Mr. Crowell, your trust is called 'the Henry Parsons Crowell and Susan Coleman Crowell Trust.' Mrs. Crowell had been dead several years when it was formed."

"Her name belongs right where it is," he said quietly and slowly. "She and I dreamed it together."

HENRY COLEMAN CROWELL

Son of Henry Parsons Crowell, and executive vice-president, Moody Bible Institute.

TWO VIEWS OF THE HOME AT SEVEN SEVENTY HUMBOLDT
WINNETKA, ILLINOIS

WILLIAM REED NEWELL
at the time of the Rush Street
Bible classes.

MILLICENT WOODWORTH NEWELL

Dwight Lyman Moody, at about the time young Mr. Crowell heard him preach in Cleveland, 1883, and about ten years prior to the founding of the Moody Bible Institute. (Hitherto unpublished photograph.)

Dr. Reuben Archer Torrey

Dr. James M. Gray

These three, with Mr. Crowell, are accorded the high places in the history of Moody Bible Institute. Their photos appear in the lobby of Crowell Hall.

# XVIII

## CHRISTIAN BUSINESS MAN
## BECOMES CHRISTIAN STATESMAN

In which our Hero learns to distinguish between things that differ, and enters an experience which changes his classification.

Churchmen who know only the baptism of John are unprepared to detect the doctrine of the Pharisees and of the Sadducees in the alias of "Sweetness and Brotherhood." They are, therefore, pathetically easy prey for the Very Rev. Mr. Unbeliever. One marvels, as he regards the modern church, over the patience accorded ordained infidels, and the tattered hope of Mr. Layman that a race of saints may be produced under men who have departed from the faith.

But Dr. Unbeliever, 1945 edition, is a very clever fellow. It is to his interests that the General Order be maintained; he is on the pay roll. Long ago, he rejected as childish the supernatural in religion. But his constituency still believes, and he must be careful not to hazard the national budgets by saying anything disquieting. He is aware that men must be kept fired up if they are to keep paying up, so he has developed a sparkling technique to that end. His public address system pleads like a prophet in the wilderness for the grand old virtue "Co-opie-ra-tion." At other times, fearful that the spotlight will be trained on his own apostasy, he skillfully drags a herring. In one denomination, for instance, he waxes eloquent on "Freedom! The heritage of Roger Williams," thus employing one great conviction of the Grand Old Order as a club to silence folks who are aware that he has repudiated every other.

Churchmen will continue the sorry victims of Dr. Unbeliever until Aquila and Priscilla have had them to one side for a more perfect expositing of the Way. (*Sketch Book*)

# CHRISTIAN BUSINESS MAN BECOMES CHRISTIAN STATESMAN

THE life of Mr. Crowell has two distinct eras which become clearly marked upon close scrutiny. In the first, which extended over a period of forty-three years, his classification would be that of *Christian Business Man,* building great commercial enterprises and amassing a personal fortune. In the second, which extended over a period of forty-six years, his classification would be that of *Christian Statesman,* building great Christian institutions, and holding his entire personal fortune as a stewardship from God. Guard, if you please, against an unfair perversion of the above analysis that would find any intimations of a lack of Christian ideals in the first period or a decrease of business acumen in the second.

Both faith and sagacity were so marked during Mr. Crowell's entire career that the division of his life will at first hearing seem to be hair-splitting. But it is not. His life had two distinct eras, and you can see it immediately if you imagine that he died at forty-two. Had Mr. Crowell died prior to 1900 he could be briefed as —no disparagement intended—just another successful Christian business man. It was his career after the age of forty-three which gave him a place in the Faith Chapter.

What made the difference? Well, it was a matter of emphasis; and this emphasis arose when some one, as in the case of the silver-tongued Apollos, "expounded unto Mr. Crowell the way of God more perfectly." The dividing line between the two periods in Crowell's life is so sharp that you can walk over to the wall calendar and put your finger on the very time it began.

One morning in the year 1896 a minister, twenty-eight, was closeted with D. L. Moody in the office of the Institute. This minister had already made a name for himself. Born in Savannah, Ohio, May 22, 1868, he came under the sound of the gospel in the ministry of A. B. Simpson, and was baptized by Dr. Simpson, 1902, in the New York City Alliance Tabernacle. People said at once concerning him, "He has a double portion of Simpson's spirit!" In preparation for the ministry, he attended Grove City College, near Pittsburgh, and the College of Wooster, in Ohio; later Princeton Theological Seminary. But his powers in preaching were so marked, churches would not let him alone; he therefore closed seminary doors behind him and became pastor, 1895, of Bethesda Congregational Church, located near the Bible Institute. The big city was immediately conscious of him as a man of unique power in Bible exposition; in fact, the faculty of the Institute decided to ask him to become assistant superintendent. That morning D. L. Moody was reporting the faculty's decision.

After some discussion, Moody, always a blunt man, pulled out a hunting-case watch and held it open. The young preacher objected, "But I do not feel competent." Moody replied, "Do you not think these men know what is necessary?" The young man countered, "I want to pray over it." Moody said, "Don't you think we've prayed over it?" He snapped the watch lid shut and moved as if to stand: "I have fifteen minutes to catch a train." The young minister said, "All right; you continue to pray and I'll accept the position." And when William Reed Newell walked out of Moody's office, he was assistant superintendent of the Bible Institute!

\* \* \*

There was a matter of affection in the young man's heart that had first claim. Her name was Millicent Woodworth. She was "a saint if there ever was one, and as beautiful as Monica." They were married June 9, 1896, and went to Northfield, Massachusetts, on their honeymoon. When Newell returned, his fame as a Bible teacher spread abroad. He began to speak in four great cities, Toronto, Detroit, St. Louis, and Chicago. He made these trips every week at tremendous physical wear, delivering the same lecture in each city, oftentimes to standing room only.

Millicent Newell, in her husband's absence, attended the Fourth Presbyterian Church of Chicago and there met Susan Crowell. The young matrons became greatly attached to each other. Millicent was mother of a baby boy, David M'Cheyne Newell, born March 23, 1898, whose name you may remember as the author of captivating fiction in the *Saturday Evening Post,* and more lately as editor of *Field and Stream.* And Susan cherished her own little son, born a year earlier. The bond of motherhood drew them still more closely together. Largely as a result of this friendship, Mr. Crowell and Susan, shortly after they moved back to Chicago into the Rush Street residence, fall of 1898, invited Dr. Newell to hold a weekly Bible class in their home. Right there, the second period of Mr. Crowell's life began!

\* \* \*

In the Rush Street classes, Newell repeated his word study of the book of Romans. The results of his teaching on both Susan and Mr. Crowell were transforming. These classes changed Susan from a nominal Christian to a flaming disciple. Her friends, as observed in the previous chapter, could not believe the difference. "She became such a living reproof to Chicago society that the Gilded Four Hundred found nice ways of letting her out." The best words to summarize the matter is to say "Susan Crowell was born again."

The effect of the classes upon Mr. Crowell was equally powerful. You could not say, however, that as a result of these classes, Mr. Crowell was born again. He was of the "twice born" ever since, as a tender-hearted boy, he was led to Christ in Pastor Hawks' study; never once in the years that passed did he decline from his early devotion. "My father courted my mother with a Bible under his arm," writes his daughter. But as a result of the Newell Bible Class, a marked difference, a magnificent enrichment, came into Mr. Crowell's life; an increment so profound that Mr. Crowell at forty-three was changed from Christian Business Man to Christian Statesman.

It is perfectly natural to desire a closer view of the teachings of Dr. Newell which drew such large audiences in Canada and the United States, and were so life-changing to the Crowells. Hereupon, you are amazed. It is easy to secure in print exactly what Newell taught in the Crowell home. The subject matter is in book form.[1] After all these years, the volume continues a press-perennial. Unlike the best sellers, it never dies out, but year after year goes into fresh editions.

Let us examine this book critically. If you seek the broad-brush glories of Ruskin, the book is deficient. Nor will you find the fluent versatility of Spurgeon, the crashing epigrams of Carlyle, or the sweetness of Cowper. Hillis' ease in coupling the facts of history with the claims of faith; the tidal-wave disorder of Cadman's rich paragraphs; the finely-hammered prose of Macaulay—none of that! Then—what?

Well, here is where you are at first perplexed. There is nothing but a study of the faith once delivered, in all-Bible language. The book, virtually a transcript of the Rush Street Classes, has page after page upon sin; the whole world is proved unrighteous before God. Rarely, Newell makes a literary reference. Greatly admiring Robert Murray M'Cheyne (you remember he named his first born "M'Cheyne") he generalizes, "A holy minister is an awful weapon in the hands of God."

\* \* \*

Dr. Newell switches abruptly from the subject of sin to point out a righteousness which unrighteous man may obtain, a righteousness God will approve; it is THE RIGHTEOUSNESS OF GOD in His Son Christ Jesus. Thereupon he surveys the mystery of justification, stating with a naivete utterly disconcerting to Dr. Unbeliever, that when a sinful man gets the blood of Jesus on his heart, God is so delighted with poor Sinner that He entirely forgets he has ever sinned.

You can take your choice, Sinner! Stay under the first Adam and be damned, or get under the last Adam and be saved! After you are saved, you can and should live above sin in this *present* life. This is done by the resurrection power of Jesus. No excuse for a Believer living shabby! Jesus puts something into our hearts and we are free from the law.

[1] W. R. Newell, *Romans.*

Furthermore, a shabby Christian has no excuse, because of the ministry of the Holy Spirit. The Spirit yearns to live in us. He reveals the Bible through us, delivers us from indwelling sin, and reveals Christ to the world through us. And salvation by the death of Jesus is an all-time, eternal, never-to-be-lost possession in spite of the Devil and the deep blue sea! [Excuse that last phrase please; your writer was so stirred by Newell's book that he added it on his own.]

Dr. Newell constantly intersperses all of the foregoing, and more, with questions, questions, questions. The answers must never be given "in their own words," but by Scripture, Scripture, Scripture!

The classes come to moments of gorgeous climax when with statement, statement, statement, and questions, questions, questions, you hear how the Christian ought to live in view of it all. He ought to be a nobleman in his conduct toward other saints, toward the world—even toward his enemies. (Questions) Especially since Jesus is coming again; and soon! (Questions) Live so you will be glad when He comes! (Questions) Stop being a stumbling block! Be as patient as Jesus Himself! Give your bodies a living sacrifice! (Questions)

*After being in those classes, you become exalted in Spirit. You feel like those old fashioned Methodists whose passing left the world impoverished. (Questions) How can we get another generation of those genuine Methodists? Answer—Scripturally!* Over and over, as the classes go on, Newell implements the faith of his hearers.

"You are living in the world's darkest time. Be on your guard! Even when Rome reigned most generally, in the middle ages, the eleventh century, she founded all her authority on what the Scriptures said. Of course, she allowed no voice but her own to interpret, *but* she quoted the Bible as the foundation of her 'tradition.' But, today! The blasphemers called 'Modernists' would do away openly with the Scripture itself. See Matthew 16:12! The iniquity of the 'Modernist' is the same as that of the Sadducees. When you find a man who speaks not according to this word even though he be the Moderator of the General Assembly, from such a one depart without delay! My time for teaching this class is short; but the Word of God will arm you in the future against the wiles of the devil."

In imagination I seek Mr. and Mrs. Crowell at the close of one of the classes in the Rush Street home. I say to him:

"My, it seems to me as if one-quarter of that class is given over to Newell's asking questions. It's questions! questions! questions! From the viewpoint of a modern dean, that's slightly adolescent. The teacher is supposed to *tell* you. Don't these questions bore you? Embarrass you? Scare you?"

"No. (Pause) No. (Pause: the quiet tones.) They are very *impressive*. Of course you have to answer him properly, or you will be embarrassed."

"Well, *how do you answer him*, Mr. Crowell?"

"In the words of the Bible. But get them right, or he will be displeased! And when you get them right, he is so pleased, and you are so pleased, the class seems like heaven."

"Tut, tut! Mr. Crowell. What are you? A lot of children? Do you just have to give a phonographic answer? No originality?"

"Well, I don't know about that. All I know is what the Bible does for me: 'Thy word have I hid in mine heart that I might not sin against Thee.'"

\* \* \*

When Mr. Crowell answers in that vein it is the end of my poor protests. I recall one of the first sentences I ever memorized as a help in shaping a literary style:

"For as the rain cometh down, and the snow from heaven, and returneth not thither, but watereth the earth, and maketh it bring forth and bud, that it may give seed to the sower, and bread to the eater: so shall my word be that goeth forth out of my mouth: it shall not return unto me void, but it shall accomplish that which I please, and it shall prosper *in the thing* whereto I sent it." [1]

Suddenly it comes upon me that the excellence of this quotation lieth not in cunning clauses for depicting the cycles of nature, but in the calm affirmation that God's *words* return not unto Him *VOID!*

\* \* \*

Mr. Crowell in the Green Court Interviews, said over and over, "I owe more to W. R. Newell than to any other man." Up to the

[1] (Isaiah 55:10, 11)

year 1898, Mr. Crowell's brand of doctrine was largely experimental. He had found Christ in the Finney atmosphere; and had obtained eternal life, which according to his church he could never lose. But his very tenderness of heart, not being perfectly instructed, made him friendly toward anything which affirmed itself "Christian." If he heard men preach who disbelieved in the atonement, or the new birth, he set aside his qualms if only now and then these men said nice things about Jesus. Up to 1898, he had no power to discern between the shades of gray that shift from White Bible Faith to Mummy-Brown Rationalism. He had yet to sense the full truth that men who discredit the Bible, set aside the blood, deny the deity of Jesus, or the fact of the resurrection are in no sense or ever, proper co-workers for Bible Christians; that however kind, light, sweet, or gentle they might appear, they were in truth the enemies of Christ.

After his Bible integration, he was able to ferret out in five minutes a man who had "reservations he didn't mention." This was important. "A dissembler who is careful about it is more dangerous than an Ingersoll."

His eyes were now sharpened to perceive something hitherto invisible; the subtle but sinister drifts in the Presbyterian Church. He began a kindly protest against these drifts, "staying in the church while he protested." And in the church he stayed until, with the elevation of Dr. Henry Sloane Coffin, he felt it was futile for him, at least, to stay any longer.

After 1898, he adopted the super tithing basis: "For over forty years, I have given sixty-five per cent of my income to God." He became "a business-priest"; a man who acted on the idea that a man's business is not chiefly his way of making a living, but his altar where he serves the King. He further realized that the release which came to his hands because of increased wealth, was not to provide him with ease, but that those hands might now be available for the kingdom of heaven.

Christian Statesman had arrived, and in good time! In the immediate future, some one must take up the little waif, the Moody Bible Institute, and give it foundations; thirty-two thousand unchurched young men under the shadows of the Fourth Presbyterian Church must be evangelized; a great new edifice must be erected; the Colportage Society of his beloved friend, William Norton, must be rigged for a world-wide exploit; scores of global missionary enterprises encouraged, counseled, and underwritten; city-wide gospel campaigns lifted against the iniquity of Chicago. . . . And in all these matters, it was as if God were saying to him, "Whom shall I send? And who will go for me?"

\* \* \*

Just at the time this chapter was coming into the book, Mr. Coleman Crowell wrote me a letter, February 26, 1945. Without comment, he said, "The enclosed slip is in my Father's handwriting. I found it in his desk."

The slip, critically examined, turned out to be an entry on a desk pad, dated September 18. Internal evidence indicates the year as 1899, when the full glory of his new emphasis was dawning. And it reads,

"IF MY LIFE CAN ALWAYS BE LIVED SO AS TO PLEASE HIM, I'LL BE SUPREMELY HAPPY."

# XIX

## MR. CROWELL JOINS THE MOODY STAFF

In which we see where his deeper experience immediately led him; and make initial observations upon how he proceeded to develop a great Christian school, just as he had developed great industries.

"Behind it lie fifty years of devotion to one Book. In that period it has centered, for a student's interval, the lives of tens of thousands of men and women. For sheer, spectacular gianthood, the Moody Bible Institute is the Mt. Everest of the Moody institutions and, for that matter, unique in the history of Christianity . . . It incarnates Moody's personality, dynamic power, great purposes, and deathless devotion to the Book. . . . Do not forget that the development of the Institute is a mosaic, the separate units representing the lives and labors of a host of Great Hearts. And the inlaying which began under the personality of Moody, while he lived, continued under his ideals after his death . . . continued by the *self*-effacement of a legion of willing Amaziahs, like Mrs. Cyrus H. McCormick, John V. Farwell, and Henry P. Crowell." (*Bush Aglow,* Chapter XX)

# MR. CROWELL JOINS THE MOODY STAFF

I F THIS chapter seems to have a limited tether, please consider
that it covers an area of book-sized proportions. Much detail,
therefore, is ruled out of bounds, and other details given but frugal
attention. The Moody Bible Institute itself will be casually observed, with but little additional comment upon its quality and
design for living than that contained in *Bush Aglow*. This chapter regiments itself completely to the general purpose of providing
"a look at the miller"; and this general purpose necessitates a
frank analysis of the state of the Moody Bible Institute at the beginning of the Twentieth Century.

*A frank analysis.* No angel should be deprived of his candle for
the benefit of another; neither should time be spent in gilding a
saint. It is a fair, though unvarnished truth, that the Moody Bible
Institute, in the year 1900, was a Syrian ready to perish, and the
indispensable factors for its continuance so far as we may humanly
judge, were the application of the industrial skills of H. P. Crowell
and the solid indoctrination of James M. Gray. The above statement is made in full view of the value of a host of other people.

Dr. Reuben A. Torrey, for instance, was a brilliant student, educated at Yale, Leipzig and Erlangen. He came to the Bible Institute in the late nineties. So great was the affection Dr. Torrey,
the scholar, held for Moody, the commoner, that in 1889 "he
joined D. L. in Chicago," becoming superintendent of the Institute, then pastor of the Moody Church. Torrey's influence on
Christian thinking is deathless; university students today are
saved to the faith by his published addresses upon such subjects as
the Resurrection. He was a great theologian, a great evangelist,

and a great teacher. But, it was not in him to meet "the precarious adolescence of Moody Bible Institute."

For one thing, "a drift toward extremes appeared in the little school—such things as divine healing. The leaven of John Alexander Dowie was making itself felt." Dowie was then in his auditorium heyday at Roosevelt and Michigan. It was a critical situation and ·Dowieism was beginning to penetrate.[1] This in time would have destroyed the Moody school. Extremes of any sort in Christian institutions run with fine fury for a time, but end with the death of the patient.

Moody, deeply apprehensive, sent for Dr. James M. Gray. As a matter of record, we know why: "Moody wanted some things stamped out, and one was divine healing; the students were running over to Dowie's like sheep." He felt Gray was just the man to stand in the breach.

Gray had loved Moody for a long time. As a very young man, he had listened to Moody many times, was even a member of the Moody and Sankey Choir in the New York Hippodrome. When he became pastor of the First Reformed Episcopal Church, in Boston, and teacher of the Bible in Gordon College, he kept in touch with Moody. He was invited to speak on the Northfield Conference program, and did so with such satisfaction to Moody, that, beginning in 1893, he appeared in Northfield several summers in succession. Soon after, he spoke for the Bible Institute, "first for a single month, then entire summers."

When divine healing threatened, Moody sent for Gray. "Gray lectured all summer, setting forth what the Bible teaches on the subject." Right then, the Institute began to settle upon those wholesome positions which today account for its wide interdenominational confidence. The following year, Gray became permanently associated with the Bible Institute.

Torrey and Gray, each of the definite executive type, soon developed tensions between them. But the problem resolved itself without benefit of man. "God took Dr. Torrey away from the Institute," Mr. Crowell said quietly in the Green Court Interviews. From 1902 to 1909, Dr. Torrey turned to his great work of evan-

---

[1] Nothing is to be gained by a bill of particulars in this matter; the files of such secular papers as the *Chicago Interocean* need not be quoted.

gelism and conducted world-wide campaigns as notable as those of his beloved D. L. Moody.

\* \* \*

Once again we stop to trace how the lines begin to intertwine. We observe how at this dramatic interval, Mr. Crowell, aged forty-five, empowered by a deeper experience, became identified with Moody Bible Institute. We quote from the Interviews, in his own words:

> "No one in particular launched our [his and Susan's] interest in the Moody Bible Institute. Our reasoning was along this line: Moody had produced Newell, and he was a great Bible student. We also admired A. C. Dixon, Pastor of Moody Church. But, *it was our wider grasp of the Bible that drew us to the Institute.* [Italics mine] Moody died in 1899. When he died, it seemed as if the life went out of the Institute. . . . Dr. Gray's being made president was one of the factors that interested me in joining the Institute staff."

On April 24, 1901, Mr. Crowell was elected to the Board of the Moody Bible Institute. On February 2, 1904, he was made President of the Board and so continued for over forty years, or until October 23, 1944.[1]

\* \* \*

Dr. Gray became dean in 1902. As a matter of fact, it was Mr. Crowell who convinced Dr. Gray that he should accept the leadership of Moody Bible Institute. Mr. Crowell never once mentioned this in the Interviews, but the Gray files show how it was Crowell, now holding the same love for Gray that Moody felt, constrained Gray to accept the office. The whole procedure was one of the sweetest pieces of gentlemanly high pressure you will find in a decade. It is a delight to envision the quiet Mr. Crowell at grips with the quiet Dr. Gray, both beloved autocrats to the fingertips; and to see Mr. Crowell come off with the field! In the following thirty-five years, Dr. Gray, "the well-groomed little man in a gray fedora," shaped the Moody Bible Institute so that it held the course without torques. Let us take the subject of prophecy as an example.

The whole subject of prophecy demands an admixture of faith

[1] Letter of Thomas S. Smith, March 13, 1945.

and common sense. If faith is missing, the heavenly horizons disappear in a modernist's black-out; and if common sense is missing, the heavenly horizons luridly glow for a Macbethian witch scene. As a means to validate prophecy and to show how it should be treated, Dr. Gray gathered in Moody Bible Institute, 1914, a group of prophetic authorities.

> "You could not gather together, if you combed the world, and promised ten thousand dollars to each of them, such a group of prophetic authorities as Dr. Gray gathered for that conference." [1]

It is fair to say that prophecy thereupon got out of its rags and entered good society.

\* \* \*

This is not Dr. Gray's biography, though we confess we would like to write it; title it *Gamaliel Invades Chicago!* But a liaison statement is perfectly in order at this point: Moody Bible Institute, thus far, has had four great figures: D. L. Moody, whose spiritual child it was; Reuben A. Torrey, who zealously guarded its infancy; James M. Gray, who set its feet in the right paths; and Henry Parsons Crowell, whose industrial skills made possible its present giant stature.

We repudiate any statement that would intimate Moody made it! Or Gray made it! Or—Crowell made it! Dr. Gray, revealing his own humility of heart, said several times, "It was the brains and heart of H. P. Crowell that made this institution." But we could not validate that statement. The only prominent thing we can see is how God in His great purpose, uses men who are disciplined to His will. Paul and Apollos felt over-honored in having a part in His program: "It is *God* that giveth *the increase.*" And that's exactly where Henry Parsons Crowell fits into this picture.

Today, you mark the stature of the Moody Bible Institute, the greatest thing of its kind in Christian history. You note the giant stride of 1946; hear the crackle of its super-powered radios; you pick up the *Moody Monthly,* styled for faith along the best lines of modern journalism; you observe the activity of the Moody Press

---

[1] Letter, Wilbur Moorehead Smith, 1943.

DR. WILL H. HOUGHTON

President (1934-    ), Moody Bible Institute and Protagonist of this Biography.

Thomas Sylvester Smith, Chicago business man, father of Dr. Wilbur M. Smith, life-long friend of H. P. C. and a member of the Institute Board since September 10, 1907.

William Norton, secretary and manager, the Bible Institute Colportage Association of Chicago, from June 26, 1897 until November, 1941; since that date, director, Colportage Division of the Moody Bible Institute; trustee of M. B. I. since June 17, 1941. Another quiet man, self-effacing, almost shy. But no man could desire higher appraisal than H. P. C. gave "My Friend, Mr. Norton. We worked things out together."

Perry Braxton Fitzwater, one of the great hearts of Moody Bible Institute. His memory and appraisal of H. P. C. are so excellent as to be indispensable to the writing of this book.

in the roar of scattered big presses:—this book is printed in Kingsport, Tennessee! You scan the average enrollment figures—

Day School............................... 1,250
Evening School........................... 1,500
Correspondence School.................. 16,000

You go into the clean severity of the hard-material lobby of stately Crowell Hall. You gaze upon four pictures gracing the wall.

Moody!    Torrey!    Gray!    Crowell!

And you think: "What good taste! What fine discrimination!"

# XX

## "AND APOLLOS WATERED"

Herein we find repeated the Divine economy that the labors of none of us are complete without the rest of us.

If comparisons, in a general way, are malodorous, they are particularly so in the economy of heaven. When one contrasts the relatively limited time which D. L. gave to Moody Bible Institute, with the two score years of Crowell's devotion; when he remembers how, humanly speaking, the life seemed to go out of the Institute at Moody's death, and how Crowell stood by until it recovered and flourished; then he finds it easy to fall for a Chestertonian epigram: "If Moody was the left hand of Moody Bible Institute, Crowell was the right."

Epigrams, however, often twisted truths, appear deformed on re-reading. We can keep out of trouble only when we remember to give every saint his candle, and—God the glory!

"Paul planted, Apollos watered, but God gave the increase!
So then neither is he that planteth anything, neither he that watereth: but God that giveth the increase."

The epigram concerning Right and Left Hands, duly humbled, needs revision: "If Moody was one hand of Moody Bible Institute, Crowell was the other." Mr. Crowell's own estimate is the truth of the matter: "The Institute is a tree of the Lord's planting, but I really think He used me for its benefit."

# "AND APOLLOS WATERED"

D R. PERRY BRAXTON FITZWATER of the staff of the Moody Bible Institute has a high appraisal of the value of Mr. Crowell to the school. Dr. Fitzwater is a credible witness from any standard you wish to apply. He is an eye-witness, bridging in his own life the left bank of Moody's day with the right of Houghton's. With calm discernment, he has watched the unfolding of the Institute from its infancy, when he first came as a student in 1898, to its present size. Dr. Fitzwater has for the greater part of his life centered his interests upon the Moody Bible Institute. After student days, he was associated with La Verne College in La Verne, California; he returned to Moody in 1913, and became assistant to Dr. Evans. He tells that he "landed the 13th day of February, 1913, and has been on this corner ever since."

His evaluation of Mr. Crowell's work is startling at first; but as you look into this West Virginian's eyes, canopied with brows as thick as Absalom's, as you observe that he pauses to give his every statement a fine hammering, you become impressed that when he says, "Without Mr. Crowell, nothing"—*that is just the way it is.*

Dr. Fitzwater is further qualified to judge in that no man enjoyed the innermost confidence of President James M. Gray more than he. The Little Giant in a Gray Fedora revealed his innermost heart to the big southerner. The foregoing authentication of Dr. Fitzwater is worth-while in view of the unique quality of the direct quotation immediately following; but there are other conclusions on these pages distinctly Fitzwater though printed without benefit of quotation.

"Gray and Crowell faced each other as they sat at a table in *Moody's Room!* Gray once said: 'Here was Henry Crowell on one side of the table, I on the other. . . . We surveyed the situation. The Institute had nothing, no prestige. It had not impressed the public, financially less. It had no money, no respect.' As those two men faced each other, they prayed. [The big West Virginian is deeply moved]. . . . Then they decided to build up an institute! [Fitzwater looks out of the office window as if dreaming.] Dr. Gray frequently said, 'It was the brains and heart of H. P. Crowell that brought this institution up, that made this Institute.'

"From the time of that historic conference, M.B.I. began to take form and establishment. It was built on a business basis. Thus for forty years, this institution has been able to tide over crises because it had a good financial standing. Call the First National Bank of Chicago if you would like to check on this!

"I'll just have to look to Mr. Crowell as the maker of Moody. Mentally, he had a well rounded way of thinking. He was always poised, keen of mind, knew how to handle a crisis. I have observed him many times. We had, in the past, two or three men who wanted to change the character of the Moody Bible Institute. Crowell appointed meetings when they asked, so as to enable them to present their viewpoint.

"Just see this layman patiently listen to their 'papers,' as they rattled and read them. He listened; asked questions. He was not a technically educated man, but by his poise, he could tell when others were, or if they had a cause. When the paper rattling was finished, the readers who presented them felt their case was a poor one. They dropped aside."

Well, Dr. Fitzwater, we can't help smiling. Remember the Autocrat's creed? "When folks do not agree with you, let them talk! Be quiet while they talk; after they've talked themselves out . . ." We venture one correction, Dr. Fitzwater: "They read their papers, and then, *they* were rattled!" Please go on.

"One of Crowell's phrases was, 'To tell by trial and error the correct policy.' As a man of judicial mind, he would get at the facts, then he made up his mind. But he never seemed to get excited. Never! Never beat the table! Never said 'now this! And nothing else!' "

Pardon, Dr. Fitzwater, he never needed to beat the table. When he made up his mind it was an approximation of the inevitable; and he knew it. He was an autocrat of the right kind. And you loved the way he did it!

"Dr. Gray often remarked the same circumstances. He watched through the years. He knew. And those of us who think at all know how M.B.I. has come to its present place.

*"Never* defaulted on an annuity.[1]

"My personal testimony . . . no month in over thirty years we didn't get a check.

"As I said in the beginning, Gray affirmed the whole thing was due to the poise and devotion of H. P. C. The Moody Board met mostly Tuesday afternoons through the years. You could be assured H. P. C. would be around. That meant one afternoon out of every week for forty years he was here and directed. And he, one of Chicago's great merchant princes!

"I heard Dr. Gray, twenty years ago, say, 'There were times when gifts slackened. I went down to borrow $20,000. *I came back with the money, but I didn't get it from the bank.'*

"No one knows how much that man gave. Every year M.B.I. expenditures must be half to three quarters of a million dollars.

"Come to this building (Crowell Hall) in which we are now sitting. In 1914 this project began with engineers drilling shafts. Through the years the funds gradually accumulated.

"When the building was dedicated, there was only a $50,000 debt.

"And that is now paid!

"That was an example of the financial soundness of Crowell. After the war hysteria, churches borrowed, lost buildings, or *defaulted!* But here was an institution so managed that when it did build, the money was in sight.

"Whatever there is of this place, the human *interest,* primarily, is Henry Parsons Crowell."

\* \* \*

Thank you, Dr. Fitzwater! In our opinion, you are one up on the best news-annalist we ever heard. Right now, however, we are going to call Mr. Crowell to the stand.

"It was the hope of Mr. Moody that his son-in-law, A. P. Fitt, would be able to stand by after Moody's death. But Fitt went

[1] Under Mr. Crowell's Big Business Background, the Moody Annuity Plan has specialized upon security and regularity of payment. In thirty-six years it has never once defaulted. The investments are used to help train young men and women for Christian service, help broadcast the gospel over Stations WMBI and WDLM. They also are used in hospital work, jail missions, struggling churches, and street meetings. The plan has an interesting catch-line slogan: "You may not be able to go yourself, but your money can start to work for you before you die, and give you a dependable income while you live."

into business leaving Gray and myself in charge. I was elected president of the Board of Trustees. I remained president. We had about two hundred and ninety students. As president of the Board of Trustees, I realized Moody did not have a number of reliable friends. It was necessary for me to keep the Institute going *until it did have reliable friends."* (*Green Court Interviews*)

"Pardon, Mr. Crowell—that new Administration Building, how much of the cost did you give personally?"

\* \* \*

Mr. Crowell was always chary about letting any one know the size of his personal gifts. He was fearful that knowledge of this sort might prove a penalty on liberality and a bounty on parsimony. He felt that it was critical for an institution to lean upon one lone man. He profoundly desired that Moody should never again experience the crisis in which he found it—lack of *a number* of reliable friends.

Therefore, even in the matter of his bequests to Moody, though he could have completely underwritten the future, he refused to do so. It is fair to say that if the fiery testimony of Moody ceased, and along with it the resultant fountain of liberality from a host of faithful stewards in all denominations, *then Moody Bible Institute could die in a single generation!*

And Mr. Crowell felt that it ought to die if the fire no longer burned. Every institution should be financed in its own, and by its own generation. If an institution did not have the vitality to refinance itself, it deserved to die; what was the sense of cathedral walls and stained glass—and a dead tenant? Furthermore, it was hazardous to give too much—endowed cats catch no mice!

The foregoing is a frank analysis of Moody for the contemporary age. Mr. Crowell left things just this way. Moody Bible Institute is still utterly dependent on folks who are led to give by reason of the fire on Moody's altars. If that fire dies—well, the question settles itself; for no Crowell money is available to keep it going, half alive. Even if its fire abides, Mr. Crowell has so arranged that it must depend on *a number of supporters.*

Administration Building

"Under the words Moody Bible Institute a space has been left where now will be carved Crowell Hall." President Houghton, Memorial Address, October 26, 1944.

Corner Stone Laying, May 27, 1938 Left to Right—President Will H. Houghton, F. J. Wielbar, Architect, Henry Parsons Crowell.

Unveiling of Tablature

At twelve noon, February 5, 1945, H. P. C.'s granddaughter, Miss Mary Coleman Crowell, pulled the cord and revealed a line freshly carved on the lintel.

"CROWELL HALL"

George Cornelius Lazear

Frank Joseph Loesch

J. Wilbur Chapman

Gipsy Smith

"Billy" Sunday

Charles McCallon Alexander

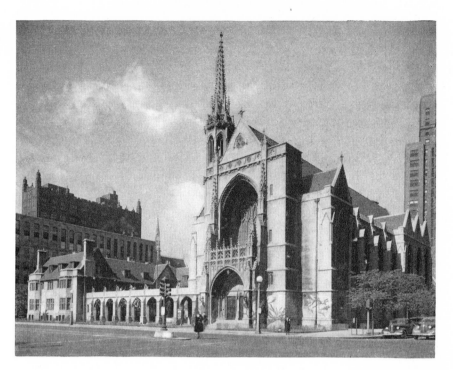

Fourth Presbyterian Church
Chicago

Rev. John Timothy Stone, D. D.

(1909-1930)

The Gates of Green Court at 2248 Cumming
Road

The Residence
(Gates and Residence face north)

The Residence
(Northwest Corner)

Well, we asked Mr. Crowell a question a few lines back. He always paused before answering. Sometimes you felt he did not hear, or forgot. But he did hear, and he did not forget. He is ready to answer now; how much did he give in financing the Administration Building?

"Well, I suppose about half."

That will have to serve as the answer; and if you are not satisfied, we have no idea how you can improve the matter.

\* \* \*

But his gifts toward building the great edifice were so significant that President Houghton felt it should be called "Crowell Hall." One day as the foundation for the Administration Building was going on, President Houghton conferred with Mr. Crowell in the Quaker offices. He urged him to permit them to cut in stone over the arch the words "Crowell Hall."

There was silence for perhaps two minutes. The typical Crowellesque reply! Then he lifted his head and said,

"No. (Quietly and a pause) No. (Quietly and a pause) Years ago, I told the Lord that if He would allow me to make money for His service, I would keep my name out of it, so He could have the glory."

Dr. Houghton's memorial address came nearly being greeted with applause when he remarked, "That (deference to Mr. Crowell's wish) was of course for his lifetime. Perhaps you have noticed that over the arch on La Salle Street, and under the words Moody Bible Institute, a blank space has been left on the stone where now will be carved—Crowell Hall."

At twelve noon, February 5, 1945, an unveiling ceremony was conducted on La Salle Street beneath the main arch entrance of the "Administration Building." It seemed fitting that "my little granddaughter" of whom Mr. Crowell wrote, pulled the cord, and the assembled throng saw a new name freshly carved on the lintel—

"Crowell Hall"

\* \* \*

After months of analysis, Mr. Crowell's Boswell, while having much admiration for the giant industries of Mr. Crowell's making, perceives that so far as Mr. Crowell was concerned, the Moody Bible Institute was foremost among his labors. The detail for proving this is too extensive for inclusion in one book. But, with broad-brush strokes you may see it in his relationship to the rise of the Colportage Division of the Moody Bible Institute, (B.I.C.A.) and to his beloved friend, William Norton. Mr. Norton is quiet, just like Mr. Crowell; so quiet that today the new students at Moody require a long time before they sense his historical and executive importance.

Mr. Norton was born in Brooklyn, New York, April 28, 1867— "born again January 26, 1885." He came under the spell of D. L. Moody, studied five years in the Mount Hermon School for boys at Northfield, Massachusetts, and was for a limited period, 1896, a student at Princeton. In June, 1897, Mr. Moody invited him to become business manager of the Bible Institute Colportage Association. He has continued at the head of this agency through its several changes until it was merged November 10, 1941, with the Moody Bible Institute. He now bears the title of "Director of the Colportage Division of the M.B.I." Mr. Crowell was elected Vice-President of the B.I.C.A., January 31, 1910, and held that office until the merger, above named. It can be said that Crowell and Norton have so effectively labored together that the colportage work is world-wide.

\* \* \*

You may see the proof of Mr. Crowell's deepest love being accorded to M.B.I. in the rise and development of the super-power radio station WMBI. And what is the station fundamentally but a projection of Mr. Crowell and his son after him? On the program printed for the dedication of the station, January 20, 1928, you will find these words:

### We Dedicate

"We dedicate this station as a witness that the Bible is the authoritative and inspired Word of God from Genesis to Revelation.

"We dedicate it as a witness that our Lord Jesus Christ is Himself very God, begotten not made, being of one substance with the Father.

"We dedicate it as a witness to the solemn truth that man is by nature a fallen creature, dead in trespasses and sins, and that in the words of Christ 'except a man be born again, he cannot see the kingdom of God.' We dedicate it as a witness to the comforting truth that Jesus Christ Himself bore our sins in His own body on the tree, and that now 'whosoever shall call upon the name of the Lord shall be saved.'

'Five bleeding wounds He bears,
Received on Calvary;
They pour effectual prayers,
They strongly plead for me:
"Forgive him, O forgive," they cry,
"Nor let that ransomed sinner die." '

"We dedicate this broadcasting station tonight as a witness to our belief in the Holy Ghost, the third person of the adorable Trinity, the regenerator of men, who dwells in the Christian believer, and who enables him by His grace, through obedience to the inspired Word of God, to live a life of victory over every known sin.

"We dedicate it as a witness that the Church is the body of which Christ is the Head, and that its mission is to carry the gospel of salvation to all men and to every nation under heaven, for which purpose it is that the young men and women in the Institute are being trained. Thousands of former students are now carrying this gospel to every known part of the world, and some of them in the past, and because of their testimony thereto, are tonight filling martyrs' graves awaiting the glorious resurrection.

"We dedicate this station as a witness to that glorious resurrection of the body when Jesus Christ Himself shall come again, personally and visibly, bringing His reward with Him.

'A lamp in the night, a song in time of sorrow,
A great glad hope, which faith can ever borrow
To gild the passing day with the glory of the morrow,
Is the hope of the coming of the Lord.'

"We dedicate this broadcasting station as a witness that when Christ thus comes 'a second time without sin unto salvation,' the Church which is His body shall be 'caught up to meet Him in the air,' and the kingdom will be restored to Israel even as He promised. It is then that Christ and His saints shall reign over that kingdom and He shall judge His people righteously and govern the nations upon earth.

"We dedicate this station as a solemn witness that as Jesus said, the wicked, that is the unbelieving, shall go away into everlasting punishment and the righteous into everlasting life."

\*   \*   \*

And you may find the evidences of his love for the Moody Bible Institute in the selection of presidents who have headed up the work. No one can doubt that Dr. James M. Gray was brought to his historic administration by the urgency of Mr. Crowell. And when Dr. Gray was evidently finishing his course, Mr. Crowell insisted that a successor be located, not frantically after Dr. Gray's death, but leisurely while he still lived. Thus, Dr. Will H. Houghton, in a curious sequence, was called long before he heard. The wisdom of this choice has abundant proof. Here is one letter from the Crowell files in which a powerful friend of M.B.I. writes, "Thank you for your wise judgment in securing Dr. Houghton as President. He has the rare ability of mastering any situation on the spot."

\*   \*   \*

We have no premiums for wilful conduct, but we never felt such pleasure in beholding a veto over-ridden as when President Houghton, abiding his time, refused to be bound by Mr. Crowell's wishes, and ordered engraved over the arch of the Administration Building the words,

"Crowell Hall."

## XXI

## THE STEWARDSHIP OF TIME

A record of some notable things which took place when a layman perceived that time, even his time, was an item of his stewardship

"As every man hath received the gift, *even* so minister the same one to another, as good stewards of the manifold grace of God" (*I Peter 4:10*).

# THE STEWARDSHIP OF TIME

THE teachings of the Rush Street Bible Class on the subjects of person and property were in sharp conflict with ideas which Mr. Crowell had for years entertained. He always felt that believers were under obligation to *live* as Christians; but when it came to such things as time and treasure, these were his *personal* possessions. The class summarily blasted this view; not only are you as a Christian under obligation to *live* unto God, but everything you have *belongs* to God. Nothing is excepted! Bank accounts, stocks, bonds, real estate—even the Belek China in one's home is the property of the Lord, and the Christian does not own a single thing in fee simple absolute. Even his time is bought and paid for! The believer is utterly impoverished; he is simply a trustee for Deity in all that he is and has.

The whole case is summed up in the Bible term "steward." You could not find a ruder word even with the help of the Anglo Saxons, who were masters of raw vocabulary. "Steward" means "a stywarden," someone who keeps his master's pen. If the term "pen-keeper for God" is offensive to human pride, that in itself is proof of the deep need of the human heart. A true Christian considers himself as having nothing of his own; he is simply a humble servant entrusted with the stys of God.

Debasing? Well, no concept has ever summered such golden harvests of character. A brief study is completely convincing that men who grasp property and say, "This is *mine!*" are on a limited tether; while the soul which exults in the idea "Whose I am and Whom I serve," has the daily ministration of angels!

Mr. Crowell laid hold upon the doctrine of stewardship with a sense of romance, and was thereby advanced from the status of a man conducting his own business, to that of a Christian entrusted with the affairs of God. Herein we find the explanation of the Crowell exploits, 1898 to 1944; exploits so vast that the record thereof, unless portrayed with severe abridgment, will read like exalted monotony. Pages of notes upon Mr. Crowell's career after 1898 are therefore distilled into the tiny vials of Revelation, and are presented in two chapters—The Stewardship of Time, and the Stewardship of Possessions. Remember that the following accounts are highly briefed.

Moody Bible Institute was one area wherein Mr. Crowell's new found sense of time stewardship found expression, of which a study has been made in previous chapters. There remain other areas to be briefed wherein he served his generation—his particular church, his denomination, his city, his nation.

\* \* \*

Stewardship ideals, in the first place, caused him to devote considerable of his leisure time to that which the worldling regards as unaccountably stupid; continuous effort "to lead others to Christ."

Mr. William Norton remembers the impression Mr. and Mrs. Crowell made upon him when he, Norton, a man of thirty, united with the Fourth Presbyterian Church in June, 1898.

He was amazed at the ardor of the wealthy young Crowells. After church service, they quietly approached prospects *in the main auditorium!* And pressed the claims of Jesus. The pastor was shocked; he felt the Crowells should be curbed. The pastor's health failed. He went to Switzerland to recuperate. But his successor, Dr. Decently N. Order, a bit liberal, heard of the Crowell auditorium scandal, and brusquely ruled, "No more personal work in *our* auditorium! Stuff like *that* must be carried on in the lobbies!" Susan and her husband kept right on—in the main auditorium!

Not only in the main auditorium, but in public, on streets, in offices, "this millionaire couple kept it up, talking with anyone and everyone about the Lord." Mr. Norton was so deeply impressed that he published a tract describing one of Mr. Crowell's interviews. He did not dare mention Crowell or his subject by name, so he titled it, "A Business Man's Experience." [1]

---

[1] This may still be obtained by writing the Moody Bible Institute.

Formal Evergreens
sentinel the
paths.

Pool with
Water Nymph

This is a formal garden.

"NOW WE WILL VISIT THE GROUNDS AT GREEN COURT"

"Brilliant, vivacious, without peer as a hostess. . . . I always think of her with an open Bible . . . tears always came to her eyes when she talked of the Lord, so deep was her love for Him" (Mrs. Henry Coleman Crowell).

Mr. Crowell paused whenever he spoke of Susan. ". . . a wonderful Christian; a fine Bible teacher; a beautiful woman."

THE CROWELLS DURING THE GOLDEN DAYS AT GREEN COURT

Well, Mr. Crowell's reserve is hereby invaded, and you shall now have names and places! William J. Robinson, a Chicago business man, was lunching with Mr. Crowell at the Union League Club. To Robinson's great amazement, as they sat under the Lincoln portrait, Crowell began to talk with him about the necessity of making a definite surrender of his life to Jesus Christ. Robinson later said: "One by one my objections fell away before Crowell's unanswerable presentation. . . . I, then and there, decided, just as I would a corporation question, to come to God . . . from that day I have been a new creature in Christ Jesus . . . all my doubts, skepticism concerning the Scriptures as the incorruptible word of God, the atonement of Jesus, were swept away . . . the thoughtless oath was gone. . . . I went back to my office and told my closest associate . . . he grasped my hand and said, 'I will start with you!'"

\* \* \*

Mr. Crowell had scruples as powerful as Moody's that no one should unite with the church until he was "born again." The following incident is a sample of the Crowell caution along this line.

A young woman, accompanied by Miss Sarah Schuster, was being examined by the Session of the Fourth Presbyterian Church. She was just about to be received for membership, when Mr. Crowell suddenly asked:

"Do you know yourself as a sinner coming to the Lord Jesus Christ who died for your sins?"

The young woman frankly replied, "I feel no sense of sin. I believe Jesus died, but I do not believe He shed His blood for me. I intend to move from Chicago. . . . I wanted to join this church so that I could be recommended to another church in the city to which I am going."

Upon this startling revelation of the girl's true state the session suggested that she await membership until she was ready for it.

Miss Schuster writes, "How I worked with that girl! Week after week! . . . One day I said to her, 'I can't go to Lincoln Park and look at the face of Lincoln without tears coming to my eyes, for I feel my unworthiness. How much less can we look into the face of the Lord Jesus Christ and not feel our guilt.'

"The girl grabbed my arm, 'Why! Is *insufficiency, unworthiness,* GUILT? Then I have it!'

"The next Sunday she hurried to the chapel 'before the devil could hold her back,' and told how she had gained the victory. She changed her mind about leaving Chicago and took a class of Sunday school children. Afterwards as I looked at that one-time, coldly intellectual girl with the poor little children she loved so well, I praised God." [1]

When this incident was brought to Mr. Crowell's attention in the Interviews, he exclaimed, "Now, that's what I mean. You have to get the Lord *right,* or you don't get Him at all. And it is unwise to make church members of folks who are making a bad start."

\* \* \*

The same care went into special Bible Classes which Mr. Crowell taught from time to time. The classes were limited-session studies, and the membership was constituted by invitation. Mr. Charles S. Bohart remembers his experience as a younger man, in the year 1920, with a class of this sort. Bohart was assistant vocational employment secretary of the Central Y.M.C.A. He arrived at the Fourth Church early one Sunday morning and was

"approached at once by the wealthy Mr. Crowell, whom I had never met, and never expected to. Mr. Crowell was so kind, so earnest . . . he talked awhile in sorrow of Chicago's crime wave and the visit was over. . . . Several weeks later Mr. Harold Dalzell, assistant to the pastor, said to me, 'You have been selected as one of a group of ten young men to receive a course of New Testament studies under Mr. Crowell.' "

Since then, years have passed, but Mr. Bohart cherishes as a state document a packet of three-by-five slips of paper, typewritten and bound with a cord. On the front he has pencilled—"Part of Mr. Crowell's notes."

One section of this document deals with the subject Resurrection of Jesus. It is a splendid arrangement of sixteen pages, brought to an earnest conclusion: "Since it can be shown Jesus actually arose from the dead, no honest man should withhold from Him the submission due to His name." Another lesson is on the New

[1] Letter, Sarah Schuster, March 20, 1943.

Birth. Mr. Crowell's notes thus speak: "It is a new creation, just as literal and actual as the first or physical birth, and far more glorious." Mr. Bohart concludes, "It was the best exposition of basic New Testament teaching I ever heard, and my whole subsequent life was changed."

\* \* \*

Time fails to speak in appropriate detail of the origin of the every member canvas, that plan of systematic giving so transforming in the work of all denominations. The every member canvas first arose in the enthusiastic dream of a young minister, Rev. George N. Taylor. Now aged in the service, "weary in it but not of it," Mr. Taylor is semi-retired in Portland, Oregon. He delights to recount his story. It was hard going to get his plan launched. Someone suggested, "Why don't you try to interest Mr. Crowell?"

Mr. Taylor said he went up to Crowell's office, "then nearly expired of heart failure when he heard Mr. Crowell saying over the phone, 'No! No! With the market as it is a million bushels is not enough. Make it two millions.'"

He never forgot his amazement that a man of such business interests would later spend months with him working out the plan which Dr. Robert E. Speer affirmed to be such a blessing to Christianity. Mr. Taylor cherishes a letter written to him years later by Crowell: "I am glad you still remember the early days when we worked together, and were able to accomplish so much for the increase of missionary giving. I am glad the Lord gave you the germ thought. . . . H. P. Crowell."

\* \* \*

The significant Laymen's Movement of the Presbyterian Church under Dr. William F. Weir found Mr. Crowell an invaluable aid. We append part of a recent letter written by Dr. Weir:

"Oh, Brother Crowell, we made men church-conscious, didn't we?"

\* \* \*

It was in connection with layman emphasis that Mr. Crowell first met a young man named George Cornelius Lazear. It was at a Presbyterian Brotherhood meeting in the Fourth Presbyterian Church. Lazear was chairman. Lazear writes:

"I called on Mr. Crowell to act as treasurer! I certainly had my nerve with me, didn't I? Asking a millionaire to keep books on a few dollars! But just like him, he agreed to it at once, and he kept all the records himself in his own handwriting . . . always did a tip-top job of rather a picayunish affair—at least for him, it was small."

\* \* \*

The Layman's Evangelistic Council of Chicago, during the time it was headed by Mr. Crowell, organized some historic evangelistic campaigns:

1907, R. A. Torrey, one month in a tent at La Salle and Chestnut.

1909, Gipsy Smith, one month in the Seventh Regular Armory, 6000 capacity: "a city-wide wave of moral reform."

1911, Chapman and Alexander in campaigns of two weeks each, on the southwest, and north sides.

In addition, the Billy Sunday Campaign . . .

To all these campaigns Mr. Crowell gave the same distinguished leadership he gave to industry.

During these evangelistic meetings, Mr. Lazear was duly penalized for his presumption in asking Mr. Crowell "to act as a petty treasurer." Mr. Crowell invited Mr. Lazear to take a permanent job—and it was not petty! He retained Mr. Lazear as the executive head of all his benevolent activities, which position Mr. Lazear occupies today. Throughout the years he has been "Crowell's right hand man, and his closest friend," a friendship still further sealed by his two sons in Cheyenne and his missionary grandson.

The barest mention only is possible of Mr. Crowell's invaluable counsel to such great religious journals as the *Sunday School Times,* of his active participation in the publication and distribution of the famous twelve volumes called "The Fundamentals," etc.

\* \* \*

The chief investment of Mr. Crowell's time-stewardship, aside from Moody Bible Institute, was in his own church, the Fourth Presbyterian Church of Chicago. An accurate record of this necessitated a special interview of Dr. John Timothy Stone, May 9, 1944, in his Florida home at Coral Gables.

Dr. Stone, Boston-born, September 7, 1868, would have accepted a call to New York City but for Mr. Crowell's urgency. Harry Emerson Fosdick took the Church, and Dr. Stone came to Chicago. Dr. Stone conceived a great plan of evangelism which was to head up in an "Invitation Committee." In the Florida interview, Dr. Stone said:

"I realized I must have the most able man I could get to act as chairman of the committee, so I asked Mr. Crowell. To my surprise, he accepted. For ten years Mr. Crowell returned to Chicago from wherever his business called him in order that he might preside at the weekly meeting of the Invitation Committee. A vast undertaking was launched, first to individually call on fifteen thousand unchurched young men living within a half-mile radius of the Church. Everything in the committee was kept secret. There were never any speeches—not even from the most eminent visitors; they just sat in and listened. I brought a brief final message.

"Scores joined; the church became great. Not only was the Fourth Church blessed, but, in a large measure, all Presbyterian Churches in Chicago were influenced. In a large way, this underlay the result of which Andrew Stevenson wrote: 'Chicago is eminently a Presbyterian city.' Scores of men now prominent in the Chicago business world came into the church as a result of this work headed up by Mr. Crowell.

"I realized the Fourth Church had to have a new edifice. When I first mentioned the matter, the bankers opposed. But Mr. Crowell stood right by me. Harold McCormick saw the vision of the new building, and he subscribed $25,-000. Cyrus McCormick subscribed $50,000. Then Madam McCormick, who had been giving a quarter of a million annually to missions, subscribed $100,000.

"Six men met to discuss the new building. I reported

$365,000 had been subscribed, and Mr. Crowell gave $100,000 of that. The building was to cost $875,000 . . . It was dedicated with $25,000 excess for endowment.

"Mr. Crowell never hastily decided anything. He always prayed and planned. He was never too busy to see me. I went to his Quaker Oats office six or eight times a year for extended conference. He was a man of God! He has been the strongest influence in my life."

\* \* \*

On the other hand, Mr. Crowell highly esteemed his pastor. In his remarks as toastmaster at the honor banquet tendered Dr. Stone, Drake Hotel, early 1934, Mr. Crowell exclaimed:

> "I view a small church at Rush and Superior Streets in dire need . . . for two years, no practical leadership . . . attendance diminishing, spiritual life at low ebb. . . . We called Dr. Stone. He changed the drift, and today I view a great church."

\* \* \*

But the toastmaster never once intimated his own part in a temple building. It is necessary to let Dr. Stone speak for Mr. Crowell:

"I was only the leader. The work was really accomplished by Mr. Crowell and other laymen like him who thought of themselves, their time and their possessions, as belonging to God. It takes great laymen to make a great church."

# XXII

## THE STEWARDSHIP OF TIME:
## SOCIAL ACTION

Mr. Crowell and a small group of Chicago professional and business men conclude that the protection of human values on the civic front is a very realistic and practical business proposition. Thereupon, for a period of thirty-eight years, 1907-1944, they pitted their skills against the vicious—politicians, king and pony sizes; John Barleycorn merchants, real estate operators, property owners, cab drivers, bell boys, physicians, shyster lawyers, police, ropers, panderers, madams, bond-buzzards, jury-fixers, loan-sharks, honkey-tonkers, snow-merchants and bindle-stiffs —with some very surprising results, even to Chicago.

"There are Christian business men who have other gifts than those possessed by Mr. Crowell. They are in great demand as speakers at conventions, etc. Not so Mr. Crowell. His skill was as a keen analyst of facts, and as an executive in getting action based on careful investigation. There are few such men in Chicago, or anywhere else. He believed in Social Service, but it had to be Christian in all vitally essential features. He could not identify himself with the merely professional types who insist on separating social service from the church. He knew the central place of divine grace in all plans for helping people." (Letter, Henry Stewart, of the Chicago Association of Commerce)

# THE STEWARDSHIP OF TIME:
## SOCIAL ACTION

CHICAGO found peculiar satisfaction in the 1942 report of Army officials, concerning venereal infection per hundred thousand population. When Chicagoans read the report they exclaimed, "Look! Chicago has the lowest rate of infected persons of any comparable city in the United States—17.5!" The average American will scarcely believe it. But the statistics were militarily impartial. The National Capital headed up the dishonor roll with 158.3!

But it is well to be chary about canonizing Chicago. Alas, the Big City has never been a candidate for sainthood; and her propriety can scarcely be called voluntary. Her good standing is the benison of a quiet and relatively small group of business and professional men, and much of the same order as the clean neck which a mother bestows upon her dear boy.

The very nature of Chicago made vice by-productial. There never was a city of more violent contrasts. You motor through the park chain on the Lake Shore Boulevard, the lake and great buildings flanking you left and right, and you love it. You ride through Halsted Street, "the human garbage pail with shabby buildings whose walls ooze filth," and you loathe it. Both of these conditions are products of Chicago's fantastic history. It is the earth's fourth city today—New York, London, Paris, Chicago. From the very outset, when it began to transmute corn into meat, to the present hour, with its big ten industries grossing a billion dollars of business annually, Chicago has been a Gold Gusher. And easy money attracts vice.

When Mr. Crowell, therefore, moved into his Rush Street residence in 1898, he found a city of such a character as to move someone to remark (likely a Los Anglean): "It is a city of pork and prostitutes, sausages and strip tease."

Sex crime may not be the chief evil that beleaguers the human family, but it is one fruit cluster by which we may adjudge the dangerous root—the love of money. Prostitution in the Windy City, if unmolested, would net the underworld a monthly income of $1,000,000. One needed only half an eye, in the year 1900, to see beneath the surface as foul a brood of varmints as have ever appeared in history. There was a great smear of city blocks, dull-red as a saloon neon, which ended up by crawling right into the Loop. Within shouting distance of the County Building there were sex shows incredibly stark. Boys attended without protest, and as a result had their consciences seared as with a red hot iron. Organized vice fearlessly sought new recruits "as inmates and patrons," from among the immature, the weak, the unstable, the lonely. Open campaigns were carried on to solicit the patronage of high school boys.[1] Thousands of the constant stream of young women coming into Chicago from surrounding small towns, seeking employment, were deftly herded into the Legion of the Damned.

In 1900, commercialized vice was firmly established in Chicago: it paid well. To be sure, it didn't pay the girls. Their bodies were as really merchandized as the meat from the Stock Yards pulley-ways. The beneficiaries of prostitution was a network of politicians, king and pony sizes; John Barleycorn merchants, real estate operators, property owners, cab drivers, bell boys, physicians, shyster lawyers, police, ropers, panderers, madams, bond-buzzards, jury-fixers, loan-sharks, honkey-tonkers, snow-merchants, and bindle-stiffs.

This alone was formidable enough to make abatement a Herculean task: but added thereto was the more formidable indifference and sour logic of Mr. John Public. Good citizens said, "You've always had prostitution, and always will. It's sensible to segregate a district, and—forget it." And along with segregations came the Four Corners of Hell.

[1] Report, Committee of Fifteen, 1945.

That was the back drop which Mr. Crowell found against Chicago at the turn of the century. But the idea of "taking it lying down" never entered his mind. He began by protesting in the circle of his church. This he found to be as effective as a pea shooter against a tank. He thereupon began to think it through, to find the will of God; and subsequently to discuss the matter with a small group of professional and business men whom he found in his city clubs.

One of these was Clifford W. Barnes. Dr. Barnes was really "a Reverend"; but he found it impossible to decide whether he was a professor, a city builder, or a social action man. Mr. Barnes, later in life, founded the Chicago Sunday Evening Club, and when he died in 1944, his friends called him "Chicago's First Citizen." The Big Bad Boys never have been able to agree with this judgment, and to this day have quite another classification. Three others who counselled with Mr. Crowell were Julius Rosenwald, Harold H. Swift, and Medill McCormick. These gentlemen, in case you do not remember, may easily be identified in *Who's Who in America,* or *Who Was Who.*

\* \* \*

In the year 1907, Chicago woke up. A series of shocking revelations indicated the city was the center of organized traffic in women. Mr. John Public began to shout, "Somebody do something!" Fortunately, somebody was ready—the five gentlemen above mentioned. They had already decided that the protection of human values on the civic front was a very realistic and practical business proposition. They immediately organized themselves into a Committee of Five, made Mr. Barnes chairman, raised a modest sum of money, and supported special investigations and prosecutions instituted through the State's Attorney's office.

They made a full-time job of their warfare against the underworld. In a short time they were giving the Chicago Bad Boys a pretty thorough working over. In 1911, they enlarged their number and called themselves the Committee of Fifteen. In 1913, the Committee of Fifteen created a Board of Directors of fifty of Chicago's civic leaders, retaining the Executive Committee of

Fifteen. The yearly records disclose Mr. Crowell's relationship: he was President of the Committee, 1915-1927; member of the Executive Committee, 1915-1944; and, on the day of his death, was to be recognized as Honorary Chairman of the Board of Directors. We hereby summarize a few of the results of the "practical business action" of the Committee of Fifteen:

*1908*: Passage of the Mann Act, a Federal enactment to prevent illicit traffic in women.

*1909*: The First Illinois State Law against pandering.

*1912*: His Honor the Mayor, being duly needled by the Committee, began to close some of the most disorderly houses of prostitution in the Red Light District. The *Chicago Tribune*, August 24, 1912, affirmed, "This came directly from a request of the Committee of Fifteen." In September, 1912, "the State's Attorney seeming reluctant about taking evidence regarding vice, his pure memory was given a profound stirring by the Committee. The Attorney thereupon decided to confer with the foes of vice." Hat in hand, he went around to the office of the Committee and ate a large helping of the well-known humble pie. The next day, 135 warrants were served on keepers of disorderly resorts.

*1915*: The Injunction and Abatement Law was enacted, and the Red Light District was obviously doomed; 500 houses were investigated by the Committee, most of which closed on notification. Some dared to stand trial, but the Committee did not lose a case which it prosecuted under the Injunction and Abatement Law. After the Red Light closed, the Vice Barons attempted to scatter the business in "call flats, and taverns and hotels." But the Committee continued the war.

*1920*: 434 scattered places in Chicago summarily closed.

*1925*: 251 more closed. "Nearly all the old time vice promoters have been put out of business, and have left the city."

*1930*: "276 places closed, including 20 call flats, and 27 massage parlors."

*1935*: "438 closed."

\* \* \*

In 1935, the Committee of Fifteen revised its charter and stated its singleness of purpose to be that of suppressing commercialized prostitution. They also warned the public, "without constant vigilance many of the older operators of vice will immediately return." By this time the Committee had proven conclusively to the nation that segregation does not segregate; that such a plan was a quack social nostrum; that medical inspection was a sorry hoax; that the Red Light was the blighted area in which the prairie fires of venereal diseases began. The Committee continued to work under its wise non-partisan policy in co-operation with public officials.

In 1943, the Committee sensed a new peril. Chicago was becoming immature again. George Sessions Perry says,[1] "Then the war came and pumped its (Chicago's) veins full of a mixture of high life and adrenalin." Strip tease waxed a little more daring on State Street; date houses were showing signs of life on Halsted.

Furthermore, "demobilization would bring far greater demands for the Committee's best efforts. Ladies of easy virtue who are expected to flood the streets as returning heroes of the war are processed must be promptly dealt with—we must not suffer a prairie fire of venereal infection."[2] Clifford Barnes remarked in 1944, shortly before his death, "There surely never was a time when the work of the Committee was of greater value." The Committee mapped out a post-war campaign. After Dr. Barnes' death, it was decided to select "their grand old man, Henry Parsons Crowell, as Honorary Chairman." The Press was notified, and on October 23 the camera men were scheduled to go over to Quaker Oats for the purpose of photographing Mr. Crowell. We will ask H. Howard Haylett, Executive Secretary of the Committee of Fifteen to finish the story:

> "Mr. Crowell called early in the morning of October 23 to inquire, 'What will we have for luncheon today? I may not arrive until after luncheon. I am badly upset, and the sight of food may bring on the trouble again' . . . later he asked to be excused altogether. . . . When I got home that night, some one phoned that Mr. Crowell had died after boarding the train to Winnetka. And this was to have been his coronation day!
>
> "I tell you, Mr. Crowell was a power for righteousness in Chicago. It was not his money, although he gave thousands. It was himself. He always came to Committee meetings. Dur-

[1] "Chicago." George Sessions Perry. *Saturday Evening Post*, November 3, 1945.
[2] 1945 Report, The Committee of Fifteen.

ing the sessions, he sat quietly, his hands folded on the table. As we were about to adjourn, some one would say, 'What do you think we should do, Mr. Crowell?' He quietly told us. We did it."

\* \* \*

If a complete account were presented of Mr. Crowell's labors in behalf of human values on the civic front, a score of other movements would have to be considered. Henry Stewart of the Chicago Association of Commerce urged that this be attempted, and he mentioned a few of Mr. Crowell's interests, such as the Juvenile Protective Association. But where would such a record end?

What of the fight against Loan Sharks who "were robbing poor people of their eye teeth?" As much space would be required to tell of this campaign as we have devoted to the fight against prostitution. We summarize by saying the sharks went out of business, and the First Industrial Wage Loan Society, later the Personal Loan and Savings Bank—was instituted, from which loan money may be had on decent rates of interest.

Or, what of the powerful Illinois Association for Criminal Justice? Many of Mr. Crowell's reforms were sponsored by the Industrial Club of Chicago, such as Jury Reform and Police Reform.

A sheaf of letters to the point, lie before me—from such men as Henry Stewart, Robert Isham Randolph, Jesse A. Jacobs. We venture to quote part of a letter written by V. W. Peterson, Operating Director of the Chicago Crime Commission:

October 30, 1945

Dear Mr. Day:

Henry P. Crowell became a charter member of the Chicago Crime Commission on February 8, 1919. The officers of the Commission at that time were: Edwin W. Sims, attorney, president; Joseph W. Defrees, first vice-president; George F. Getz, second vice-president; Joseph R. Noel, banker, treasurer; John R. Burgess, assistant treasurer; W. Rufus Abbott, president of Bell Telephone Company, secretary. Mr. Crowell accepted chairmanship of the Committee on Police. He was elected to the first Board of Directors at the first annual meeting of the Commission in 1920. The membership of the Commission then was ninety-five. That year he was elected first vice-president of the Commission and a member of the executive committee. He retained chairmanship of the Committee on Police. He was appointed member of a special Committee on Membership in 1923. In that same year, 1923, Mr. Crowell asked to be relieved of his duties as vice-president. He was a member of the Commission until January 18, 1934.

As chairman of the Committee on Police, Mr. Crowell did valuable pioneer work. He called numerous meetings of the committee to which were invited police officials. He held many personal interviews with Police Chief Colonel John J. Garrity; Percy B. Coffin, president of the Civil Service Commission; Colonel Leroy Steward, Major Funkhouser and others. The committee's findings were responsible for many improvements in police work.

It might be of some interest to you that Colin S. Gordon, vice-president of the Quaker Oats Company, is now a member of the Chicago Crime Commission.

The lobbies of the exclusive Chicago and Union League Clubs, to both of which Mr. Crowell belonged, were the places where Mr. Crowell and his crusading friends frequently met to discuss plans against Chicago crime waves. In 1943, by reason of advancing years, Mr. Crowell wrote to the Chicago Club resigning his membership. The Club responded in a letter which Mr. Crowell deeply esteemed; the Club declined to accept his resignation: his name was retained as an Honorary Member—*their first and only*—free of dues!

Time fails to detail the practical usage to which he applied his membership in his several golf clubs—the Indian Hill Golf Club of Winnetka; the Onwentsia Golf Club of Lake Forest; the Augusta National Golf Club (the "Bobby Jones Golf Club"), and the Augusta Country Club. "He played just an ordinary game, liked the courses; and—was able to talk things over with key men." [1]

Mr. Crowell's rule of thumb for social action was "adequate legislation, in harmony with Christian ideals, and backed up by courageous citizens." His biography could well have been written

---

[1] An example of his golf-course cabinet sessions was his Augusta games with President Warren Gamaliel Harding. But when the President suggested a stake of fifty cents a hole, Mr. Crowell, who likely had the money, quietly declined.

about that thesis. But he would not have it that way. He never put the premium on this phase of his life. However, it did amuse him no end to observe the way the Devil "hightailed" it when decent men resisted him. "It was very impressive."

# XXIII

## THE STEWARDSHIP OF MONEY

He makes a princely fortune as a servant of God, then disposes of it as a steward of God.

## A SHEAF OF LETTERS

(Relevant to this Chapter, if you look deeply enough)
"How consistently and richly you have lived your life . . ."

Janet Grieg Post"

\* \* \*

"Do not forget to tell of Mr. Crowell's ideals in the biography; how hour by hour he sought to be led by the Spirit of God."

William F. Weir

\* \* \*

"How fortunate it was that your work on the biography was started in time so you could have a personal acquaintance with Mr. Crowell. He must have given you an inspiration and an insight into his character that could not possibly have been obtained from any of his associates regardless of how intimate their friendship had been."

George Curtis Fretz
The Quaker Oats Company
Akron, Ohio

# THE STEWARDSHIP OF MONEY

O N THE subject of money, it is difficult to think of anyone who spoke with greater discernment than Richard Theodore Ely, Head of the Department of Political Economy, John Hopkins (1881-1892), and Professor of Political Economy, the University of Wisconsin, 1892-1925. This solid little man with a head well-set on square shoulders, labored on his various definitions until they were excellent with hammer marks, and they gave the impression: This is the last word.

The conventional definition of money, "a medium of exchange," he found inadequate. Money had to be more than that; it must have an *intrinsic* value, otherwise it was *fiat* money, ground out with a mimeograph like German marks. In the highest sense, Professor Ely affirmed, "Money is a store of value. To be *sound* money, it must have value in itself independent of government promises."

One great reason for Ely's conviction was that the fruits of hand and head and heart were worthy of safe storage, just as safe as governments can provide. In the long last, money was the hire of merit condensed into a reasonably indestructible form. More to the point, a man's money was in a mystic sense the man himself.

Now, let us apply Ely's clear-cut dictum. In the study of his Bible, Mr. Crowell came to feel that not only was he God's steward so far as his person and time were concerned, but he was also a steward, and a steward only, of the stored values which resulted from his labor. Nothing really belonged to him! It was the King's! This may be a fine place to remark that the gangrene of money possession is totally negatived for the man who holds wealth as a stewardship. On this thesis, Russell H. Conwell fired the hearts of thousands who today are commercial leaders with the ambition to "get rich to the glory of God."

The possession of money is a perilous thing unless it is held as a stewardship. There are many attitudes held by men towards their wealth, whether it be *much or little!* The lowest, no doubt, is the one which got to itself divine contempt; that of the churl who said, "I will build greater barns, and I will say to my soul, Soul, thou hast much goods laid up for many years. Take thine ease! Eat, drink and be merry!" This attitude makes any man a progger, even though he be a Cardinal.

A step higher (but still inadequate) was the philosophy of John Coney, silversmith. He put his economic surf board down on the gold-tides of Boston, at the turn of the eighteenth century, and went flying for a Midas ride. Everybody was getting rich, and in consequence, beaten-silver hungry. They craved silver for personal adornment; silver for their tables; silver for their churches. John saw mere money making had a rather cheap aspect so he assayed to sanctify his bank balances by declaring, "He was as diligent in God's work on the Lord's Day as he was in his own on other days." The angels knew what John meant. He ran a fence around "his other days" and put up a sign for God to read, "No trespassing!"

A still higher level, and a minimum safety level, is the practice of tithing. Singularly enough, the purpose of God in establishing tithing was not to finance His Kingdom, but to provide His people with a prophylactic against cacoëthis aurendum, (the desire for money). And we have yet to find a tither, young or old, who is in danger of the rust of riches. Even though the tither keeps nine tenths, what he keeps becomes "clean money and free from the root of evil." Immediately following Crowell's conversion in 1865 he began to tithe; and as a young business man he tithed with unswerving fidelity while his great enterprises prospered. "And he was blessed in all things."

But, here is the highest level of all, the stewardship level, which Mr. Crowell saw and accepted immediately upon his deeper knowledge of his Bible. Not only did *the tenth* belong to God, but the *nine-tenths* which he kept! And since the nine-tenths which he kept belonged to God, it was romance to present special gifts of love *above the tithe,* and to handle what he kept as a trustee for Deity.

\* \* \*

"Mr. Crowell, remember: One condition of writing this biography was that when questions are asked, the answers will be supplied."

Mr. Crowell remembered. He smiled.

"Very well, then: What has been your average rate of giving?"

For the first time in his life perhaps he broke silence on the subject:

*"For over forty years I have given sixty to seventy per cent of my income to God!"*

"Over forty years" dates the beginning; his deeper knowledge of the Bible.

"But," he continued earnestly, "I've never gotten ahead of God! He has always been ahead of me!"

\* \* \*

Mr. Crowell's letters are here at Cedar-Palms, a sacred trust. The hundreds of thousands which he *loaned* are recorded; and alas, a great deal will never be repaid. The vast totals of his gifts cannot even be conjectured. There was some reduction in his giving of late years, due to the tax program of the Administration. But the pensions which Mr. Crowell provided for disabled friends, old servants, old ministers, missionaries, etc., were continued, even though that continuance was quite a problem.

The last five years have been trying years for American business men. We note with regret the passing of that rugged individualism which made America great, and the infiltration of Parlor-Pink into American politics. Mr. Crowell, as other business men, puzzled his way through the taxations avalanched upon business by sour economies, Russian adaptations, and senseless extravagances. But, in spirit he was free! E. W. Oman, high in American financing wrote:

"Dear Mr. Crowell: The peace and strength in your soul in this trying period, which though in this world is not of this world, are continually a source of strength to me." Along this same line, another business man wrote, "But as to Mr. Crowell; I never saw that man with his hackles up."

\* \* \*

Mr. Crowell's high standards in the management of big business were an inspiration to the thousands who knew him, or knew about him. The respect accorded him by the world made you remember a John Plowman adage—"Men look at weather cocks, but they don't steer by them." George F. A. Nelson in a letter to Moody Bible Institute on the question of investments, paid tribute to men like Crowell in words that are a classic summary:

> "I have one other reservation about all investment-counsel organizations, and that is, the success of any such firm or banks is always due to one, or two, or three individuals. . . . If any of these persons die, leave, or *take to drink,* the organization may no longer be any good. Ability to make money is a gift, and it is relatively a rare gift. When the gifted individuals are no longer present, or take to drink, it (the gift) is often more of a danger than a help. . . . City records abound in the stories of big firms that in the twenties were of such merit that no better places existed in New York. Now, a few individuals have left or died and these firms are of little use to us. . . ."

Panegyrics have been frugally used in this book, even for the Autocrat himself; but at this point we cannot help observing how the thunder of Crowell's silent fidelity was a powerful factor in giving character to his several business enterprises. You cannot help thinking as you encounter the high type personnel in these corporations, "Well, I have a good idea as to how this came to pass." We remember Jack High Heels once saying, as we walked the cactus, "A ranch's appearance is part of the owner."

Before we conclude this chapter, a few words about goat's wool. The Crowell correspondence files have many missives from members of the Crack Pot Family. Some are refreshingly fantastic, and some provide you with a pain *au beau milieu.* One letter could be exhibit A for the dictum, "It is easy to be generous with another's goods."

"Give all your money away at once (this man wrote). Communism is coming. *The Methodist bishops say so!* Give your money away before it is confiscated!"

The writer then let it be known he has some fine suggestions to make when Mr. Crowell started the distribution. . . . There is a mass of letters with oily tongues, "Dear Beloved and Grand Mr. Crowell." After three pages of oleamen, the writer lays his pen aside and put out his hands, palms up. . . . Alas, how expensive it is to be a rich man! So long as a man is wealthy, even though he be pagan, he is attractive; and a man of means can seldom know if he is really loved. No matter how great the labor shortage, a rich man can always secure a regiment of claquers.

\* \* \*

This book again yields to the law of contemporaries, therefore but a fringe of Mr. Crowell serving millions may be recorded. However, comfort may be had in remembering, "From the foot, you can tell it is Hercules." His gifts will likely never be recorded beyond the pages of this book.

\* \* \*

More than a hundred great Christian enterprises are listed in the Sketch Book; works into which he poured princely sums, and of which no one man will know all. The great forward movement in systematic giving, for example, received from him $7500 annually for a number of years. Then there were continuous gifts to particular enterprises totaling in forty years millions of dollars. Such as (just a few where no harm can come from publicity):

> The Chosen Mission; missions in Sao Paulo; Brazil Colporteurs; Garibaldi Center; Korean Bible Commentary; Korean Evangelism; ten thousand dollars for prison visitation; Italian Missions in the United States; The Family Altar League; tract publication; mountain missionary work; Blue Ridge Missions; radio programs, a score of them; Bible translations; Bible commentaries in foreign language; Medical Missions to China; the Washington and Jane Smith Home for the Aged . . . add to this, his private financing of physicians who gave their services to the city's poor; hospitalization of worthy folks; private pensions, gifts to assist youth in getting an education . . . etc!

Go on until you have named a hundred more! Then add thousands of dollars privately given to young women in training as nurses; young men in training for the ministry; pensions for the widows and dependents of famous evangelists and ministers; thousands to rehabilitate young people trying to beat back from a bad start.

But a sense of restraint lays hold. Always in the writing of this book, I was conscious of two obligations: one, to be pleasing unto Crowell's King, and, the other, not to be displeasing to Mr. Crowell.

\* \* \*

It is in order, however, to print and preserve several quotations as samples of the letters of gratitude he received.

One woman, whose eyes were blinded and whose friends were few, received "as from heaven itself the means for treatment." Then came the day when she saw men as trees walking! Clearer and clearer her sight! At last she sat down and wrote in a good firm hand:

> "Dear Mr. Crowell: I hope very soon to come to the Fourth Church in order to get a good look at you from a distance. Please pardon my joy at the thought of it, for you know you helped me get my eyesight back and how can I do otherwise than look at you with an enthusiasm which is well nigh adoration?"

\* \* \*

Another, a woman whose hearing was restored:

> "Dear Mr. Crowell: Now I can hear *you,* every word. But I do not have to hear you. I can just sit and look at you and love you for what you've done for me."

A third is a group of letters written by a famous missionary during the month of January, 1944. In one letter this missionary writes in that lonely vein which every devoted worker some day feels:

> "I am due to retire at the age of seventy next October (1944). The doctors say I must be careful . . . my heart . . .

but during the war everyone is overloaded. I feel I must carry on."

Two weeks later, he becomes reminiscent of early labors:

"The flood gates of memory open and remind us of the Sunday thirty-two years ago when you took me home with you after the morning service, and just as we were sailing to India, you cabled to the Board your gift of $5000. Oh, Mr. Crowell, I can truly say you are a man sent from God into my life! Without that gift, I question if we would ever have had the Agricultural Institute. Your gift created confidence in the Board, who were not quite sure the Institute was a thing they could support . . . your gift gave confidence to the missionaries; your gift enabled us to get the land. So, I never think of you without prayer and thanksgiving to God. . . .

Sam Higginbottom"

\* \* \*

"How much in all, Mr. Crowell, do you estimate you've given to missions, welfare work, etc?"

After a long, Crowell silence, he replied, "Well, I've never even let myself in on that."

He looked out the window over the lawns of Green Court. I knew what he was thinking. He was remembering a boy, broken in health, hurrying with a full heart from a church service years ago, vowing to his Creator:

"Oh God, if you will allow me to make money to be used in Your service, I will keep my name out of it so You will have the glory."

## XXIV

## HOME IN AUGUSTA

Mr. and Mrs. Crowell find a climate "not as hot as Florida nor yet as cold as Chicago." They purchase a Governor's Mansion in Georgia.

"After she went home, folks wanted me to move over to New York. I even made a try at it. I know you won't understand, but she wasn't there at all. When I came to Maricopa, my heart filled up: there she was again! In the little cabin under the rim of Camel Back, in the brilliantly flowered Candle of the Lord. Yes, mysteriously in the tints on the barren hills, rose-red from the dawn of creation, and in the Arizona-blue of the skies themselves." (*Jack High Heels*)

# HOME IN AUGUSTA

To THE soft-spoken people of Augusta, Georgia, Henry Parsons Crowell was one of their citizens; his home was in their midst. Never mind about the beautiful estate in Winnetka, Illinois; "it was like a hunting lodge or a summer cottage so far as Mr. Crowell's affections were concerned. He was obliged to be in Chicago part of his time on account of business, but when he was free, the trains couldn't carry him South any too fast."

Mr. Crowell loved his home in Augusta as much as did its original owner, the Honorable Charles Jones Jenkins, who built the first half of the Green Court Mansion.

\* \* \*

A deepened sense of friendship developed as the biographical labors proceeded; and this friendship occasioned considerable time spent in the Georgia home. These extended visits with Mr. Crowell in the Southland provided the necessary "color" for portraying his home life.

The following excerpts from our correspondence files will be of interest. All these letters are dated in the early part of 1944:

(To R. E. D.)
"In one of your letters you said that soon after Easter you would like to plan another visit with me in Augusta . . . apparently for a few days. But, as we have grown to know each other, a few days will not answer . . . we should prolong a few days into at least two weeks. The spring season is opening . . . the leaves have come out on all the trees . . . many flowers are blooming. . . . H. P. C."

\* \* \*

(To Deborah)
"I am looking forward with great pleasure to your coming to Augusta. . . . I trust not for two or three days as before, but

for two or three weeks. . . . I have learned to love you and your husband, which is the reason for my speaking so plainly. . . . H. P. C."

\* \* \*

(To both of us)
"I do hope you can make more than a few days visit in our final conference. . . . H. P. C."

\* \* \*

(Deborah to R. E. D.)
"Mr. Crowell's letters are very precious to me, and the consciousness of his love toward us is most pleasing. . . . You must not fail to plan your work so as to go to Augusta, and I hope you can make more than a few days visit in what he calls 'our final conference.' This expression 'our final conference' grieves me deeply. I feel he has a premonition he might not be with us much longer. . . . Deborah."

\* \* \*

(To both of us)
"I appreciate a letter recently received from Dr. Day, stating that you will arrive at Green Court on April 19, 1944, and will continue as my guests during the balance of the month . . . each one of us will be happy and contented over the outcome. . . . April is always a month of charm and beauty . . . we can enjoy sitting on the porch, or walking about the grounds to look at the flowers and points of beauty. There is rivalry between the months of March and April; for different azaleas come into bloom, and then disappear within a brief space of time. . . . We have over thirty different kinds of azaleas, and each one has a charm of its own. . . . Therefore, to see all of them, it will be necessary for you to be my guests in the Southland *on several occasions . . .*"

\* \* \*

(Deborah to R. E. D.)
"Once again on receipt of Mr. Crowell's letter, I was made to feel we must give Mr. Crowell as much time as possible. . . . You can easily see he loves his Augusta home best. It must carry many precious memories of HER. . . . I was most sensitive concerning Susan at Green Court, but at Winnetka, not at all. I couldn't see her at Winnetka, but it was easy for me to see her always at Augusta. I believe he wants you to see Green Court when it is at its best; when the azaleas are in bloom, that it might have first place in your book. . . . I think

he wants you to do some of the writing there. . . . I can't help feeling deeply moved by the last sentence in his letter: 'Thank you for all you are doing and the happy relationship that is ours! Devotedly yours!' How my heart is moved by his closing words, 'Devotedly yours.' . . . Deborah"

\* \* \*

One indeed could not be in Green Court without becoming aware of Susan . . . you felt a tug at the heartstrings as you walked among her *azaleas,* for they indeed are *her* azaleas, though she died nearly a quarter of a century ago. . . . You thought of Susan over and over as you saw the loved objects d' art which she and H. P. brought back from their European trips; placed just about where she liked to see them when she was alive. . . .

On Easter Sunday night, therefore, we boarded the Empire Builder at Seattle for Chicago; took the Dixie Flyer south to Atlanta; continued on the Southern to Augusta. We didn't know it then, although our hearts were filled with misgivings; no, we didn't know it then, but that was to be our last visit to Green Court when the beloved host was there. For when he left Augusta in May, for the Chicago-interval, he was never to return. . . .

\* \* \*

Deborah was right; Mr. Crowell did want Green Court to have first place in his life story. Therefore, we have no interest in presenting an abbreviated account of his Georgia home. The chapters in this section shall be unabridged. We want you to have your heartstrings pulled just as ours were when we walked with our gracious host among *her* azaleas . . . we want you to envision her and her womanly excellence, just as we did. We want you to note his poignant memories of her though he masterfully concealed his feeling. We want you to know, for H. P. C. and his Susan were one—body, mind, and spirit.

\* \* \*

At the turn of the century "Susan's health was not the best," so they began to look for a place with a friendly climate, "not as hot as Florida, nor as cold as Chicago." Once, in the Interviews, Mr. Crowell said: "From the very start, we asked the Lord to direct us and He brought us to this place."

"This place," as in Shakespeare's loved lines,
"Hath a pleasant seat!
The air sweetly and nimbly recommends itself
Unto our gentle senses!"

To better understand the Augusta home, let us take a look at the city itself. . . . The turgid Savannah River, which forms the boundary between Georgia and South Carolina, executes its labor in a line as wobbly as Methuselah's signature. The course at one point totters eastward, then southward, then westerly, forming a giant, quivery water-bow. Early settlers liked this curve so well that they snuggled the edifice of the Episcopal church right in the elbow of the river, apparently that the city might be in the Savannah's affectionate embrace. But the river at times becomes too affectionate, so protective dykes have been created to hold it back. Stand on the dyke just above the charming old church building and its beautiful grounds. There is the Southern Railroad bridge, its stone feet cloyed in driftwood. Look over to the South Carolina bank; half a dozen bare-footed negroes fish and dream; better dream and fish. They have in mind a hot catfish sandwich; and it's not a bad idea, if you ask me.

Look over the city; it is indeed an attractive spot. Woodrow Wilson selected it as a capital place in which to be born, and Bobby Jones prefers its excellent golf courses. Into this city on the Savannah come men and women who have tethers long enough to go anywhere they wish. But they winter in Augusta.

They can never tell when the blazing fury of a thunderstorm will strike, with torrents of rain and flashes of lightning. But there is something about the city that holds the winter guest. So, he comes again the next year, and the next, knowing that here is one place in the U. S. A. where no one is in a hurry; where folks even talk that way; where one will have time leisurely to drink tea in dearly-quaint old southern drawing rooms. The visitor returns to Augusta. He continues to grumble about the climate "so hot, muggy, and sticky"; but he returns just the same.

\* \* \*

Augustans have achieved a British insouciance toward their city. The dusky and the dingy are conjoined and intermixed with the elegant and the aristocratic, with no particular preference for either classification, thank you! The dusky and the dingy are the precise places where great things took place, and that makes them as lovable as your old negro Aunt Beulah. In fact, the Augustan does not care for things Yankee-new; like the British girl who felt Stanford Chapel might become a very charming edifice after five hundred years.

You go into a temple of musty smells, called the public library. You desire more information about Mr. Jenkins. You feel you would like to tear the building down next week. But the Augustan is horrified! That building was something else before it was the library!

You learn that the Honorable Charles Jones Jenkins was an aesthete, with a penchant for carefully landscaped grounds, and rare flowers. You discover also that Mr. Jenkins was, casual-like, an Augusta lawyer, and a very talented one at that. He advanced to Legislator, Attorney General, State Senator, Judge of the Georgia Supreme Court, and finally Provincial Governor of the State (1865-1868). He had a strong affection for Augusta, purchased a plot of about six acres in the West Forest, laid out the grounds, erected a fine residence, and called it "Green Court."

\* \* \*

Mr. Crowell and Susan visited Augusta in 1908, and discovered Green Court. She exclaimed, "Harry, this is just right. We can *live* here and spend our summers in Chicago!" They sought God's guidance in the matter. It seemed good! Better every minute! She liked the few azaleas which Governor Jenkins had bedded along the border paths. Later, those azaleas were, under her direction, to become the ancestors of the floral aristocrats which you may see today. *Yes, it was good!*

So they purchased Green Court in 1909 and settled down while their son Coleman was growing up. In due time, they just about doubled the Governor's original structure, taking care to duplicate his architecture, even to the fireplaces. They built additional curving walks, added a sunken garden and a colony of fine shrubs and trees. . . .

It always seemed like Heaven! That's right, Heaven! Whenever a couple bases their home on the will of God, it gets something over and above Georgia Januaries. Here they abode for nearly fifteen years; or, until that June day in 1922, when she entered the house not made with hands, leaving behind a lonely-hearted man who continued his residence there until October, 1944 . . . with her azaleas for remembrance.

\* \* \*

As the years go by, a man and his wife shape and color that little area around them, which they call home, and in a mysterious sense, even the sky above. Oliver Wendell Holmes remarks that the soul of a man "has a series of concentric wrappings, like an onion."

Let us exposit Holmes' statement like a text. First, is his personal feeling, his own body. You get that by thinking of his face. The one he had at twenty was given to him; the one at forty, he made for himself. Then, the next layer is his home. When he first buys it, or gets it from the contractor, everything needs going over, even though it be brand new! At first it is hard and cold; it has to be mellowed down. That mellowing, as many of us have found, is really the "projection of ourselves into the outer layer": a new hedge, a new plant, a repaired trellis, a brave touch of paint. After awhile the home becomes a projection of the owners.

And now walk with us about the grand old place; let us admire its curving stairs, antique furniture, beautiful trees. And we shall not be surprised if you suddenly think as we did,

"Well, I feel as if I had met Susan and Harry walking in their garden in the cool of the day."

# XXV

## GREEN COURT

And now you visit a southern home, whose guest register records a host of names, rich and poor, great and small!

"When we return to Philadelphia, and experience rain, wind, cold and ice, Augusta's weather, the lawns of Green Court, and the flowers are truly longed for. However, green grass and azaleas are not what we really miss . . . We miss you, Mr. Crowell! . . . just to think, you have given yourself to Dr. Erdman and myself year after year! . . . I can hear your voice asking the blessing at the table, a blessing so different from any others. . . ." (*Letter, Mrs. Frederick Erdman*)

# GREEN COURT

BATHOS, Queen of Literary Disorder, has always inspired a
wholesome fear. Therefore the account of the Crowell home
in Augusta is placed toward the close of the book so as to insure
the good wine for the end of the feast . . . Let us walk through
the big gates at 2248 Cumming Road and make our way directly
to the mansion. Please do not ask to tarry beside the curious and
exotic banana bush which sentinels the front steps; and do not
ask to walk over to some one or other of the azaleas clumps,
glowing with pastel shaded blossoms. The azaleas shall be reserved for more leisurely display, like angels' lanterns, in the
next chapter.

Let us mount the high steps sweeping upward from the gravel
drive to the noble old veranda, fifteen feet wide, which forms
"a gracious margin around three sides of the house." Take time
to regard the delicate iron lace running from the top of one
porch-column to the next. Governor Jenkins secured this "metal
braid" in New Orleans. Proceed to the front door. You may
notice how from continual retouching the warm-stone paint is
thickly piled on the porch floor, like a boat deck. Enter the
front door, flanked with its charming "peek-panes."

A spacious hall fifteen feet wide sweeps through the center
of the house from the wide front door on the north side to the
French doors overlooking the formal garden on the south. The
hardwood floor in the hall is highly polished, and there's a place
for everything, that is, everything which belongs there. Don't
put your grips down! If you do, Anthony will remove them as
soon as you let go of the handles. While we are in the business of
warnings, permit us to spare you another *faux pas.* When the
mail comes, never receive it from the postman, even to remove

your own! That is just not done! Wait! In due time Anthony will bring you what is yours on a silver tray. It would be satisfactory to Mr. Crowell if you took your own mail, but dark Anthony exudes a cool butlerian disdain toward all such misconduct . . . At the left, just as you enter the front door is the east parlor, a smallish room, replete with cases, old books, good chairs and a fireplace.

This parlor has a special assignment. It is the Green Court chapel. There you will come each morning, and sit in your appointed place, while Mr. Crowell conducts devotions. Everyone in the house will be there, *in his place,* including the servants . . . Just back of the east parlor, separated by French doors with cynanide panes, is a downstairs guest room. Large French windows open out of this room onto the veranda. The veranda, adjacent to the guest room, is screened; mind you, Augusta does have mosquitos! Good prints, picked up here and there, are on the walls. (But if you aim to create a Wilshire Boulevard effect, you wouldn't want them for yourself.)

There is a massy, dark secretary, a fine highboy, and a noble four-poster. . . . Just north of this lower guest room, a wide hall traverses the house east and west; south of the hall is the spacious dining room. But, come on; you are not going in there—*yet.*

\* \* \*

To the right as you enter the front door are the west living rooms, a great double room with fireplaces. The south fireplace was built by Governor Jenkins, and the north, in duplicate, by Mr. Crowell. Everything in the west living rooms is complete and in order: books, busts, and sofas; heavy chairs, flowers in interesting vases resting on tables with Percheron legs. Old French prints of French gentlemen "adorn" the walls; photographs on tables, and plenty of bric-a-brac. In the southwest corner of the west living rooms, there is a desk on which lies the guest book. Glance through its pages. What an array of great evangelists, professional men, captains of industry, college students, authors, politicians! And what an array of comment these guests have scribbled after their names; some clever, and some, alas, otherwise. . . .

A dainty staircase, mid-house, ascends just a bit too steeply to the upper floor. In making the turns, the tread width narrows down to nothing-at-all on one side; watch your step if you value your dignity! Governor Jenkins installed that wood lace, as dainty as a spider web, in the stair-guard, and capped it with a fine, curving walnut rail. But do not lean on the rail! It is to look at, not to lounge on!

\* \* \*

On the second floor level, there are a number of guest rooms. Every one of them, being under the roof, is an ideal place to listen to a Georgia thunderstorm slash the windowpanes and to hear the waste water gurgling down the soil pipes. On the northwest corner is a guest room, master size, whose windows look out over the great lawns. The wallpaper is a refreshing pattern, which Mr. Crowell will tell you was selected by himself. . . .

The room on the southeast corner belonged to the master himself. It is lighted by great windows facing south, east and north. There is a table covered with new books, fresh from the presses, most of them autographed by their authors; a fine, large old flat top desk; a typewriter and desk, and another four-poster bed. In this room, day by day, Mr. Crowell managed his great business interests via private wire; dictated to his secretaries. Prominently displayed on a small table is the photograph of Susan, which you will find facing page 121; and beneath the photograph a chaste little vase bearing an azalea . . . You can't help being impressed "by the grand old place." It is the home of a gentleman and his lady; vast, hospitable, homey, and winsome.

\* \* \*

Now we will visit the grounds. The main drive, surfaced with well-rolled gravel, comes in calmly from the front gate on a slow curve, that innocent deception for giving a sense of ample space to rather narrow bounds. But not too narrow; for Green Court covers about six acres! The curve permits Denton Bench to bring the Chrysler right up to the front steps. The drive, like the Savannah River, (after which we suspect it was modeled) then goes off again on a gentle curve to the garage and servant's quarters. The garage, with its over-head apartment; Denton's cottage, etc., are all nicely screened from house-view by noble trees.

. . . A menage as large as Green Court required the presence of a number of servants, of several classifications, all "white" save Anthony and Cornelia; and all paragons of efficiency.

\* \* \*

Edward J. Lofving, ("Eddie") the gardener, really owns the trees. As in the case of nearly all the people who work for Mr. Crowell, he has been in his employ for years. Get him to talk about the Green Court Oaks; the Quercus akin to the Beech family; the Robur Pendunenculata, the Robur Sessiliflora. Everybody who visits Green Court is certain to hear Eddie praise a pair of Darlingtons on the west of the mansion. The Darlington is a dainty aristocrat of the swamps. Its leaves are so small, so fern-delicate, one can scarcely believe they are Oak trees.

Eddie will fairly stroke the giant Hackberries which stand in a stately row behind the mansion. He will tell you the Hackberry is a member of the Elm family; that Georgians call it the "Sugar Berry." (By the way, no dates ever tasted racier than their buckshot-sized seeds.) He will tell you the Hackberry makes good fence timber; that its roots provide fine dyes. He will inform you that Augusta is "just in the Magnolia Belt; had the city been twenty-five miles east, it would have been out." And he will inform you that Augusta is in the Hickory Belt, too. There is a great Shagbark.Hickory on the grounds to illustrate his point.

\* \* \*

Regardless of season, this Hickory is an aboreal beauty, lifting its giant symmetry on the northwest corner of the grounds; one hundred and twenty feet of living glory, supported by a thirty-inch trunk! In the spring, spike-like flowers appear in rusty-wooly. In the fall, the leaves turn to hammered copper, and it bears a harvest of white nuts with charming shells, crinkled like the skim of boiled milk.

"You ought to hear the negroes sing as they gather the nuts," says Eddie, the gardener. "Mr. Crowell lets the darkies have them free. Every fall they come with baskets and gunny sacks, and carry away bushels of them."

Come now to the formal garden just south of the mansion. Centered in it is a slightly sunken pool, around which proper yew trees rise in proper lines along gravel paths, fretted with violets and pansies. There is a bronze fountain mid-pool, looking like a cherub playing in the water.

\* \* \*

All about the grounds you find walks concealed in the shrubbery, like a secret trail in Big Basin. You walk along azalea-bordered paths, edged with beautiful shrubbery. Every now and then paths emerge into the open, and run alongside broad lawns of California rye grass.

\* \* \*

An entire morning has been given to inspection and you now feel tired, maybe hungry. You go to your room. Presently Anthony knocks at the door, "Dinnah in ten minutes!" You assemble in the west living rooms with the other guests, so as to enter the dining room in formal procession. Quite ceremonious! Yet perfectly natural in this home. You enter the dining room, charming in old silver pieces on the mantle, and oversize bronze fireplace equipment faultlessly polished. Anthony stands by the service door of the room stiff as a Swiss guard, deftly removing the service as used, and replacing it with the next course.

The graceful bouquets scattered about are the craftsmanship of Cornelia, Anthony's dusky wife. (Anthony and Cornelia, by the way, have two brilliant daughters, splendidly educated, who are public school teachers.)

Deborah whispers, "Wonder what kind of China service we will have today? We've been here a week and no service has been used twice!"

"That's so," I reply, "but I was wondering if they'd have another Georgia baked ham."

\* \* \*

After dinner, everyone retires to his room awhile, to write, read, rest or what-you-will.

Life in Green Court, you will decide, was bounded by well guarded formalities. True! Yet no visitor ever esteemed them burdensome. You loved them all! The wife of Eddie, the gardener, wrote a poem depicting the day's round at Green Court. She composed these verses as an affectionate tribute to Mr. Crowell on the occasion of his eighty-fifth birthday, and he cherished her poem in a docket of his valuable papers. No wonder! Mrs. Lofving's lines, though meter cripples, conceal their deformities under the fine lines of true feeling!

### TO MR. H. P. CROWELL, ON HIS BIRTHDAY

This is the birthday of one we love;
And so we wish this love to prove
By sending roses, pink and gay,
To brighten and sweeten the happy day.

First comes Sara, who likes to be sure
That things are right and nothing poor.
Then there's Eddie, who loves to till,
And keep "The Garden Spot of the Hill."

Next comes Denton, a happy soul,
Whose chief desire, as a part of his role,
Is to keep the Chrysler shining bright
And see that no part gets too tight.

Mrs. Remington looks after his health,
Which means much more than golden wealth.
Hilda uses the spoons and beaters
To keep in trim the grateful eaters.

Ruth is busy all day long,
Doing her part to keep him strong.
Gertrude, in her allotted spot
Has to be sure that dust is not.
Margaret, this time wants a part,
Because she's been here from her start.

Anthony next comes in the line,
He serves the food when its time to dine.
Cornelia, too, puts in her hours
In doing a lot of things with flowers.

And so, each one would have a part
(And every bit comes from the heart)

In making happy by what they do
The man who's lived so long and true.
(The Gardener's Wife)

*    *    *

Thank you, Esteemed Lady of the Gardener! Your praise is praise indeed. You have furnished a very choice epithet for the beloved autocrat, every bit from the heart!

"The man who's lived so long and true!"

# XXVI

## GREEN COURT AZALEAS

Wherein you learn something of the Flowers of the mansion and discover that the chief blossoms nurtured in its serene climate were not of the vegetable kingdom.

"My Beloved is gone down into his garden . . . to feed . . . and to gather lilies. *I am my beloved's, and my beloved is mine!* He feedeth among His lilies." (*Song of Solomon*)

# GREEN COURT AZALEAS

THIS is a proper place for a bit of patter about azaleas-in-general, scientific and otherwise. The books affirm, "The azalea is not botanically separated from rhododendron, and belongs to the Heath family (Ericaceae)." Once again you are introduced into a nature family of amazing size: over fourteen hundred species of azaleas! The Madrone Tree in the Coast Range behind Los Gatos is a member of that family! And so is the Manzanita on the foothills of Shasta!

Can you bear a little-more-in-general about azaleas? A further word as to the number of species—you will never know exactly! The Americana type, for instance, lists over twenty-five members; one man says "fifty"; Hylander, "one hundred!" But when you visit the Singing Tower in Florida, they will tell you, "There are over two hundred types here at Mountain Lake."

The characteristics of the plants vary so largely that fixed formulas are impossible. Some varieties have evergreen leaves; other, deciduous. Some are odorless; others exude a dark muskiness as rich in romantic suggestion as a perfume ad in a teen-age magazine. Some put up their flowers in terminal, umbel-like clusters; others, well, they are as diversified on this point as the scintillating little cinerarias—simple and double, and neither!

As to the names of some prominent types—the Amaena and Kemsferi can live even in New Jersey; the Occidentalis prefers California; the Viscosa likes swamps—and then there is the Indica, the Rhombis, the Vaseyi, the Austrina, splendid for the South; the Calendulacea, the Hispida, the Arborescens, Undiflora, the Pontica Senensis . . . Some are two feet tall, some thirty . . . Friends, this is getting involved, let's talk about color.

231

Their faces vie with each other and with the prism. Yellow, red, orange, and copper, pink and purple, apricot and salmon, white with red edges, orange-red and flame . . . Let's talk about structure.

\* \* \*

No fixed pattern is followed in the blossom-architecture of the various types. The stamens, for instance, which happen to be the gentlemen members in the blossom house, are diversified. Some stamens are short, juicy little rods ring-grouped in the flower cup, as in the case of the saffron-colored Mollis. Other stamens are long and pendulous, and stick way out like the whiskers on Spookie, our cat, as in the case of the golden Austrina. This is getting more and more involved. Let's talk about azalea culture.

\* \* \*

The azalea is fussy as to climate. You may see that in the California cousin, the rhododendron, which flourishes in the Redwoods of Mendocino. The azalea watches the thermometer like an anemic old gentleman. If the air gets dry, like Arizona, it moves out. Or cold, like Alberta, it never moves in, unless it can get a hot-house apartment. It likes nights of sixty-five degrees, and days of eighty degrees. But it will pine away at temperatures below thirty-five degrees. The azalea loves humidity and sulks if it doesn't have it. Palo Altans, remember that, when you fuss over your puny plants! If the azalea humidity of Augusta moved into the Santa Clara Valley, you would move out.

Moreover, the azalea is decidedly foot-conscious. No taste at all for tight shoes; so the gardener stands them in fibrous peat soil, there they may freely move their root-toes. They even enjoy moist sox; but these sox must never be wet. Further they like a little acid in the soil, as fair maidens with a taste for lemonade.

The old-man diseases which annoy them are thrips and spiders. Having a tendency to become stringy, they must be cut back, cropped while young, if the plant is to remain attractive. Dear me! If one is going to grow azaleas along his gravel walks he will have to give up business, or hire a gardener like Eddie, the floral symposiarch of Green Court! For fear someone with a small degree of scientific knowledge concerning azaleas will suddenly de-

Exotic blossoms
border the
paths . . .

And catch the eye at the turn of the lawns.

The blossoms are
many-colored. This
coral-tinted beauty
heralds Augusta's
April

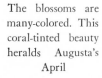

THE AZALEAS OF GREEN COURT

Some azaleas are almost as tall as trees . . .

Others are kept low-growing . . .

And there is a great company of middle-sized beauties.

THE AZALEAS OF GREEN COURT

tect the author's ignorance, this analysis is swiftly concluded. Azaleas? *Well, my friends, they are very impressive!*

\* \* \*

You now realize as you walk among Susan's azaleas that here is a realm of mystery. You are amazed to think that you have never entered the fringe of the subject. But, she, as a Vassar girl, mastered a respectable fund of information. She knew that her plants were descended from originals, some of which came from the hills of the Orient, some from the Berkshire Mountains. The marriages of these plants were performed by gardeners, who sensed that Chinese and Massachusetts rhodos had always been attracted to each other, but never could mature their romance without a kindly human hand. Just as there are certain words in the vocabularies of the world that have always been in love with each other, but never could get together without the kindly offices of a poet. These winsome children of the azalea romances glow like flashing jewels, banked along Susan's garden. And when she went home, Mr. Crowell found he was as deeply in love with them as she; better, he was in love with them because she loved them. They were her azaleas!

\* \* \*

But Susan's floral azaleas which glow like Chinese lanterns in the beds of Green Court, are the symbols of a more glorious flowering. Mr. Crowell followed as we walked with him in the garden. Suddenly, with no apparent relevance, he said: "She was a beautiful Christian character! She had a Bible class here. It became a center for men and women who had a definite interest in Christ. It made its impression."

"It made its impression!" We always did relish Mr. Crowell's naive understatement. It made its impression, indeed! Go where you will in the churches of Augusta, and you will find a host of the right-hand workers whose faces brighten up on every mention of Green Court; whose spiritual integration stems from its influence. There is scarcely a church in Augusta that has not profited by the spiritual fervor emanating from Green Court. Sunday school teachers, officers, devoted members in astonishing numbers will tell you frankly that their deeper experience began at Green Court.

Just a wisp of examples which *do refer to persons living and dead.* . . . Charlie and Margaret occupy an imposing home. He heads a large business. They are a singularly consecrated couple. Their letters in the file always begin "Beloved Father Crowell." You can see that they looked upon Mr. Crowell with the adoring eyes of the children of John, walking in the faith. . . . Here are Donald and his wife. You are now in the upper circles of Augusta. What a testimony this couple makes to the modern world! But —they will tell you themselves—they were born again at Green Court. . . . Mrs. Y— is a woman in the prime of life; she is a tower of strength, not only in her own church, but throughout Augusta. She quietly says, "I never knew my Lord until Susan Crowell revealed Him to me." . . . These are just a few samples!

Later, others came who helped the Crowells spread a Christian summer over the City of Augusta. Conspicuously among these were Mrs. George Rounds (Tryphena Cecelia Schnobly) and Mrs. Anna Mabel Utley. Early in life, Mrs. Rounds was private secretary to Miss Frances Willard. When Mr. W. E. Blackstone organized the Chicago Hebrew Mission in 1887, Mrs. Rounds was elected secretary and treasurer, then superintendent. Mrs. Utley is described as "for years Mrs. Rounds' beloved companion and assistant." These two women so deeply impressed the Crowells with their knowledge of the Word and evangelical fire, that the Crowells became heavy contributors to the Hebrew Mission. Finally, "the women grew old in the service; weary in it, but not of it!" In 1919 Mr. Crowell suggested to Mrs. Rounds and Mrs. Utley, "I would like to have you retire and make your home with me in Augusta."

They moved to Augusta; but, did they *retire?* We shall see! Mrs. Rounds, aided by Mrs. Utley, immediately started Bible classes in the Green Court Chapel and in the East Living Room. The influence of these classes permeated the entire city. In the years that followed, more than three hundred persons were saved, as well as a great number of others who were brought into a deeper experience.

We append one story as an example. It might be titled "Deb-
utante Becomes Dean of Women in a Bible Institute."

\* \* \*

Miss Katherine sat in the lobby of Boston's Bellvue Hotel as she
told her life story; a story which would make a worthy chapter for
Begbie's *Twice Born Men*. She frankly appraised her early life:

> I was a cigarette smoking, cocktail drinking, small town,
> rich girl. My father, an Augusta lawyer, was educated abroad;
> he was a brilliant agnostic who for a pastime read Juvenal in
> the original. He and Mother never went to church. Sunday
> was a day for cocktails. Our home picture was—*horrible!*
> French novels were my reading. At seventeen, I received a
> volume of Ingersoll and came to the conclusion "There is no
> God." At nineteen, I was an Augusta debutante, country
> club type. Then the "rounds" began; Europe, Paris every
> summer, until I was ready to die with ennui. I finally re-
> ceived some help from the Oxford groups. Remember the
> strange history of this cult? But a time soon came when the
> groups could do no more good for me. I lapsed into despair . . .
> Right at this point Miss D— said to me, "Let me take you
> over to see Mrs. Rounds."
> "What can *she* do for me?"
> Miss D— practically dragged me over to Green Court.
> When I laid eyes on Mrs. Rounds—that did it! What could
> that old thing do for me? Why—she looks mildewed! That
> terrible old shawl . . . that awful hair-do!
> But I didn't know that for seven years the prayers in the
> Green Court Chapel had ascended for my salvation. I couldn't
> understand it. Presently my revulsion for Mrs. Rounds began
> to change, against my will, into a deep respect . . . One day
> my heart turned liquid within me. Jesus Himself stood before
> me, and I wanted to adore Him . . . Augusta society life
> grew stale, dreadful to my heart . . . I could not even remain
> at home . . . went out into mission work and hardship. . . .

Today? Miss Katherine is Dean of Women in one of America's
greatest Christian schools.

\* \* \*

We started in to talk about floral azaleas but we end with better things. We have heard a Voice saying, "I am the Rose of
Sharon, and the Lily of the Valley. And thou hast ravished my

heart, my spouse! Thy plants are an orchard of pleasant fruits: camphire and spikenard, trees of frankincense, myrrh, aloes and all gracious spices!"

Our hearts cry out with joy as we behold what the King can do with springs shut up, and fountains sealed! "The winter is over! The flowers appear on the earth! The time of the singing of birds is come!"

The Central Utility Buildings cover a village-sized area

The Manager's
Residence
"Sometimes it's Sum-
mer," says Bob—

"and sometimes we have
a May blizzard."

THREE VIEWS, WYOMING HEREFORD RANCH

# XXVII

## MR. CROWELL TAKES OVER AN ESTANCIA

Herein we see what happened by reason of our Hero's double life. So far as the public could see, he was plighted to giant factories. But, furtively as it were, he also cherished a love for wide Open Spaces. So—in 1912, his "division" betrayed him! He got himself a nice little cattle ranch in Wyoming.

For twenty-two years Hereford cattle were his avocation. His enthusiasm over the progress of his herd was equal to that of a country clubber over an improved golf score. Mr. Crowell's notes clearly reveal the reason why he became a cattleman:

"There is a magnetic power and inspiration to be found in the taking of a herd that is mediocre, and building it into one where imperfections are difficult to find, and where the strength and uniformity of every animal is so noticeable as to excite admiration." (*Sketch Book*)

# MR. CROWELL TAKES OVER AN
# ESTANCIA

UPON first learning that Mr. Crowell was the owner of one of the five great cattle ranches in the United States, one is surprised no end. But it was a perfectly natural outcome of his tastes evidenced from boyhood. There is no time where his beginning of interest in livestock may be dated. Lying before me is a letter in longhand, written at South Williamstown, Massachusetts, in his twelfth year, 1867:

> "There is a little boy came here last Tuesday from Troy; his name is Henry Jones. He has got a very beautiful little pony and phaeton which he is going to keep here . . . I had a very nice ride on the pony the other day."

You are captivated by his affection for livestock. A preceding chapter has portrayed him, still a boy, heading his famous Percheron parade down the Red River of the Dakotas. You see him later, a very young man, putting his oatmeal business into the side line of making stock feed. That in itself is a chapter-length story that has been boiled down paragraph-length in the Cedar-Palms Kettles. Here is the digest.

Conditions changed rapidly in the salad days of the United States. Almost immediately after big ranches "snaked their fences out over the ranges and ruined them," the big ranches themselves were blighted—crumbled into little farms. The reason for this was the rising cost of acreage. With little farms came the necessity of intensive farming to make a living, and intensive farming always means dairy cattle. Everywhere things were changing! Changing! [1] Razor-back hogs were chased back into

[1] The amazement with which each generation views its "Shifting Scenes" is an old story. A historical perspective and frosty temples enables one to hear with equanimity the startled cries of adolescents over "Our Changing World!"

the brush, and replaced by better porkers; poultry became a farm staple, "so as to make productive value equal to land appreciation."

Mr. Crowell and his associates "were alert and ready." It was not long before by-products, once thrown into the river, were "fixed up" for the market. Furfurol, for instance; but if you want to know about that, ask the man at the service station who sells you a quart of oil for your motor. The "edible wastes" were balanced, vitamined and packaged so prettily "that even the roosters were intrigued."

\* \* \*

The farmers in those days were also looking for "better milkers," and soon began to look for "better meaters." Enter the Hereford like the prima donna of a butcher-shop opera!

The Hereford! No apology is offered for this bucolic aside. Mr. Crowell was so deeply interested in livestock that he marvelled over men who were not. He knew about Herefordshire, that tiny eight hundred and forty square mile valley on England's Wye, whose Hereford cattle did more for the country than the haughty cathedral. He knew about the cattle experiments of one family in particular, there in the Wye Valley, which resulted in the appearance of an animal as surprising to them as the potatoes which bore his name were to Burbank. That animal was "Mr. B. R. Hereford the First."

Mr. Crowell knew how breeders in England began to register the bovine descendants, and how breeders continued to keep up the blue books in the United States, until the annals of human aristocracy look simple when compared with Who's Who in Cows. . . . He knew about Patrick Henry importing a few head. . . . He knew about that great Chicago merchant, John V. Farwell, owning a Hereford herd as a hobby. . . .

He could tell you, if he thought you were really interested, about Hereford history in the United States . . . Gudgell and Simpson who, on becoming old men, let their herd scatter before reaching perfection (that was something to be watched) . . . of the Mosell Brothers who produced a superior herd, decided to sell out, start over; auctioned their herd, then went broke "on poor notes." (That was something to be watched, also; never let go

MRS. TRYPHENA CECILIA ROUNDS AND MR. CROWELL

Mrs. Rounds, formerly of the Chicago Hebrew Mission, and Mrs. Utley,
her constant companion, made their home in old age at Green Court. They
organized Bible classes in the west living rooms, through which scores were
saved, and every church in Augusta blessed.

MRS. ANNA MABEL UTLEY

Susan's azaleas were but the symbols of a more glorious
flowering that came of Green Court.

Big bovine beauties beneath the willows along the creek

Amiable giants with no hay in their horns

"Old Type"

"New Type"
(W. H. R. S. Prince Domino C)

Well, Mr. Crowell, you certainly did get yourself a ranch and there is no need
of trick photographers to prove how good your Herefords are.

Robert ("Bob") Wells
Lazear, manager, W. H. R.
He dresses the part. Six quart
Stetson, skin-tight sun-cloth
pants, a Hollywood coat . . .
but you wouldn't care to rile
him up.

When Mr. Crowell
made his last visit
(1944), he drove over
the ranges to see the
animals grazing. "Bob"
dressed up city-style to
be photographed with
Mr. Crowell.

Mr. Crowell admired the great creatures. "It was very impressive to see what
the boys were doing."

"They have a painting of Mr. Crowell in the Saddle and Sirloin Club in recognition of his contribution to agriculture. That's quite an honor" (Bob). Portrait by Joseph Allworthy, the Portrait Gallery, Saddle and Sirloin Club, top floor, Livestock Record Building, Chicago Stock Yards.

of your first-line animals.) He knew about Hazlett in Kansas who did some fine things but was disappointed upon finding his time was too short. (You have to watch that, too. Someone must take up the herd where you leave off, and he must be under-written so that he can go on with the work.)

And he could discuss in a fluent way why the Hereford is such a superior animal, that is, if you have meat in mind. If you want a dairy animal, then do not consider Herefords. But if you are seek-ing an animal that needs no "babying"; an animal so rugged it can thrive on snowy prairies or in the super-heated canyons of the Mogollons; an animal that can prosper where other breeds grow lean and starve; an animal that can give you a mountain of good eating as tender as cowboy beef—then, sir, you are looking for Herefords. It's the top-grade grazer for the beef steak platters of the world.

\* \* \*

We append a bit of Hereford propaganda at this point. On a long transcontinental summer afternoon, two pullman porters were talking, one of them fresh from Harlem, the other "breaking him in."

"What kind of cows is them?" said the Harlem boy, greatly excited.

"Why, *Herefords.*"

"Herefords! You sure gets no bread with *them.*"

"What do you mean, no bread?"

"Well, they is certainly One Meat Ball!"

We do not hope many of our gentle readers will get the subtler refinements of this tale; but that is not necessary.

\* \* \*

The Hereford is indeed an amazing animal in a score of ways. The gentlemen cattle, for instance, never appear to have hay in their horns; they are boys with amiable dispositions . . . They have a way of ennobling every view, whether knee-deep in Kentucky blue grass, or in the boulder-strewn canyons of Yavapai. But—why *do* Hereford breeders always photograph *their* cattle knee-deep in something or other, barn hay, or packing-box ex-celsior? And why do they photograph *other* breeds standing on places as bare as Inyo? *Why?* We don't know unless the owners of other breeds cannot hire fancy photographers.

\* \* \*

It was not surprising, therefore, when the time came that Mr. Crowell was eagerly ready to take over a Wyoming cattle range. For one thing, he had loved Wyoming ever since the time, years ago as a lad, broken in health, he changed cars there. "He seemed to feel so much better right away; something about the West."

Then there was another circumstance:

"I loaned some money to a Denver friend who wanted to go into the cattle business. He secured a big ranch near Cheyenne and started to develop a herd . . . but he was not successful. . . . Then, I had to take over the herd and the property in compensation for the money loaned."

"Wasn't that a hard turn, Mr. Crowell?"

A whimsical light came into his eyes: "Well, I was sorry for my friend . . . tried to save him . . . but he wanted out . . . *and I always wanted a cattle ranch!* I always thought I would like to see if I could improve the breed."

\* \* \*

Now what do you think of that! This city dweller, boy and man, always wanted a cattle ranch. "But, Mr. Crowell, didn't you remember Gudgell and Simpson, the Moselles, and Hazlett?"

"Yes, I remembered. But I didn't expect to make money. I was just interested."

"All right, Mr. Crowell, it's your money."

\* \* \*

The ranch which he took over, and subsequently enlarged, should satisfy anybody with city-lot phobia. It was fifty-five thousand acres of semi-arid country, a mile high, just east of Cheyenne! Fifty-five thousand acres gently waving toward the horizon like a ground-cloth which you are spreading on the lawn! An empire, untroubled by trees, save where gnarled old willows betray the course of Crow Creek, which in its cross-ranch meanderings require fourteen lineal miles! . . . Scattered over this domain, uncrowded and serene, are the buildings and the stock . . . great barns, corrals . . . a charming home under the willows for the manager . . . pretty little buildings for week-end guests . . . a breeding herd of one thousand giants, fifty breeding bulls, "something never known to exist before"; big bovine beauties along the creek . . . another fifteen hundred animals as family members . . . and for good measure still another twenty-five hundred "ordinary" cattle . . . all spaced out in contented herds on the gentle billows of your ground square.

* * *

Well, Mr. Crowell, you did get yourself a cattle ranch! And we are bound to admit after seeing animals like your Prince Pharaoh, and his bundly little sons and daughters, there is no need of trick photography to prove how good *your* Herefords are!

# XXVIII

## HE HIRES A MANAGER

Herein you see him take on a green hand to manage
the ranch; the new manager takes off his college cordu-
roys, puts on a six-quart hat, and makes it a super-ranch.

"The problem was to find a leader who would gather efficient men to head the departments of the W. H. R., men who would be loyal and devoted to those in authority over them. To bring the Hereford industry toward higher standards and more perfect developments, a human organization had to be created. The key man for the organization was the manager. He had to be efficient, he had to love men, he had to command the loyalty and devotion of those under his authority. He had to be a man of faith." (*Notes, H. P. C.*)

# HE HIRES A MANAGER

THE report that Mr. Crowell, city-man, had taken over the Wyoming Hereford Ranch was received by cattlemen as "just another of those things." Some wrote him letters of friendly caution. Even the boys at the Ranch, to tell the truth, had their tongues in their cheeks. But when the new owner went into action —Tom Smith of Chicago is still laughing about it:

> "Hereford raisers, you know, have A, B, C and D grade animals. Mr. Crowell said at once, 'Get rid of C and D.' The hands were startled, 'What's that, Mr. Crowell?' 'Get rid of C and D.' It sounded like disaster. 'But, Mr. Crowell, no one has ever done it; look at that big ranch, the Bar—' *'Let's get rid of C and D.'* [Quiet tones: the Autocrat has gone into action.] They got rid of C and D and put their fingers in their ears so as to shut out the crash."

The next thing he did was no help for restoring confidence. He hired a foreman who had no experience behind him! Mr. Crowell's line of reasoning for this revolutionary selection is to be found in his 1940 speech before the Saddle and Sirloin Club in their Chicago quarters at the Stock Yards. The occasion was the hanging of an oil painting of Mr. Crowell, executed by Joseph Allworthy. This honor was bestowed on Mr. Crowell, "because of his contribution toward agriculture in the development of the Hereford industry." The portrait was unveiled at an honor banquet. It was a colorful occasion. The quiet Mr. Crowell, standing below his own likeness, "stormed the cattlemen with a speech so mild you wonder how he did it." Mr. Crowell's draft of that speech in his own hand, lies before me in Cedar-Palms. We will let him tell you just why he hired a green hand as manager.

I am sure it is not necessary for me to explain why I became interested in cattle, or how I became owner of the

Wyoming Hereford Ranch. Gladly do I admit that I am interested, and willingly to confess that I am thrilled and fascinated with the problems I have been forced to face during the eighteen years of my experience in the great Hereford industry. [We have it on fair authority that the smokers looked up intrigued and applauded this opening sentence.]

Our mutual friend, John Clay, gave me some good advice in those early days. He sympathetically warned me that there was no money in the raising of cattle for breeding purposes.

He was a wise man. [Laughter.]

If he were living today, I would thank him for his counsel, and—go into the cattle business. [More laughter.]

When the original herd was transferred to me, it brought with it no human organization of value. In fact, but one man came who knew cattle . . . we were truly fortunate in having Mr. Rossman with us until old age caused him to retire. The problem was to find a leader. . . . Should he be young, middle-aged, or old? Should he be thoroughly imbued with the industry? Or, young, inexperienced and capable, an independent thinker, courageous . . . ready to find new ways?

We decided in favor of the young man. We believed more could be accomplished than through someone set in his ways of thinking, and fixed in his judgments. It was not long before the young man we needed appeared in the person of Robert Wells Lazear, a graduate of the University of Michigan, trained as an engineer, strong, active, virile, a lover of nature, and—an intelligent Christian.

For many years we have worked in perfect harmony; the forecast of him has proved true. The inexperience of youth has changed into the ripe and rich experience of middle age. His knowledge of cattle has steadily broadened and increased . . . his judgment of an animal either young or old is not surpassed by any and equalled by few. Gradually, there has been gathered about "Bob" (as we call him) a group of talented men capable of managing the difficult departments of the enterprise . . . men who have caught his spirit, entered his ideals, becoming motivated by his vision of lifting the herd to surpassing excellence. . . .

\*      \*      \*

As a matter of fact, two Lazear brothers, Robert Wells Lazear and Edward Tuthill Lazear, sons of George Cornelius Lazear of Chicago, arrived to manage the W.H.R. when Mr. Crowell took

Unfinished Torrey-Gray Auditorium where the Memorial Services
were held, October 26, 1944.

Torrey-Gray Auditorium as it will appear when completed

Monument on the Crowell plot, Lakeview Cemetery, Cleveland. Here, October 28, 1944, Mr. Crowell's body was buried beside his loved ones.

it over. But Edward, with a heart set on the hustings, left the ranch, and by dint of grim application rose in the legal profession. He lives in Cheyenne today, partner in the firm, Loomis and Lazear, attorneys for the State of Wyoming for the Union Pacific Railroad, and "a likely man in Wyoming's future." He continues to handle the legal end of the ranch affairs.

Mr. Crowell's address reflects the man and his methods, all the way from Quaker Oats to Moody Bible Institute. Mrs. X— of Boston wrote: "My beloved husband was with Mr. Crowell for years beginning in Ravenna. Mr. Crowell was slow in giving his confidence, but when he did, he went the limit." The human organization was everything to him. He wanted men untrammeled by the past; men whose slogan was, "What's new?" Moreover, so far as he could arrange, the men were to be intelligent Christians —"Man for man, a Christian will always go further."

* * *

Very well, we will now present Bob Lazear! We wish space permitted a proper introduction of the first lady of the W.H.R. Bob manages the ranch, and Mrs. Lazear manages! . . . We wish space permitted us to present also the family that has come into their home under the willows; two boys who stay by the ranch, and a third who is a foreign missionary.

As to Bob, if his biography were ever in order, it could be titled, "Don't Fence Me In! The story of an Ann Arbor Insurgent." He dresses the part. Skin-tight pants of sun-cloth, and a sufficient stock of them to have a fresh-pressed pair day by day. There is just a hint of high-heels on his polished yellows; a brave shirt, barred like a Dominecker rooster. A hat, five-quart variety, studiously old, so as to offset any wrong impressions the rest of his get-up may create. The hat says, "Don't get me wrong; I'm no dude." His eyes are sharp-focussed, and the only way you can tell he is a bit sore is that he smiles sweeter. If you know men, you will be chary about riling him. He has a marked evangelical fire; a sort of Puritan in high-heels. You sense it when he talks about Robert, Junior, and Robert's wife Eleanor, who are flaming evangels of the Cross in Colombia, South America. Bob is quite a bit of all right, Hollywood coat and all. At least Mr. Crowell thought so:

"He manages herd, ranch, and business on a Christian basis. Ranchers take his word. They send orders for animals with sight drafts attached."

\* \* \*

Bob Lazear should some day confide to the world his treasury of W.H.R. stories. The years have provided a store of westerns just as good as you will find anywhere. There was, for instance, the fellow of questionable standing (circumlocution for "rustler") living down in Weld County, who

"actually came up into our pastures and stole some of our best two-year old heifers. It took months to run down this case. We finally came across a country school teacher who reported:

" 'I was driving home one weekend past an abandoned group of farm buildings . . . some men were cropping the ears of the cows and dehorning them. When I came up, the men jumped on their horses and rode away, so that all I saw was a few cattle with bleeding heads, and some horns piled at the end of the chute.'

"We patched the story together . . . tied the guilt on the right man . . . we prosecuted the case with Ed doing a grand job of prosecution. Our cattle were not branded but tattooed in the ears. The culprit thought that by ear-cropping and 'under-bidding' he would be able to eliminate the marks. Ed based the case on one animal where the tattooing was set a little too high . . . the man was duly 'put away.' Mr. Crowell was concerned about the man's family . . . but we think they got along better without him than they did beforehand."

\* \* \*

Just one more, please! That story of a Wyoming spring blizzard—

"Our winter months are usually enjoyable enough."

[That's right, Bob, stand up for Wyoming!]

"Well, they are admittedly not as pleasant as *Sunny* California. . . .

"But when those spring blizzards hit us, we do get into it. This one came along about May 8. Our cattle drifted with the storm. The cattle milled around when they got to a fence, until the snow built up under them so they could jump over and go on to the next. We gathered cattle for days following the storm, picking them up as far as twenty miles away.

But on the final check-up we found twelve or fifteen cows had lost their calves in the storm.

"We never did find the lost calves. Several years later, I was way over in western Colorado, three hundred and fifty miles from where the calves were lost. I crawled up into the portal of a little one-man coal mine, and walked down the sloping shaft. There in the privacy and secrecy of the black walls, the operator asked me,

" 'Did you lose some calves in the storm a few years back?'

"I immediately pricked up my ears! The operator told me how 'a dry farmer' had seen the cattle drifting by when the storm was abating on the second day of the blizzard. He caught the calves, used some old milk cows as foster mothers, and sold them for veal. But it didn't do him any good. The N. R. A. had to help him out of the country."

\* \* \*

The manager's affection for Mr. Crowell is in good keeping with Mr. Crowell's affection for the manager. Bob delights to tell you the account of the honoring of Mr. Crowell by the Saddle and Sirloin Club. "When the portrait was hung (he loves to recall) there was a large delegation of Quaker officials."

Mr. Crowell was accustomed to making an annual visit to the ranch—except in 1942.

"How did that happen, Mr. Crowell?" "Well, George Lazear was very ill, and I did not want to go without him."

\* \* \*

Bob Lazear's letters make somewhat of a log of Mr. Crowell's annual visits:

August 9, 1943

"Father and Mr. Crowell arrived here last Saturday on their annual visit."

September 2, 1944

"Yes, indeed, Mr. Crowell spent his usual two weeks here at the ranch in August. His daughter, Mrs. Herrick of Cleveland, as well as Mrs. Herrick's daughter, Anne Frances, were here. . . . Father and Mother were also here, so we had a good, old, rousing reunion. . . ."

You can say that again, Mr. Manager! During the 1944 visit, Mr. Crowell in his eighty-ninth year, was ubiquitous. Accompanied by Bob, he walked along the brook, under the willows; drove out to see the great animals grazing on the ranges; visited barns, buildings and corrals.

"How did you enjoy your 1944 visit, Mr. Crowell?"

"Well, it was very impressive to see what the boys are doing."

It was also very impressive when the totals of the October sale appeared on the comptometers—$200,000! John Clay back in 1912 never figured that way when he advised, "There is no money in raising cattle for breeding purposes." Mr. Clay would have been equally astonished could he have known that W.H.R. proceeds would be credited to the Number One Trust, of which more will be said.

# XXIX

## AND FORMS A TRUST

Herein you will find how human foresight may go far
in assuring the unbroken development of economic gains;
and how the works of man may be helped in following
him.

There are instincts in nature so selfless that upon beholding them one feels—"This is holy ground." The partridge, for instance, fluttering as if wounded, exposing herself to gun fire, if only she may divert attention from her little brood of chicks. The same selfless attitudes appear in the hearts of men. Some, feeling death may not be far away, have secretly placed special love gifts in a deposit box for *her* to find when he is gone. This is the forethought of those about to die! One may observe it particularly in the provisions of conscientious men for securing the fruit of their labors to the next generation. (*Sketch Book*)

# AND FORMS A TRUST

DURING the passing years, Mr. Crowell noted with satisfaction how the W.H.R. developed and matured. But, he noted also that "problems became more serious with each advancing step" (H. P. C. notes). That, naturally, was to be expected; progress on higher levels always required a ten times bigger heave than the same gain on lower. To illustrate: Mr. Crowell and his associates, Bob Lazear, and the other co-workers, observed as they advanced in cattle breeding "the problems became not only serious, but mysterious." It suddenly dawned upon them that another permanent addition should be made to the staff; a resident physician, so to speak; "a man experienced as a veterinarian and possessed of a wide knowledge of genetics. Their acquaintance with men of this field led them to approach Dr. Harry E. Kingman."

The matter was proposed to Dr. Kingman, and they found he, too, had been dreaming of the development, somewhere, some day, of a superior herd. He was therefore delighted to become one of the W.H.R. staff. He at once applied himself to the pioneer task of building up a medical technique and an equipment for cattle breeding. The results in a few years have come to surprising proportions, amazing indeed to visitors who see the same skills devoted to cattle as to human beings. There is, for instance, one goodly building which the hands humorously call "The Maternity Ward"; and a medical building so complete that they have dubbed it the "City Drug Store."

The human organization continued to build up. Ernest Green and Tony Holmes were put in charge of the breeding herd. Art Killian made it his business to have the animals properly groomed as show cattle. Art Harrod became transportation manager, so that the animals travelled in carlot comforts. Dave Stevens was made foreman. These, with a good-sized colony of workers and their families now constitute the Wyoming Hereford Ranch village.

\* \* \*

Of course, to quote H. P. C.'s notes, "The herd was always the magnetic center of the ranch, and the reason it existed . . . the thought of every one employed turns to it; its welfare is the vital interest of each and all." The standard practice was adopted of holding the herd at twenty-five hundred animals, and the breeding part of the herd at one thousand.

> "Every animal was registered, and its case history meticulously recorded. They were kept in the best of health, strong, clean, free from T. B. and Bang's disease, which so often brings disaster . . . if new animals were purchased, they were kept by themselves and tested before being allowed the freedom of the ranch. . . . And furthermore, every animal was a pet! No yelling at them! No swearing! The W. H. R. knew 'it is the eye of the owner that makes an animal fat.' "

\* \* \*

You would *expect* years of such practice to bring results. Mr. Crowell's notes have an exultation a little unusual for him:

> "We like our breeding herd, and are filled with rejoicing over the changes that have taken place. Eighteen years of thoughtful, careful, patient, exacting labor to change the cow herd from what it was when we started to what it is today. It has been slow, but by degrees the irregularities have disappeared and the desired uniformities appear in evidence."

\* \* \*

Just how good *did* the W.H.R. herds become?

Well, W.H.R. bulls have been the champion carloads at Denver fifteen times in the past nineteen years. A big sheaf of letters are on file here in Cedar-Palms written by owners and managers of some of the greatest cattle ranches in North America and the world—surprising letters, voluntary letters from such outfits as the Crapo Farms of Swartz Creek, Michigan . . . George Pollock of Sacramento . . . Chester Crozer of Cincinnati . . . Oliver Wallop of Big Horn, Wyoming . . . and E. L. Scott of Phoenix, Arizona.

Praises also from the ends of the world! There is (unless the Japs
came across it), a herd in the center of China, selected by the
Chinese Government as "the best we could find." From Southern
Rhodesia Mr. Black of the M'Gutu Farms writes that "W.H.R.
animals seem to be at the head of a majority of Rhodesian herds."

\* \* \*

Eighteen years! Fine progress! It is now 1930 and yet, the work
is far from finished. Mr. Crowell's notes make mention of the
ultimate goals:

> "Still further changes are to be made. We know that we can
> improve the breeding herd still further for we are doing it
> year by year. . . . Younger men in 1948 inspecting the cows
> on the W.H.R. will be as surprised at what they see then,
> as we are today over the changes we have seen in the past
> eighteen years. There *may* be a limit beyond which we cannot
> go, but we have not discovered it yet!"

\* \* \*

Well, Mr. Crowell, eighteen years is a long time! You are now
seventy-five; in eighteen years you will be ninety-three! Had you
ever thought, Mr Crowell—?

He had not thought much; at least, not too much. He was never
one to make folks about him uncomfortable, as many older people
do, by pathetic references to "my short time on earth." So far as
one could tell, his eyes were always set to the future right up to his
ninetieth year. His interests were in making history, not reviewing it. . . . And yet, if you were near him, watched him closely,
you could see the forethought of those about to die beginning to
appear. It first came to view in the provisions of his magnificent
arrangement, the Number One Trust, which was formed in 1928.
And thoughts of the end, though closely concealed from the eyes
of men, were occasionally entertained. For instance:

On a certain chill November day in 1943, we had lunched in
the Union League Club, and stood on the draughty corner beside
the Board of Trade Building. It wasn't good for him to stay there
long, so I said,

"Goodbye, Mr. Crowell."

He didn't go. It was embarrassing. I said again, shaking his
hand,

"Goodbye, Mr. Crowell, and I'll see you at Green Court next April."

He held my hand just a moment longer than conventional.

"But Brother Day, April is a long time."

I turned aside quickly to hide my face! Was he thinking . . . ? I wished he had never said it! On the train to New York, and down to Florida, I kept swallowing that dreadful lump; over and over hearing him say, "April is a long time!"

* * *

You can see how the forethought of those about to die increased in Mr. Crowell's mind until it resulted in action. . . . He suddenly appeared at the W.H.R. one day in September, 1938. . . . Bob, somewhat puzzled, drove him over the ranges; they stopped at a fair vantage point to view the land. The men talked quietly for a time; talked of the work that had been done, and the achievements yet to be made. Bob having for some time entertained the sobering thought that his own life was beyond mid-station, and the herd was far from perfection; and, being moved by Mr. Crowell's mental disquietude, suddenly made a surprising statement. Surprising in that while Bob was not an old man, what he said was not a young man's reaction. He sensed that the ultimate perfection of the herd was not for him, Bob Lazear; time was too short. And it grieved him to think that the plans for Hereford perfection might be broken off if he should die.

> "Mr. Crowell, my reward in life is not going to be in the form of money or wealth or fame, but I would like to leave behind me a name that is untarnished, that might be an inspiration to others, and an accomplishment in my field of endeavor that would result in benefit and blessing to everyone interested in the Hereford industry. But at my age, I cannot expect to see all of the plans that we have formed and the hopes and ambitions satisfied."

* * *

They drove back to the house under the willows. Bob never dreamed how deeply his words had touched his chief. On the Streamliner, City of Denver, as it flashed toward Chicago, Mr. Crowell thought continuously:

"Bob is now a middle-aged man! How rapidly the years have passed since he began as the young ranch manager! What a joy he has been! I've found in him a man who is more of a royalist than the king! He is more interested in my purposes than I am."

On that train journey and in days following as Mr. Crowell kept thinking about the matter, he saw:

"There were obstacles, many. But the most serious one seemed to be *time*. Given time, Bob would be practically assured, and when assured, in his unselfish way, he would pass both benefit and blessing on to the Hereford industry . . . *In so doing his ambition as well as mine would be satisfied.*

"The solution began to appear. There were two things I could do. One was to take advantage of certain concessions offered by the National Government to organizations with notable public service goals. By these provisions, such organizations were permitted to form a twenty-five-year trust, under unusally favorable conditions so as to perfect their ideals. Ten years ago I had settled the problems incident to my personal fortune by forming the Number One Trust. Now I should do as much as I could, as much as the Government would allow in case of impersonal entities, and make the W. H. R. over into a twenty-five-year trust. The decision was reached and approved by Mr. McKinzie, our lawyer, and the Ranch was transferred to a trust, so formed that the U. S. Government approved it. Now Bob would at least be favored with twenty-five years of additional security to perfect the herd.

"But in less than twenty-five years, Bob might die! In that case, the trust arrangement would come to nothing. There was one other thing I should do for Bob. For Bob? *Yes, for Bob!* For it was a matter more highly cherished by Bob that the herd be perfected whether he lived or died, than it was to me as the owner. I knew what I could do; I would take care of the second thing at the Saddle and Sirloin Club Banquet." (From H. P. C. notes in lead pencil.)

\*   \*   \*

He stood beneath the oil painting [1] of himself as he brought his address to a close. Now was the time to take care of the second thing! He dramatically turned to R. J. Kinzer:

[1] This painting referred to is "now in the Portrait Gallery of the Saddle and Sirloin Club on the top floor of the Live Stock Record Building, Chicago Stock Yards." Letter, William E. Ogilvie, Secretary Saddle and Sirloin Club.

"If Bob should die before the trust terminates, I will expect you, Mr. Kinzer, or someone else of the American Hereford Association, to lead a movement to conserve the herd and the W.H.R. for the general benefit of the industry to which Bob has devoted his life. All of us today are striving for a superior race of Hereford cattle. I dare make this request not only for ourselves but for the industry, and for the nation."

\* \* \*

Mrs. Jack London once remarked, "You have a lot of fun writing your books, don't you?"

"Yes, Mrs. London, but I have even more fun scouting for the material."

And no scouting for the Cedar-Palms books has been more delightful than the Cheyenne Journeys incident to the writing of *Breakfast Table Autocrat*. There at Wyoming Hereford Ranch, we found a goodly company of new compadres, men and women of the friendly West. Especially Bob!

\* \* \*

Frequently we dream of those fifty-five thousand acres gently undulating over the treeless sweeps towards the Wyoming horizon; dream of Crow Creek meandering, willow-bordered, across the scene; dream of the hundreds of Hereford beauties peacefully grazing up to the sky line. It all seems an appropriate background for H. P. C. Ah, but he was as much at home on the great open spaces as he was in the towering white canons of city streets! You feel like suggesting to Mr. Allworthy,

"You could well have made the cumulous clouds in Wyoming skies the background for your oil painting of Mr. Crowell; and for the foreground, diminutive-like, you could have sketched in the cattle on a thousand hills."

And when one thus dreams of H. P. C., projected as it were upon the western glories, Mr. Crowell seems to speak to the men of America:

"Take your time! Take your time! Find the will of God! For the precious things brought forth by the sun, and the chief things of the ancient mountains; the precious things of the earth and the fulness thereof are secured unto the nation by men who are—*Intelligent Christians!*"

# XXX

## THE LEAVEN OF THE SADDUCEES

He locates the real fifth column in the Church and decides not to leave his beneficence in fee-simple-perpetuo; he inquires about a trust so fashioned that thieves cannot break in and steal.

There are some ferments, esteemed *"so good for you,"* that they are linked to a detective serial and their virtues are plugged in a radio program. But there are other ferments—not so good: "Beware of the leaven of the Pharisees, and of the leaven of the Sadducees." The former is identified as "Hypocrisy," and the latter as repudiation of the authority of the Scriptures. The leaven of the Pharisees is not particularly deadly, just annoying; a sort of spiritual tinea tonsurans.

But the latter! Ah, it is more perilous to the faith once delivered than boll weevil to a cotton crop. Its presence means—*war*. When and in whomsoever it appears, complacency ceases to be a virtue in Zion. The Dominie was not narrow; he was simply battle-wise when he wrote, "You'll have to excuse me as a speaker on your program. These men on your program do not preach the gospel we are standing for at Moody Bible Institute."

The Leaven of the Sadducees does a thorough job with Faith. It not only takes her life, but runs away with her assets. This generation needs a reprint of Ernest Gordon's *The Leaven of the Sadducees.* It is not pleasant to read how Faith lies poisoned and dead; less pleasant still when Gordon describes how the vandals make off with Faith's assets; her endowments, her treasury, her church edifices and her colleges. But he did not design his book as a document on sweetness and light. It is a battle cry. (*Sketch Book*)

# THE LEAVEN OF THE SADDUCEES

THE memorabilia of Mr. Crowell's life discloses that his faith began and continued to the end without modification. A reporter might well have written, "Here is a man almost ninety years old who affirms the same religious views he held as a lad. Evidently progress in modern thinking means nothing to him." If such comment were written in sarcasm, Mr. Crowell esteemed it praise; he had no desire to change. He was not unfamiliar with so-called "progress in modern thinking." His documents prove he followed the liberal trends as critically as a professor—as you shall presently see. But he selected to stand fast.

You will also note how his reactions toward Modernism shifted from hurt-surprise upon first meeting "Christians" of unbelief, through an extended period of conciliatory pleading, then earnest protest. Finally, an utter break with the whole dismal business.

The contemporary church is now in the third chapter—Earnest Protest. . . . This is called "fighting it out on the inside." It is the era in which the Occupied Journals are approved, though with misgivings; and the Progressive Leader is still permitted the pulpit, though you feel worse than silly about it afterward. Mr. Crowell's life is a sort of Twentieth Century Pilgrim's Progress, in which you see how he began by taking everyone for granted and ended with a courteous disclaimer of fellowship with Modernism no matter how discreetly it labelled itself.

As Mr. Crowell was filing his case history—casually as it were, no comment—I began to suspect that either he had an inscrutability which made Mona Lisa a child; or that the dear brother was just—*naive*. The latter most likely; for one does not expect *a layman* to detect the nuances of unbelief—many dominies cannot.

Then, I began to suspect he was "taking his time" with me;

working me over just as he did American cereal boards. On a number of occasions he handed me dockets with the remark, "Here are a few papers that may be of help to you." The documents had two types of material in them: one, praise in abundance; the other, specimens of the subtleties of unbelief. At first, I reasoned, he wants me to find the praise. But that did not square with the estimates I had to form of him. Then, I reasoned, he wants me to see how the leaven works. So, I thought, I'll try out some of this oatmeal-board technique myself—on Mr. Crowell.

He handed me a letter, a very apprehensive letter, written by a member high in the Sanhedrin. The real purpose of the letter was to "allay" Mr. Crowell; to quiet him by leading him to think that, after all, the writer was "sound." This the writer assayed to do by means of equivocation, sprinkled with fine stage grief:

> "My dear So and So: A mutual friend has written me a letter which has filled me with great sorrow. . . . It is to the effect that . . . I am not sound!
>
> "Of course, I do not know exactly what they mean by 'sound.' If they mean that I believe the Bible to be the word of God, and the supreme rule of faith and life; that I believe in Jesus Christ: that God's word became flesh and dwelt among us; that He is God manifest in the flesh; that He died for our sins according to the Scriptures; that He rose again . . . *then I am sure that I am sound!*
>
> Affectionately yours,
> Such N. Such"

\* \* \*

I thought, "Surely Mr. Crowell could not have been taken in by *that!* I'll find out." I mentioned the letter. For awhile, Mr. Crowell said nothing, just smiled. ("You're on your own, young fellow.") At last he said,

"What do you think of it?"

I let go:

"Mr. Crowell, if I were looking for a top example of verbal thimble-rigging, *this is it!* Why doesn't the man say, 'I believe this,' and 'I believe that,' instead of running the pea under the shells? As a matter of fact, his utterances at other times prove that he does not believe a single one of the things for which he so earnestly portrays himself as standing condemned."

Mr. Crowell smiled, ended with a quiet chuckle, "Well! I'm glad you noticed it."

\* \* \*

Another incident in proof of his keen discernment: He handed me a memo filed with him after his break with the Presbyterian Church, pleading in effect, "Come back now into the church. You have made your protest and satisfied your conscience."

"What do you think of it?" he asked.

"Have you made up *your* mind?" I parried.

"Well, yes."

"Very well. Remember I am your biographer, not your counsellor. But since you have decided—that memo sounds to me just as if Tetzel were saying to Luther, 'Now you've done it! And you ought to feel better. Putty up the nail holes, go home, and be a good boy.'"

He chuckled, "Well, I'm glad you noticed it."

And I said, "Mr. Crowell, you make the writing of your biography a delightful exercise."

\* \* \*

No purpose is served by too much detail upon the reaction of Mr. Crowell's Bible faith to Modernism. But we venture a brief review of his case history. As a boy, he joined the Second Presbyterian Church by way of "the old fashioned Bible faith that filled the Presbytery of Cleveland in Finney's day." That was all he knew. He vaguely felt uneasy when he began to hear things that sounded "off." But the men who made him feel uneasy were called "Christians"; so he kept still.

When he united with the Fourth Church of Chicago his misgivings increased. He did not know that the mixed currents which troubled him were set up in the Unitarian pastorate of David Swing. It was something he could only sense, not define. So he kept still. . . . He felt very badly when the minister from Colorado ruled personal work in the Main Auditorium had to stop. But he kept reasonably still. Then came the Bible classes in his

own home, his adequate experience of Jesus, and the sudden dis-
covery that the disquietude he felt during church services was
caused by an unsound man in the pulpit. Therefore, for nine
years, he and Susan quietly dropped out.

> "We were not pleased with the character of the instruction
> we received in the Fourth Church, and we were delighted
> with the way Newell taught the Bible. We really began to un-
> derstand and know the Bible. A little later we began to go to
> Moody Church, without removing our membership. A. C.
> Dixon was then pastor. We did not return to the Fourth
> Church until John Timothy Stone became pastor." (*Green
> Court Interviews*)

In those days, Dr. Stone filled his heart with joy. "The Pastor's
continuous challenge was to bring men to Jesus." Mr. Crowell
never once said a word about some things in the pastor's subsequent history, but his files carried the story.[1]

Mr. Crowell began to take a prominent part in the wider circles
of Presbyterianism. "He was a Presbyterian by ancestry and
choice." But he could not help seeing that the Presbyterian Church
was moving in a dangerous direction. . . . He protested, kindly
and earnestly, continuously. It never entered his head in those
years that he would some day be obliged to sever relationships—
"he was fighting on the inside." Though a man may be quite a
nuisance who "fights on the inside," yet from an hierarchic administration of church economy, that is just the place to keep a
troublesome giver, "fighting on the inside."

He began to notice not only in the Presbyterian Church, but
in all evangelical churches, a sharp practice he would never have
tolerated in Quaker Oats. Monies and institutions provided by
devoted people for promoting sound doctrine were being pirated
by men who did not believe a thing the donors believed, and who
excused their acts on the ground that "faith is progressive, changing."

[1] One filing was the public approval of his former pastor for *The Autobiography of
Dr. Shailer Matthews*: "A great religious leader; no one will read this volume without
spiritual uplift." Adjacent to this comment was a Crowell memo: "Dr. Matthews was
not only a modernist, but a radical modernist, the head of a divinity school where hundreds have lost their faith, and where today not one teacher believes in the Virgin Birth,
the Vicarious Atonement, or the Resurrection of the Lord Jesus Christ."

"Mr. Crowell, you know the only evident difference between these gentlemen and Jessie James is that Jessie rode a horse."

"I'm glad you noticed it."

\* \* \*

He knew exactly how these gentlemen "took over the colleges." The thin edge was driven in by the practice of hiring a teacher (or a pastor) on the ground that he was a great scholar, without any care being exercised to find if he were a great believer. For his part, he could not see how any thoughtful person would give two straws to sign a man up merely because that man "was a brilliant student." The results were uniformly disastrous.

> "Louis Aggasiz strolls through the (Harvard) college yard smoking his cigar in sublime disregard for law and order. President Walker sometimes wondered how such men, Aggasiz, Gray, and Pierce, had drifted into professorships in a college that was designed to turn out ministers of the gospel. None of these men could be called *atheists*. Yet, everything they said and the way they said it, was upsetting to boys reared in good orthodox surroundings . . . curiously the old morality was disappearing with the old religion." [1]

Christians even become so blunted as to be calm when a Unitarian is appointed a professor of theology. What unsophisticates believers are! The day when a college takes a Unitarian would be followed by the day when the Unitarian takes a Unitarian; and at last the Unitarians would take the college! For unbelief is predatory, red in tooth and claw. If anyone should protest against the Unitarian on the faculty, and should propose to "drop him," Modernism will sound all its big bronze alarms.

"Academic Liberty! Academic Liberty! Roger!" (As in Williams.)

\* \* \*

Mr. Crowell knew, too, old age had to be watched. Old age could become a softening down period. Softening down wasn't bad if it affected the heart; but the head! He had heard Softened

[1] *Yankee From Olympus,* Catherine Drinkwater Bowen. Little, Brown and Company, Boston.

Septuagenarians piously say: "We have lived long enough to find people are *not always* villains! Often they are just mistaken." Then he watched them walk off "arm in arm with the devil."

He was greatly amused—and concerned—over the way the fetish of evolution had become established in so-called Christian colleges. Evolution, Mr. Crowell thought, should wear cap and bells! It was really funny. How could anyone take it seriously! Aggasiz drew a portrait of an undiscovered fish from a single scale! And Barnabus, the evolutionist, proposed to construct a complete Molleyosaurus with nothing more to go on than a fossil fish bone which he deducted had been stuck in the gullet of the great pre-historic monster!

Mr. Crowell finally realized that all attacks on faith were essentially the same; *the discrediting of the Bible as the inerrant and perfect revelation of Truth and the Will of God.* That was the Leaven of the Sadducees, whether it was the innuendoes of a maturing mind, or the broadside blasts of an endowed professor.

The integrity of the Bible, he felt, was the issue to be maintained no matter where it led! You can see in his own life just where it led him!

He began his Christian life by holding the Bible as true and authentic history.

Then, he began to feel that this belief was a necessary qualification for every gospel worker.

Then he realized the case could be lost if it were not implemented at this point. No general worker should be kept on church pay rolls who did not accept the Bible as true and authentic history. Moreover, no one should be tolerated in *high authority* who did not accept the Bible as true and authentic history.

To his amazement, he saw that even with these precautions, Faith was still losing the battle!

He realized that not only must Faith be careful to select workers and leaders who are Bible believers; but *these workers and leaders themselves must be intolerant of unbelievers in office!* If they were tolerant it could bring defeat just as effectively as if they themselves were infidels. Therefore,

*FAITH MUST NOT SUPPORT MEN IN AUTHOR-
ITY WHO, THOUGH THEY ARE THEMSELVES
BIBLE BELIEVERS, ARE TOLERANT OF OTHERS
IN POSITIONS OF TRUST AND AUTHORITY
WHO DO NOT SO BELIEVE.*

\* \* \*

This was the identical conclusion which he found in a letter
from Wilbur M. Smith.

> "Dear Mr. Crowell: I was asked if I would participate in a
> program of a series of services . . . upon inquiry I found there
> would be on that series men whose names are definitely classi-
> fied with the modernists . . . men who could not be invited
> to outstandingly conservative pulpits. . . . This made it im-
> possible for me to accept. . . .
>
> You as President of the Board of the Institution I serve
> would wish a copy of my reply. . . . I cannot afford to be
> publicly associated on any platform with men of this sort. . . .
> These men do not believe the things we believe. They do not
> preach the gospel we are standing for here at Moody Bible In-
> stitute . . . they are not holding up Jesus Christ as the only
> Saviour from sin, and the only begotten Son of God. *I know
> the pastor of the church where these meetings are to be held is
> a true believer . . . but the presence of men who are liberals
> makes it impossible for me to accept the invitation.*"

\* \* \*

Mr. Crowell saw that the battle against the Leaven of the Sadducees was being lost in Christendom today by reason of—

*Tolerance toward believers who were tolerant toward unbe-
lievers.*

And this meant—all-out war!

\* \* \*

Well, he did not want war to that extent—at least, not yet.
Perhaps it might be avoided. Although the church was in a sorry
mess, it might still be adjusted *from the inside.*

But he could do something immediately. He could better protect his own fortune from the thefts of the Sadducees after his
death. It gave him a stifled feeling to contemplate his estate being
"captured," *and used against the gospel!*

As a man of world-affairs, he saw how this sort of thing was happening every day. Courts had a queer way of ruling that Christian properties always belonged to "the church that remained," and "go-outers" could take nothing with them. Therefore, if a church or a denomination became apostate, so bad that believers had to get out, they always went out penniless.

Evidently, then, the thing to do was not to leave a great sum in permanent tenure, neither to a church, nor to a school, nor to a denomination. Some way must be figured out so that, after his death, his fortune could be kept intact, and the interest parcelled out from time to time to gratuitants *on the basis of sustained loyalty to the Bible as true and authentic history.*

That sounded like a trust. He would confer with his attorney, Mr. Loesch.

# XXXI

## BENEFICENCE AD VITAM AUT CULPAM

That is to say, there's a string to it; and bad children suddenly find the gratuity has folded its tents like the Arabs, and has silently stolen away.

Long time has produced certain convictions; clear-cut convictions. One is, that the chief asset of Christian institutions is a faith-vitality sufficient to refinance, if need be, in every generation. The other is, that permanently to underwrite Christian institutions without wholesome restraints is to invite the depredations of infiltrators. The best way to handle the matter is satisfaction on annual inquiry. That is to say, beneficence, particularly in large brackets, should be *ad vitam aut culpam.* (*Sketch Book*)

# BENEFICENCE AD VITAM
## AUT CULPAM

MR. CROWELL, therefore, in the year 1929, conferred with his counsel; he wished to take care of his personal estate in good time, before the sun and the moon and the stars were darkened. One phase of his forethought was to provide for his loved ones, his own flesh and blood. A second was a benevolent and endowment trust to take care of people who had spent years in his service, "almost like his own folks"; also, to provide for the education of certain persons. (The Wyoming Hereford Ranch Trust had not yet been formed as we have already noted.)

"Well, Mr. Crowell, how about the rest of your wealth? The great remainder after matters of affection are cared for?"

"That's the point. I want the rest of it to go to the work of the Lord Christ Jesus. But I desire that it be protected from the wiles of evil ones, who are much interested in the loaves and fishes but not at all in the faith once delivered."

\* \* \*

He called into conference his long-time friend and legal advisor, three years his senior, Frank Joseph Loesch. Mr. Loesch had made a notable record in public service as specialist in estates and trusts; as Counsel-at-Chicago for the Pennsylvania Railroad, and as bomber-in-general against thuggery of all sorts. Mr. Loesch was, on that account, just the man to help Mr. Crowell guard his estate against ecclesiastical termites. Mr. Loesch's unusual sagacity was evidenced in his very phraseology, one specimen of which is his famous term "Public enemy."

Mr. Crowell stated his desires to Mr. Loesch:

"I would like to leave the bulk of my personal fortune in such a way as to protect it for many years to come from theft. Could a trust be fashioned so that the income thereof would be appropriated from time to time to such institutions only as are loyal to the Faith?"

His lawyer-friend laughed good naturedly: "Yes, Mr. Crowell, you want a trust to be executed so that its benefits will be *Ad Vitam Aut Culpam*."[1]

\* \* \*

Now that is something! But if one decodes the lawyer-talk, Mr. Loesch was saying in effect, *"Quamdiu se beni gesserit."* If any reader is still in the dark, the lawyer's first Latin meant "For life, without fault"; and his second, "So long as he behaves well."

We venture to predict that this procedure will become a standard device for thousands of well-to-do Christians who with a feeling of helplessness have watched mission budgets raided, church property "appropriated," colleges stolen. The highly invulnerable method of protection which Mr. Loesch worked out is the administration of a properly conditioned trust by *five secret trustees*. These trustees reaffirm by signature each year their *own* total agreement with the terms of the trust—no reservations! Trustee Boards both gratuitor and gratuitant show unhappy tendencies to become "carnal" toward the original terms of the trust, and have need to be perennially sensitized, replaced or—fired! The trustees are self-perpetuating, secretly appointing others of like mind to fill vacancies. They never make appropriations in perpetuo; and no beneficiary is ever encouraged to conclude that an appropriation made to him is permanent. If any beneficiary evidences a drift toward Modernism—then, no more appropriation.

\* \* \*

"Well, Mr. Crowell, that makes me think of a song recently on the Hit Parade."

"What's that?"

"No Letter Today!"

"I don't know anything about the song. But for such institutions as expect help from the Number One Trust, the plan is very impressive."

[1] It is of interest to note that Mr. Loesch died in July, 1944; Mr. Crowell, in October, 1944.

The Loesch plan is not one hundred per cent protection against monetary thrips. Eternal vigilance is the price of many things besides liberty. And eternal vigilance is particularly in order when it comes to the raids of Unbelief upon the Treasures of the Temple. Unbelievers slogan their piracies with plausible cries of "Academic Liberty," and the like; but their "liberty" is one with the liberty of Herr Göering's in making his art collections. No, the Loesch plan is not one hundred per cent safe, but it will do until we hear of a better one.

Mr. Loesch and his staff drew up a trust so impervious that in 1943 the Federal Government stopped to admire its crack-proof armor.[1]

\* \* \*

Mr. Crowell named the Trust "The Henry Parsons Crowell and Susan Coleman Crowell Trust," or "the Number One Trust." My readers will sympathize with the limitations under which I have worked in dealing with the intimate details of this trust. The only detail of the trust which Mr. Crowell wished to have printed is Article Two. However, you may see in Article Two those standards of Christian faith which he, a great merchant, industry-builder, Christian statesman, felt ought to be upheld for all time—"the faith *once* delivered!"

### THE HENRY PARSONS CROWELL AND SUSAN COLEMAN CROWELL TRUST
### ARTICLE II

The objects and purposes of this trust shall be to aid Evangelical Christianity by the disbursement of the net income of said trust fund among Christian and Christian-educational corporations, foreign and home missionaries, boards, churches and Evangelical Christian organizations, having for their purposes the teaching, advancement and active extension among mankind of the doctrines of Evangelical Christianity.

By Evangelical Christianity or the Evangelical Faith, the donor means what is expressed succinctly under the following five heads:

(1) God is a person who has revealed Himself as a trinity in unity, Father, Son, and Holy Spirit—three Persons and yet but one God.

---

[1] Certain agents, in a recent year canvassing income tax sources, demanded a tax sum not far from $100,000 from the Number One Trust. Their labors came to a water-haul.

(Deuteronomy 6:4; Matthew 28:19; I Corinthians 8:6)

(2) The Bible, including both the Old and the New Testaments, is a divine revelation, the original autographs of which were verbally inspired by the Holy Spirit.

(II Timothy 3:16; II Peter 1:21)

(3) Jesus Christ is the image of the invisible God, which is to say He is Himself very God; He took upon Him our nature, being conceived by the Holy Ghost and born of the Virgin Mary; He died upon the cross as a substitutionary sacrifice for the sin of the world; He arose from the dead in the body in which He was crucified; He ascended into Heaven in that body glorified, where He is now our interceding High Priest; He will come again personally and visibly, to set up his kingdom and to judge the quick and the dead.

(Colossians 1:15; Philippians 2:5-8; Matthew 1:18-25; I Peter 2:24-25; Luke 24; Hebrews 4:14-16; Acts 1:9-11; I Thessalonians 4:16-18; Matthew 25:31-46; Revelation 11:15-17; 20:4-6; 11-15)

(4) Man was created in the image of God but fell into sin and in that sense is lost; this is true of all men; except a man be born again he cannot see the kingdom of God; salvation is by faith in Christ only; the retribution of the wicked and unbelieving, and the reward of the righteous, are everlasting; and as the reward is conscious, so is the retribution.

(Genesis 1:26, 27; Romans 3:10, 23; John 3:3; Acts 13:38, 39: 4:12; John 3:16; Matthew 25:46; II Corinthians 4:1; II Thessalonians 1:7-10)

(5) The Church is an elect company of believers baptized by the Holy Spirit into one body; its mission is to witness to its Head, Jesus Christ, preaching the gospel among all nations; it will be caught up to meet the Lord in the air when He comes to set up His kingdom.

(Acts 2:41; 15:13-17; Ephesians 1:3-6; I Corinthians 12:12-13; Matthew 28:19, 20; Acts 1:6-8; I Thessalonians 4:16-18)

## XXXII

## THE INTOLERABLE YOKE

He had so often read a certain passage, "be not unequally yoked together with unbelievers" that at last it patterned his life.

"It is often said by friends of 'liberal' clergymen who wish to improve their reputation with orthodox people, that they have 'returned to the evangelical position.' This should be good news; but if the clergyman under discussion continues to live and work in a seminary where the textbooks, the books written by the other professors, and himself, the magazines, and all that is in, or left out, of the lectures to the students—are all saturated with the same theological poison which came from Germany, and destroyed the Protestant church in Germany and made Germany what it is, then the statement displays incredible ignorance or immeasurable effrontery.

"If a man had any belief in the divine origin, inspiration, or authority of the Bible he would leave a liberal seminary as quickly as if the other professors all had smallpox." (Memo from the Crowell Files. It could be titled *Wisps of Wild Fire* and handed to Boreham for a footnote.)

# THE INTOLERABLE YOKE

THE Number One Trust was consummated in 1929, and in the fourteen years that followed, Mr. Crowell continued as a member of the Presbyterian Church, "at times dismayed by its tendencies, and always ill at ease about it," but with never a thought of departure. He might have continued a Presbyterian—might have "died in the fold" but for the crisis of May, 1943.

One day in the latter part of the month, Mr. Crowell, returning from lunch at the Union League Club, bought an afternoon paper at the entrance of the Board of Trade Building. He stopped for a moment to look at a headline:

"Dr. Henry Sloane Coffin
New Presbyterian Moderator
Elected on First Vote Cast"

His eye caught a bit of detail in the article: "The nomination was made by Dr. George Arthur Buttrick of New York and seconded by Dr. Harrison Ray Anderson, pastor, Fourth Presbyterian Church of Chicago." He walked into the elevator, heart and head light with a sense of defeat and weariness. This was it! This was—War!

\* \* \*

He sat at his office desk throughout the early part of the May afternoon, looking out through open windows. Jean Val Jean's struggle with conscience over the avowal of himself was not one whit more poignant than Mr. Crowell's: What was now the proper course for him? Conscience said, "There is nothing to do but to break with the Presbyterian Church. This is the intolerable yoke." His temperament revolted against conscience; there must be sufficient extenuations so that an open break could be avoided.

279

But what *were* those extenuations? The Presbyterian Church had been in a ferment since January over visible political moves to elect Dr. Coffin as moderator. It was a plain issue. Could a modernist be elected to head up the Presbyterian Church, North? And the brutal truth stood up too solid to be dissolved; the modernists had won.

\* \* \*

During the entire month of June, the problem was never out of Mr. Crowell's consciousness. He had for years tried to fight from within; he had even challenged the "Come Outer" appeals of Dr. Charles Gallaudet Trumbull, as embodied in his tract, "Betrayal of Foreign Missions." But now he saw Trumbull was right. If Trumbull were alive, he would immediately call him long distance at Philadelphia and say, "Brother Trumbull, I was wrong."

\* \* \*

As never before, his inbred habit of careful deliberation asserted itself. In June, he ceased attending church on Sundays; he shortened his office hours so as to be alone. Extended periods at Winnetka were given to prayer. He had never before been "conscious of the years"; but now he felt very definitely an old man; a bewildered old man searching through long periods of prayer and meditation to find his way. What was the will of God for him?

Perhaps he ought to advise with friends. He quickly decided against that. He knew that many who affirmed loyalty themselves would beg the question with a plea for "denominational loyalty," or a bromide of "it will come out all right. Be patient."

Natural inclination moved him strongly. If he withdrew he would no longer be a recorded Presbyterian; he would sacrifice nearly seventy-five years of cherished associations. It meant breaking with the Fourth Church, into which he had poured the vigor of his middle age. It meant that the Number One Trust would not be available for Presbyterian enterprises. That did not really have much significance; it was God's money. But, so long as *he* had it, he was responsible as a steward to see it did not fall into the hands of unbelievers.

Natural inclination said, "You are now an old man; weather

it out." Then he looked at a letter lying before him, from another "old man." The letter was as the voice of God:

"I am surprised at Christian men who are not quite willing to go all the way; who think they have a church or a school or a Bible class which might be jeopardized if they made the full testimony expected of them. So to save their institution, or organization, they hesitate about going the whole way."

Thereupon he recalled the biographical interview: "Thousands of American business men will say, 'If God can use Mr. Crowell, I want Him to use me. I would like to know just how Mr. Crowell went about the matter.'" People were now looking at him, not as the builder of great industries, but as a steward of God. What he did in this crisis would more profoundly influence men than what he did as the builder of an industrial empire.

\* \* \*

In order to insure wisdom in his decision, he was under obligation to begin by examining afresh the evidences that Dr. Coffin "had departed." And when he did this it was apparent that Dr. Coffin, point by point, was conclusively a modernist. Before him lay a number of Dr. Coffin's printed statements. Quotations made from spoken addresses were of no value; but when a man goes into *print,* that is something else! . . . Even in his printed statements, Dr. Coffin often concealed his own views. In *Religion Yesterday and Today* he contrasted the views of different eras, but he did it so skillfully, no one could say which views he approved.

But there *were* passages wherein Dr. Coffin was explicit concerning his personal views.

As to the Virgin Birth: "My own country is in the throes of a belated theological controversy due to the persistence of an obsolete and unprotestant view of biblical inerrancy . . . it has focussed on a single point, the Virgin birth of our Lord. . . . No New Testament writer combines pre-existence and miraculous birth."

As to the Atonement: "The revolt from various theories of the atonement has been due to their un-Christian views of God. . . . A father whose wrath has to be appeased is not the Father of Jesus Christ. . . . Such a God freely forgives. . . . Certain widely-used hymns still perpetuate the theory that God pardons sinners because Christ purchased that pardon by His suffering. . . . Forgiveness that is paid for is not forgiveness. . . ."

*As to Miracles*: "Some preachers discard passages wherein the miraculous is prominent . . . they do not feel intellectually honest in employing them. Others use them, but give the impression of being ill at ease with them. Others, to the bewilderment of some of their hearers, use them as though they were handling a matter-of-fact modern history. . . . The modern preacher may not feel he knows exactly what lies behind the tradition of many of the biblical miracles. Let him use them for that purpose (that is, the modern preacher does not ask his hearers to reproduce the miraculous experience in literal form, but to urge them to apprehend a spiritual principle)."

*As to Presbyterianism*: He hoped the day would come when ministers and other office-bearers would not be required to accept the Scriptures as the supreme standard of faith and life. . . . He remained a Presbyterian, not because he believed it was better, but because for the present he could most usefully serve in it. . . . People pass readily from one communion to another. There *are* genuine differences—the differences between an infallible type who believe in an inerrant book, and, the experimental type who believe in the progressive leadership of the Spirit within.

*As to the Bible*: "Liberalism is opposed to external authority because it obstructs free response to truth. Tradition declares it [the Bible] verbally inspired and inerrant . . . verbal inspiration cannot be asserted of a collection of writings which frequently contain divergent accounts. . . . The Protestant Reformers did not regard the Bible as an external authority. . . ." Etc.!

Well, there you are! What need of further proof? *This was the Leaven of the Sadducees!* And this man was now Moderator of the Presbyterian Church, North!

\* \* \*

Thus for the entire month of June, the Winnetka Home housed a man agonizing before the Throne of Grace. His world had turned upside down. The temper of the Church today was obviously not what it was when he found Christ as a Cleveland boy. It was the exact picture of apostasy Dr. Newell had described forty-five years before in the Rush Street Bible Classes.

At last the subject cleared; the modern church had changed, but the Word and the Testimony were just the same! And would be forever!

For several days he tried to prevent this conclusion from its inevitable sequence. Sometimes he switched off the bed lamp as if to shut it out; but even in the darkness the inescapable sequence remained. He had put up a fight in the Church, and had lost. He ought now avow himself! He must avow himself! *He would avow himself!*

\* \* \*

Curiously, when that decision was reached, the peace beyond understanding flooded his heart. It was good to do the will of God, and this was the will of God! Now he felt different! He was himself again! "Take your time!" Others had talked and acted. Now he knew so far as he was concerned, there was a great gulf fixed; he was not responsible for it. Tomorrow, he would avow himself. . . . In a moment, sound, peaceful sleep was upon him.

In the morning he called in his secretary and dictated:

Dictated June 25, 1943
Mailed June 28, 1943

Dr. Harrison Ray Anderson,
Pastor of the Fourth Presbyterian Church of Chicago, Illinois
126 East Chestnut Street
Chicago, Illinois

My dear Dr. Anderson:

Some of the decisions made at the one hundred and fifty-fifth General Assembly of the Presbyterian Church of the United States held at Detroit, Michigan, in the latter part of the month of May, 1943, have been so unexpected and startling as to cause me to remain at home on Sundays that I might study the full depth and meaning of them under the direct guidance of the Holy Spirit.

The conclusion that I have finally reached is not in harmony and sympathy with the decision of the Assembly in electing Dr. Henry Sloane Coffin, the President of Union Theological Seminary of New York City, as Moderator of the Assembly. In arriving at this decision, I believe the delegates have made a serious error and one difficult to understand. The commissioners or delegates to the Assembly are picked men, chosen because of their character, ability, and fitness in meeting and understanding all of the problems that will have to be considered while the Assembly is in session. It is assumed that they know the Bible and its deep and valued truths, for most of them must have taught classes in the Sunday school and used its truths in personal work. With this preparation, and possessed of clear minds and devoted, prayerful souls, how could a majority of them cast their ballot for a man known to be an outstanding modernist for many years, as well as the President of the Union Theological Seminary of New York City ever since 1926?

Dr. Coffin was elected on the first vote cast, a very unusual happening, which means that no questions were asked and no discussions took place. To be Moderator of the General Assembly of the Presbyterian Church North is to occupy the place of highest honor within the gift of the Presbyterian denomination. Why should this honor, exalted as it is, be conferred upon a modernist, talented, intelligent, and forceful though he may be, instead of upon a conservative member of the Presbyterian denomination whose faith has never been questioned and who has never faltered in his loyalty, devotion, and obedience to our risen Lord and Saviour, Jesus Christ?

I have protested against Modernism before and have done many things that I have hoped might check it, but the present issue and its apparent popularity indicate that the trend is now stronger than ever before.

There is one further protest that I can make and as I have been led to it through prayer, communion, and fellowship with the Lord Jesus Christ, I make it known to you. I desire to sever all relationship that I may have with the Presbyterian denomination. I hereby resign from membership in the Fourth Presbyterian Church of Chicago and retire from the office of Elder in said church, which service of love I have prized for many years. I also release the occupancy of Pew 32 which I have held for myself and family ever since the opening Sunday when the first services were held in the new church building.

I have received many blessings because of my membership in the Fourth Presbyterian Church that have been rich and full as the years have passed, and my heart is filled with love for many dear ones that I have worked with in various ways so it is difficult to say "good-by."

The appeal of Modernism appears to be gaining strength as revealed by the General Assembly at its last meeting and it leaves the Presbyterian denomination standing on dangerous ground, for there is a vast difference between conservatism and Modernism in the interpretation of Scripture and in being loyal and true to the well defined standards left us by Jesus Christ, our risen Lord.

Something should be done at once to stop this drift toward Modernism and I have thought of nothing better than for me to withdraw from the church as a definite forceful protest against changing standards and the weakening of the church's loyalty and devotion to Jesus Christ. I can serve the Lord elsewhere with a clear conscience, warm heart, and responsive love that will keep me ever in close union and fellowship with my Saviour who loves me and gave Himself for my salvation and that of all who come to Him by faith.

I shall continue to remember you, Dr. Anderson, and the members of the Fourth Church in prayer.

Hopefully yours,

H. P. Crowell

HPC:MD

\* \* \*

Thereupon he wired:

"Come to Winnetka."

The stigmata of the month's anguish were upon him. For the first and only time, *he looked like an old man*. But he was calm; at peace.

"Read this, and tell me what you think."

"Have you sent it?"

"Yes."

"Well, Mr. Crowell, then I can speak. This is exactly what you had to do, or your biography would have collapsed."

"Well, if I ever found the will of God, it was in this matter."[1]

There was a long silence. Presently Mr. Crowell looked up and smiled:

"I wonder what Dr. Newell would think of this?"

[1] After Mr. Crowell made this decision, he never spoke of it to others, and his Church concealed it. He said to me, "Every man should form conclusions like these by the guidance of God, in the light of his own experience, and for himself."

For some reason he did not desire personally to tell Newell; he wanted Newell to find it out.

"I don't know, Mr. Crowell; but I'm on my way to Florida. I'll go by and see."

\* \* \*

Gray moss hung from the wires and orange trees of Orlando. It was Florida-sultry weather. The windows were open, and the stimulating trills of mocking birds came into the room.

Dr. Newell, now such a one as Paul the aged, sat and listened, his heavy brows and leonine head bent in attention. When the narrative was completed, he sat awhile in silence. Then:

> "Mr. Crowell always had a clean desk. This one would drive him crazy. [And it would at that.] Crowell is orderly, sane; the most sane man I ever saw. One year he failed of Quaker Presidency. He went quietly about his business; then they re-elected him. He has no quirks, no twists. My son David, editor of *Field and Stream,* is devoted to him.
>
> "I am not surprised at his decision. When I regard his fidelity to God and to His Word, it just looks like a step of consistency.
>
> "But, personally, I'm so happy I could shout! I never said or wrote a word to him! He did it himself!
>
> [A burst of mocking bird trills fill the room.]
>
> *"THIS IS THE PROOF OF MY MINISTRY!"*

\* \* \*

Returning through Chicago, west bound to California, I went up to the Quaker offices:

"I told Dr. Newell, Mr. Crowell."

"What did he say?"

"Well, Beloved, (Forgive me for saying what I did. It still seems the appropriate thing.) *Dr. Newell was very much impressed.*"

# XXXIII

## "AS THE STARS FOREVER!"

Portrait of a man who declined to grow old.

"And they that are wise shall shine as the brightness of the firmament; and they that turn many to righteousness as the stars for ever and ever" (Daniel 12:3).

How winsome are the aged if they be righteous! The evil days come not from growing old, but from growing old impiously. (*Sketch Book*)

# "AS THE STARS FOREVER!"

WHEN Susan died, June 17, 1922, Mr. Crowell was in his sixty-seventh year; "the Lord gave us thirty-four years of precious fellowship." When he died October 23, 1944, he was in his eighty-ninth year. The twenty-two years between these dates define the period in his life which is commonly tagged "old age." But no one who really knew Mr. Crowell had mental liberty either to call him "an old man," or to think of him as such. As Rabelais would put it, such an epithet applied to H. P. C., was "above the pitch, out of tune, and off the hinges."

In what particular was H. P. C. ever an old man? We venture at this point to try him by three of the canons commonly applied De Senectute.

## I

The first is a marked physical decadence: the man is obliged to slow down; he becomes "afraid of that which is high and fears are in the way." How about Mr. Crowell? To be sure, he did not play tennis as he did in Greylock; in fact, he *would not* play tennis at all. Many a man has ruined the rest of his life by an hour of grand-standing with a racket trying to demonstrate how boyish he is. No tennis, now! It was smart when you matured to put away high school exercises. But, it was amazing to find this man at eighty-seven still heading the Quaker Oats Company, keeping regular office hours! It seemed incredible that up to eighty-nine he walked, as a rule, over to the Bible Institute Tuesdays and presided at the two hour sessions of the board. He walked, almost every day, the seven long blocks from the Board of Trade Building to the Northwestern Depot. You miserably walked with him on a humid afternoon, fervently wishing he would spend some of his money on a taxi!

And you should have seen the Crowell stride! He walked right through Octogenerian Valley with his feet slightly angled out. Not straight in line like an Indian or a Boy Scout. That stance is fine for a jungle-walker, real or fancied; but deadly to the savoir-faire of a genial soul. He finished each step with a little, almost imperceptible forward kick. That was something he never lost. Had a camera man caught him at twenty-seven walking into his new mill at Ravenna, he would have laughed, "Look! the Crowell kick! Something jaunty about it." And in 1944, he would have thought: "Still the Crowell kick. It seems to say, 'This old world's a very good place to walk around in.'" (Watch yourself, reader, or before you know it, you will be finishing your steps, right and left, with a little terminal kick. And it will not look good on you.)

His reserve power, for his age, was baffling. During the Green Court Interviews, there was a preliminary fear of overtaxing him. But each morning at nine, he cheerily said, "Shall we go to work?" At two P.M., "Shall we go to work?" At eight P.M., "Shall we go to work?"

"Old Man Crowell!" You are not talking to me! At the end of the week it was Boswell who came up *hors de combat,* not Johnson. . . .

There is a letter to Rev. George N. Taylor, his Every-Member-Canvas friend, written in 1943, in which he speaks of his physical condition:

> "I am glad to report that I am keeping well and able to carry on in all branches of life much to the surprise of many, who think that I should take less interest in the activities and efforts that are being put forth for making the Lord Jesus Christ known to men. The Lord is evidently preserving this body of mine to enable me not only to be interested, but also to be active; therefore, I have the satisfaction of co-operating with younger men, and at times guiding them, because of my experience, as well as the things I have learned."

He frankly ascribed "the preserving of this body of mine to the treatment of my physician of many years, Dr. Frederick Erdman of Germantown, Pennsylvania. Dr. Erdman does wonders by controlling the circulation of the blood." You look at the ruddy

vigor in the face of this man almost ninety and think Mr. Crowell's physician had an ideal patient, one whose moderation worked
in harmony with the treatment. "When thou sittest to eat, put a
knife to thy throat if thou be a man given to appetite." Anybody
would look fine, feel fine, if he had his food weighed and served
him on a plate as did Mr. Crowell—*no seconds!* Many a man gets
a new lease on life by a slight attack of diabetes; he graduates
from gobbling.

## II

The second evidence of old age is a blackout of interest in the
future, or even in the present. The old man at the window pulls
down his shades, and nought more is heard from him save the
low-grinding mills of rumination. Were the Autocrat's ears to the
past? You should have heard him, like a Goodfield reporter,
cheerily inquire, "What's going on in the world?" then read
aloud from the latest Washington Forecast.

On the afternoon of October 17, less than a week before his
death, Mr. Crowell presided at the regular Executive Committee
of the Board of the Moody Bible Institute. He opened the meeting
by remarking, "I would like to take a few minutes." He then
began to talk about *the future of the Institute!* For forty-five
minutes he outlined his hopes for the place of the Institute in a
world like this.

"For one thing," he said, "we must not overlook the drift to
Modernism so visible in organized Christianity. As never before,
the Moody Bible Institute has a responsibility to give forth the
true gospel. There are two particular phases of this responsibility:
we must preserve sound doctrine in the years ahead; and we must
get the gospel to the ends of the earth. We have a large student
enrollment this year; and there has been a significant growth in
the circulation of Moody Monthly; the enlarged radio program
of WMBI is very gratifying. But Moody Bible Institute must
think in terms of still greater things for the glory of Christ!"

President Houghton sat spellbound, forgetful of taking notes!
A week later, when Mr. Crowell lay dead, the president sat down
to prepare his notable editorial. Tearfully, he wrote, "As Mr.

Crowell spoke, there was little or no mention of the past, but abundant reference to the future."

## III

A third evidence of farewell to youth is a sense of boredom when others are talking. "Old men" are poor conversationalists; they either grab the spotlight or turn off their attention. Listen, Patient Reader! If you insist on doing all the talking (mostly about yourself); or, if prevented, sit wool-gathering, alas! you're old, whether nineteen or ninety!

Let us see how H. P. C. acted when interviewed. No doubt interviews fit into the prayer, "Lead us not into temptation." If there is ever a time when a man is in danger of letting go, of strutting up-stage, mouthing great lines, it is when seduced by reporters. We now let you in on a Crowell interview. There he sits (bless his heart!) eyes blue, not faded; quiet, but alert; voice dry, pleasant; sentences, close clipped, not involved. He has a white, tooth-brush-efficiency type mustache, clipped as closely as his sentences; carefully groomed hair; brown suit, *pressed;* brown tie, brown woolen sox. Just right. (Brown today, some other scheme tomorrow.)

You think, "Well, Mr. Crowell is a good-looking man." You then felicitate, if you have rounded fifty, "Men never become really good looking until they are a little along in years." But you also think, "How winsome are the aged, if they be righteous! The evil days come not from growing old, but from growing old impiously."

The reporters inquire, "What books do you read?"

"Well, I like this one by Kenneth Wuest—just received it; or this one by Dr. Wilbur Smith."

"Do you read all those books, Mr. Crowell?" (pointing to a flock, book-jacket-fresh from the presses.)

"Well—no. You see I study chiefly human nature, men. What books do you gentlemen like? Did you ever read Proverbs? . . ."

The reporters are leaving. One of them suddenly exclaims, "Say! we didn't interview Crowell; he interviewed us."

Mrs. W. T. Weir said to her husband one afternoon, following luncheon with H. P. C. at the Union League Club: "Mr. Crowell has none of the usual traits of older people."

\* \* \*

His voice you would never forget. Holmes observes that man does not commonly realize what kind of a voice he has. That has a curious modern confirmation. Record man's voice for him on a radio disk, run it back, and every time he will say in amazement —"Do *I* sound like that?" As a general rule people do not have amiable voices. Voices are mostly thin and strident, high and quarrelsome; annoying no end, like ma-ri-a's from Naples. But H. P. had a beautiful voice. It was dry, but warming; a man's voice; but so much woman in it. . . . If you listened closely, you could hear Lillie and Susan. . . . When you talked, he said at recurrent intervals, "Yes. Yes." Just a little up-slide on the tone. It didn't mean, "I'm amazed!" or "I doubt you"; simply, "I'm following you. I'm interested. I get what you're saying. Please go on."

No, you could never forget his voice. One day Mrs. Coleman Crowell requested just before luncheon at Green Court, "Father, *you* return thanks!" The kindly voice began:

"Our Heavenly Father . . . Thy mercies are new every morning and fresh every evening. We acknowledge Thee to be the giver of every good and perfect gift. We accept this food as from Thy hand, and ask that we may be strengthened by it. May we use that strength in Thy service. May these evidences of Thy love draw us into deeper, richer, and fuller fellowship with Thee. This we ask with thanksgiving, for Christ's sake."

The voice seemed a gentle touch on your elbow, urging you, though your eyes were shut, to look up and see the King in His beauty. . . . Often in the months that followed, when you felt sorry he was gone, you seemed to hear the words again—"Thy mercies are new every morning, and fresh every evening." Tears filled your eyes; but, oh, what a fine cleansing for the lenses!

\* \* \*

The prayer habits of this layman would shame clergymen who have fallen into the evil habit of opening their days with an office key and closing them with a letter for the late mail. His was a life where Devotion held Priority Double A one. President Houghton had a striking division in his Memorial Address—"Certain Things Taken From His Pockets."

Among these things were Scripture notes and Scripture references in Mr. Crowell's own hand. We were never much impressed with men who are professionally pious; men with reversed collars; men who mount trains and immediately flourish a Bible. (We've often wondered if they really read them!) But we are impressed on thinking of a great business man night by night, mounting the Winnetka train, taking a small brown Testament from his pocket, depressing it so as not to be seen of men—reading, worshiping.

You may sense his judgment as to the value of habitual devotion by a few words copied from his own notes; his remarks to a graduating class at the Moody Bible Institute.

> "Before presenting the diplomas to the members of the graduating class, I have just a brief word of caution for them concerning their devotional life. Some of you may think, perhaps all of you, that no word of caution is needed; that your love for the Bible is so great . . . your prayer hour so sacred, so delightful. . . . If this thought is in your mind, it is there simply for the reason you have never measured your strength against the insistent, impelling, and compelling power of steadily accumulating activities. The more competent you are . . . the stronger will be the temptation to take time for these activities that belongs to your devotion . . . something must be given up . . . reluctantly and slowly you lessen the time set aside for devotions . . . then comes curtailment of power. . . . I plead with you, remember this last word or warning from the Institute! . . . Refuse to lessen the devotional period, no matter how severe the pressure! . . ."

* * *

"Then comes curtailment of power!" Right here is disclosed the secret of the man who declined to grow old; his inner man was renewed from day to day. Ponce de Leon could really have found that Fountain of Youth had he known where to look! It's location is revealed! See Province of Isaiah, District Forty, Thirty-One: "They that wait on the Lord shall renew their strength; they shall mount up with wings as eagles!"

Come now to his last days! . . . During the week of October 15, he arranged for a Cleveland visit October 25; he planned to spend some time with Mrs. Herrick; some with his biographer. They would walk together along Sheriff Street, sit in the public square. But somehow, he felt unaccountably weary; well, he would do his best to overcome that sense of exhaustion.

\* \* \*

Sunday morning, October 22, he attended the services of the Winnetka Bible Church, and heard his young friend, Rev. Milford Sholund.[1] Gipsy Smith, who with Mrs. Smith, was a house guest of Mr. Crowell at Winnetka, made a few remarks during the service. . . . (No one was more greatly loved by H. P. C. than Gipsy Smith. "We labored together for the Lord nearly forty years.") After the meeting, Mr. Crowell shook hands all around, and remarked that "it was a blessed service; the choir music was most beautiful."

At the noon meal in Winnetka, the conversation turned to the Second Coming. Gipsy Smith exclaimed, "How wonderful, without dying, to be caught up in the air to meet the Lord!" Mr. Crowell made a response so peculiar that every guest looked up in amazement; and remained silent for a time.

"Yes, that would be wonderful. But it is more wonderful, so far as I am concerned, to be raised from the dead upon Christ's appearance. For, the dead in Christ shall rise *first* at His coming!"

\* \* \*

Monday afternoon came at last and he was glad of it. He stood up, his head light with fatigue, for the walk to the Northwestern Depot. As he passed along the office corridor, Quaker workers noted, "He looked pale. . . ."

He wearily sat down in the train seat, opened the little brown Testament to read. . . . The train jolted to a stop almost immediately after starting. Some one had noticed that an aged man had completed his journey before the train left the station. . . .

A little later the phone bell rang in Hotel Cleveland: "This is Mrs. Herrick—Father—went home—this evening—just after he boarded—the Winnetka train."

[1] Howard Stanley Berglund, Buyer and Superintendent of Buildings, M.B.I., supplied these details.

Golden October never provided a more beautiful afternoon than that of the twenty-sixth. La Salle Street seemed to float in an Indian Summer haze. Inside the unfinished Torrey-Gray Auditorium Mr. Crowell's body lay in state. . . . Mr. Edward Boulter, the Winnetka gardener, grouped the floral tributes of Autumn chrysanthemums into beautiful masses about the coffin. He glanced at me and quietly said, "I've been with Mr. Crowell over forty years." I watched Mr. Boulter deftly emplace the pastel-beauties, and noted that now and then he furtively wiped his eyes. I remembered Mr. Crowell once saying, "Mr. Boulter is so zealous!" Yes, Mr. Boulter *was* zealous—*for Mr. Crowell!*

\* \* \*

The building was filled with men and women from all points of the compass, and from equally differentiated walks of life . . . Ed and Bob from Cheyenne . . . Donald and Bothwell from the South . . . hundreds of students; Chicago men-of-affairs; ministers; labor union men, for Mr. Crowell was a member of the Labor Union! Voted in and certificated so that he could lay the corner stone of Crowell Hall . . . now and then, a tattered figure from the poverty-fringe of the Big City; these quietly, but unashamedly wept as they looked into the casket, then went on. . . .

\* \* \*

The words of President Houghton's Memorial Address were as apples of gold. As he neared his conclusion, he referred to the Sir Christopher Wren inscription in St. Paul's Cathedral—

> "If you seek his monument,
> Look about you."

Look about you!

A panorama of the beloved Autocrat's life seemed to unfold. . . . I saw a lad, broken in health, walking beside Cleveland's Lake Front crying out in his heart, "O God, if You will allow me to make money to be used in Your service, I will keep my name out of it so You will have the glory." . . . I saw a man in his fiery forties write on a desk pad, "If my life can always be lived so as to please Him, I'll be supremely happy." . . . Then I saw again the exploits-for-glory which this man did during forty-six years, and among them beheld the rise of a powerful school. . . . Then I seemed to hear sainted Dr. Gray exclaiming, "It was the brain and heart of H. P. Crowell that made the Moody Bible Institute!"

Look about you, indeed!

Thereupon, I *did* look. For a moment I was dismayed to note that his memorial service was in the basement of an unfinished auditorium. He who deserved the greatest auditorium in Chicago!

Then I smiled; this, too, was just as he would have wanted it. Two hundred and fifty thousand dollars were in the treasury toward completion of the Torrey-Gray Auditorium; two hundred and fifty thousand more were needed. Of course that money could have been borrowed—*No! it could not!* Mr. Crowell disapproved of Christian institutions contracting debts, great or small. Then, he could have finished it himself. No! he *would* not!

I seemed again to hear him in Green Court, "Mr. Day, I never want to see Moody Bible Institute as it was when I came to it— no reliable friends." He knew if he gave too much, it made reliable friends unnecessary. He wanted M.B.I. to have ten thousand reliable friends.

\* \* \*

The mourners as they filed by the coffin noted in Mr. Crowell's right hand, resting over his heart, a tiny, brown Testament. At my request, the mortician, Mr. John L. Hebblethwaite, removed it and handed it to me. It was the Testament Mr. Crowell had carried for years. Inside, on the fly leaf, was a written inscription,

"H. P. C.
With love
C. M. A.
Chicago, October 15, 1910"

Charlie Alexander! I wanted to write something else into the little book before the mortician replaced it. I wanted to write:

*"They that be wise shall shine with the brightness of the firmament; and they that turn many to righteousness as the stars forever!"*

# XXXIV

## THE AZALEAS BLOOM AGAIN

Wherein we perceive that the floral glories of Green Court have reappeared in the hearts of men.

"And I heard a voice from heaven saying unto me, *Write!*
"Blessed are the dead which die in the Lord from henceforth!"
"Yea," (saith the Spirit) "that they may rest from their labors: and THEIR WORKS DO FOLLOW THEM!"

# THE AZALEAS BLOOM AGAIN

JANUARY 27, 1945, was a day of silence at Cedar-Palms. We looked at the photograph of Mr. Crowell in its place of honor. This was his ninetieth birthday . . . We had counted so much on spending this day at Augusta with him. . . . Disappointment and regret, however, roused dreams whereby we seemed to return to Augusta and to Green Court. . . .

\* \* \*

The train puffed slowly through Georgia swamps, whistling at cows on the tracks; past shabby southern shacks with pathetic little gardens; a world of negroes, mules and hogs. Finally, Augusta. It was heart searching to go out to Green Court . . . like returning to Cedar-Palms when Mother lay cold in death. . . .

Deborah said, "Let's walk in the garden. You know how much he loved the azaleas." So we walked. What a joy could he have walked with us on his ninetieth birthday! We walked silently. Then Deborah said, "Somehow these azaleas now suggest more than Susan. They were *his* azaleas, too."

Memory reviewed the entire scroll of friendship with H. P. C., unfurled it beginning with the first biographical discussion in the Quaker offices . . . subsequent interviews, consummated in Green Court fellowships . . . his letters, glowing with kindness! . . . The first delicate intimation of parting that November afternoon when we stood in front of the Board of Trade Building; "But, April is a long time" . . . Yes, it was a long time; too long . . . Now, we had naught save memories, and *their* azaleas!

I was suddenly roused from this sorrowful reminiscence: "Did you ever think these are not the only azaleas he had? His azaleas are blooming again, *all over the world!*"

Suddenly a host of others walked with us in the garden, a

301

great company in whose lives the flowers of heaven had appeared; men who once lived, lived now, and were yet to be born. Yes, his azaleas are blooming again, all over the world!

\* \* \*

They are blooming again in loyalty to great convictions, where that loyalty is expensive. It is hard to be a young pastor in these days of denominational Feudalism. The young pastor has a little family; he has covenanted to witness to the truth as it is in Jesus. . . . He suddenly discovers this loyalty might be penalized. . . . Men are often rated today not "because they love not their own lives even unto death," but on the score of a mysterious virtue called "Co-opie-ration." Some day the young minister may desire a new pastorate. If he has been too annoyingly fervid, he may get nothing at all. In that case, what of his children? his wife? Perhaps he would be wise to quiet down; become a pulpit Gibeonite hewing wood and drawing water. Then he hears of the Acts of H. P. C. and writes a letter:

> December 23, 1943
>
> "Yesterday it came to my attention that you had done some-thing that required real courage . . . due to conditions in your denomination, you severed your connections. . . . I am (a young pastor) . . . I have admired you, expected the best of you. . . . I have never been disappointed in you. . . . Again, you prove your real worth. . . . It was hard for you as a business man to take that step. But it proves Christ is first in your life. . . . *And He shall be first in mine!*"

They bloom again in higher brackets of American leadership. Here is an excerpt from the letter of a man so prominent in the public eye, we could not print his name:

> "The first time I heard your name was about twenty-five years ago when I used to take my mother to the M.B.I. She was a Baptist, but liked Moody Institute because she liked evangelicism (sic). In those days I did not give a great deal of thought to Moody Institute except that you were a main leader . . . but I did not know much about *you*. . . . I have seen Moody grow. . . . I have come to realize that you have had in mind all the time that if we are to preserve the influ-ence of Christian religion in this country, as it was understood

by pioneer Americans, then we must depend on religious evangelism rather than political evangelism. [This is a fresh and startlingly new phrase; typically a layman's phrase, so he hastens to explain.] Take Union Theological Seminary, for instance: They emphasize political evangelism. I can name several of the faculty who are working hand in hand with the Communist movement. . . . The Chicago Theological Seminary is another illustration of intellectualism leaning more toward political than religious aims. . . . You have had in mind religious evangelism; *leading souls to Christ*. And that is the only sort worth keeping. *And the sort I have come to esteem through you!*"

\* \* \*

The Crowell azaleas flower today in a thousand leading business men. This from a great Chicago merchant:

"I saw you, when I was a young man, walking along Michigan Avenue. I was so attracted to you that I followed you, not once but several times. . . . You became to me a clear burning torch. . . . Mr. Crowell, your biography should be written and given to every young business man in America. I know others will be as blessed by your Life Story as I have been."

\* \* \*

A rising young Chicago attorney writes:

"As I dictate, I look at three photos hanging in my office, my Father, John Alexander Clark, and—yourself! These three men have been the best influences in my life."

\* \* \*

A young man upon being informed he was to receive the honorary degree of LL.D.:

"The degree really belongs to you, Mr. Crowell! How much I am indebted to your personal and kindly interest!"

\* \* \*

"An old man" writes:

"I listen to Radio WMBI. You do not speak over the radio. But every day I thank God for H. P. Crowell. You fill my little cottage with beauty."

Again . . . but the letters here in Cedar-Palms are baffling in number. The very files containing them seem fragrant with Rosemary. Why go on? The azaleas of Green Court are indeed blooming again, in hundreds of corners, all over the world! And they shall continue to bloom until Resurrection Morn!

\* \* \*

On this twenty-seventh day of January, 1945, we stand looking at your photograph, Mr. Crowell! How beautiful indeed the aged when they are righteous!

We desired to be with you today. . . . But—this is not the end.

The sweet reassurance of D. L. Moody's farewell rings in our hearts—

"Good Night, Beloved! and
WE'LL SEE YOU IN THE MORNING!"

# APPENDICES

A. The Memorial Services
B. "Through The Bible" (Amos R. Wells)

## ORDER OF SERVICE FOR
## HENRY PARSONS CROWELL
October 26, 1944, 2 P.M.

Choir—For God So Loved the World, *Stainer*
Prayer—Dr. William Culbertson (Dean, Moody Bible Institute)
Scripture, message, and prayer—Dr. Will H. Houghton (President,
   Moody Bible Institute)
(Scripture read—I Corinthians 15:12-20, 51-58; 3:9-23)
Choir—"Still, Still with Thee," *Mendelssohn-Bartholdy*
Benediction—Dr. Culbertson (Hebrews 13:20, 21)

## HENRY PARSONS CROWELL
*President Houghton's Memorial Address*

It has been my sad duty to preside at the funeral service of three
great men whose lives were intertwined with that of the Moody Bible
Institute—Dr. Torrey, Dr. Gray, and now Henry P. Crowell. In October, 1928, when I preached Dr. Torrey's funeral sermon, I little
dreamed of having personal identification with the Institute. But how
grateful I am for the privilege of side-by-side service with Dr. James
M. Gray for eleven months, and Henry Parsons Crowell for just eight
days short of ten years.

It is probably not important to my hearers, but I record it as an
historical fact that these have been the ten happiest years of my life,
due largely to the encouragement, vision, and loyalty of the man
around whom we gather to pay this final tribute of love and respect.

It has never been my custom to eulogize in such a service as this,
for I have understood it to be the minister's responsibility to address
the living and remind them that they too must go the way of all the
earth. But this occasion is so unusual it will not be thought poor taste
to make personal reference to this great soul, now departed.

There is a sense in which we could be considered selfish for confining our remarks to the relationship Mr. Crowell bore to the Institute. There are other realms in which he held high place: the Quaker Oats Company, which had so many years of his life and so much of his affectionate interest, and of course the realm of his family, where he loved his children and grandchildren and was loved in return. But these friends will be understandingly sympathetic if this proves to be almost entirely a tribute to his relationship to the Moody Bible Institute.

Henry P. Crowell was the most Christlike man I have ever met, bearing to the full that distinctive mark of the Christian—humility. He exemplified and illustrated in his daily life and his contact with men the life about which so many of us talk, and some of us desire. He loved men, whether or not he agreed with them. He was keen of intellect, clear in memory, and wise in judgment, even this far, in his eighty-ninth year.

Many, many messages have been received from those who have been touched by this noble life, and who would be here today, were it possible. Time forbids reading these, but there is one telegram so significant it must be shared with you. Addressed to the son, H. Coleman Crowell, it says:

"IN YOUR GREAT SORROW YOU HAVE OUR DEEPEST SYMPATHY," and it is signed ELEVATOR OPERATORS AND STARTERS, BOARD OF TRADE BUILDING.

What a revelation this of the humanity of this man, who, going in and out of the Board of Trade Building, always had a smile and a word of greeting for elevator operators and everyone else. In his eyes men were men, all alike before God, and each accountable for himself to God.

At Lincoln's grave these words are to be found:

> "His grave a nation's heart shall be,
> His monument, a people free."

It cannot be said that a nation mourns the passing of Mr. Crowell. He so sought to keep himself out of sight in all his work for Christ that comparatively few have recognized a king in disguise. Those of us who knew him saw the royalty shine through. And he would not have wanted the plaudits of the world. He would much prefer the approval of the Lord.

Without wishing to take anything from the records of past Institute leaders, in all honesty the admission must be made that this man has been more responsible than any other for the success of the Moody Bible Institute from early times to this good hour. The continuance of the school, the sending forth of multitudes of young people with the gospel to the ends of the earth, the radio ministry, and all the other varied activities, were made possible largely by the devotion and generosity of this consecrated servant of Christ.

Who can doubt that last Monday evening, among those who welcomed him in the glory were some who were there because of his part in the training of the Christian workers who brought them the gospel. Perhaps he has even had an opportunity to report to D. L. Moody on the state of the Institute. Surely he has been able to give a good account of his stewardship. Imagination, not discouraged by the Scriptures, suggests there has been for him a warm welcome from his old friend Dr. Gray.

But what makes possible such a character as Mr. Crowell? We understand that there are many high qualities of human goodness in the man, but we recognize also something beyond these qualities. Are there not business men—young business men—and some of our students in training, who are asking this question at the moment? The answer is clear and unmistakable. If you could ask him, his answer humbly would be in one word—Christ.

I hold in my hands certain things taken from his pockets, the day he departed. There is here a poem on "Christian Victory"; a clipping, "How to Become a Christian"; a tract, "To Walk with God"; some Scripture notes in his own hand; Scripture references, and that familiar poem of Annie Johnson Flint—

> Christ has no hands but our hands
> To do His work today;
> He has no feet but our feet
> To lead men in His way.
> He has no tongue but our tongue
> To tell men how He died,
> He has no help but our help
> To bring them to His side.
>
> We are the only Bible
> The careless world will read;
> We are the sinners' gospel,
> We are the scoffers' creed;
> We are the Lord's last message,
> Given in deed and word;
> What if the type be crooked,
> What if the print be blurred?
>
> What if our hands are busy
> With work that is not His;

What if our feet are walking
    Where sin's allurement is;
What if our tongues are saying
    Things His lips would spurn;
How can we hope to help Him,
    Or hasten His return?

Believing in Christ as Saviour at an early age, and then yielding his life to Christ, he found sustenance and joy in fellowship with Christ through His Word and prayer. The great questions that determined everything in his life were, "Is this what He wants me to do?" or "Will it glorify Him?"

We pay this brief and incomplete tribute to Mr. Crowell, with the full understanding that it was the grace of God thus revealed in his life. We would not unduly exalt the instrument, but we thank God for what He did in and through the life of His servant.

If you have ever been in St. Paul's Cathedral, London, you have probably had called to your attention the inscription to the architect, Sir Christopher Wren, which ends—"If you seek his monument, look about you."

Fitting it is that this service should be held on the premises of the Moody Bible Institute, for we can repeat the Wren inscription and make present application—"If you seek *his* (Henry P. Crowell's) monument, look about you"—not merely in the cold dead stones of a new Administration Building, but in the living stones of young lives here built upon the one foundation, Jesus Christ.

Probably the hardest moment for me in this service is just now, as I try to recount a personal, intimate experience.

The foundation for the Administration Building was going in. The architects were at work on detail drawings of the face of the building. One day I sat with Mr. Crowell in his office, and asked him if he would permit us then to cut in stone for the arch of the Administration Building the name, Crowell Hall. He bowed his head in meditation. There was silence for perhaps two minutes. Then he lifted his head and said, "No, no; years ago I told the Lord that if He would allow me to make money to be used for His service I would keep my name out of it, so He could have the glory."

That of course was for his lifetime. Perhaps you have noticed that over the arch on La Salle Street, and under the words Moody Bible Institute, a blank space has been left on the stone where now will be carved—Crowell Hall.

It is selfish of us to mourn in such an hour. Of course we are going to miss him dreadfully, but there is for us the knowledge that he is with Christ. The body, to be taken to Cleveland, there to rest in Lake View Cemetery, is only the garment of the spirit, the tenement of clay in which he lived for nearly ninety years, but Henry P. Crowell still lives!

Those of us who have had fellowship with him here in Chicago have been accustomed to an annual break in that companionship, when for the winter he would take up residence in his Augusta home. Oh friends, let us realize he now has but transferred his residence to his heavenly home.

> "For all the saints, who from their labors rest,
> Who Thee by faith before the world confessed,
> Thy name, O Jesus, be forever blest.
> Alleluia!

> "Thou wast their Rock, their Fortress, and their Might;
> Thou, Lord, their Captain in the well-fought fight;
> Thou, in the darkness drear, their one true Light.
> Alleluia!

> "O may Thy soldiers [today], faithful, true, and bold,
> Fight as the saints who nobly fought of old,
> And win with them the victor's crown of gold.
> Alleluia!"

## THROUGH THE BIBLE

(One of Mr. Crowell's Favorite Poems)

I supposed I knew my Bible,
    Reading piecemeal, hit or miss,
Now a bit of John or Matthew,
    Now a snatch of Genesis;
Certain chapters of Isaiah,
    Certain Psalms (the twenty-third!),
Twelfth of Romans, first of Proverbs—
    Yes, I thought I knew God's Word!
But I found that thorough reading
    Was a different thing to do,
And the way was unfamiliar,
    When I read the Bible through.

Oh, the massive, mighty volume;
    Oh, the treasures manifold;
Oh, the beauty and the wisdom
    And the grace it proved to hold!
As the story of the Hebrews
    Swept in majesty along,
As it leaped in waves prophetic,
    As it burst to sacred song,
As it gleamed with Christly omens,
    The Old Testament was new—
Strong with cumulative power,
    When I read the Bible through.

Oh, Imperial Jeremiah
    With his keen coruscant mind;
And the blunt old Nehemiah
    And Ezekiel refined!
Newly came the minor prophets,
    Each with his distinctive robe;
Newly came the Song idyllic
    And the tragedy of Job;
Deuteronomy, the regal,
    To a towering mountain grew
With its comrade peaks around it,
    When I read the Bible through.

What a radiant procession
　As the pages rise and fall!
James, the sturdy; John, the tender,
　And the myriad-minded Paul!
Vast apocalyptic glories
　Wheel and thunder, flash and flame,
While the Church Triumphant raises
　One Incomparable Name;
Ah, the glory of the Saviour
　Never glows supremely true
Till you read it whole and swiftly,
　Till you read the Bible through.

You who like to play at Bible,
　Dip and dabble, here and there,
Just before you kneel aweary
　And yawn through a hurried prayer;
You who treat the Crown of Writings
　As you treat no other book,
Just a paragraph disjointed
　Just a crude impatient look,
Try a worthier procedure,
　Try a broad and steady view;
You will kneel in very rapture
　When you read the Bible through.
　　　　　　　　　*—Amos R. Wells*

# INDEX